KU-513-402

To Kevin and Donal O'Shea,
brothers, not friars

The Friar of Carcassonne

Revolt Against the Inquisition in the Last Days of the Cathars

STEPHEN O'SHEA

P

PROFILE BOOKS

First published in Great Britain in 2011 by
PROFILE BOOKS LTD
3A Exmouth House
Pine Street
London EC1R 0JH
www.profilebooks.com

First published in the United States in 2011 by
Walker Publishing Company, Inc., New York
A division of Bloomsbury Publishing

Copyright © Stephen O'Shea, 2011
Maps copyright © Jeffrey L. Ward, 2011

10 9 8 7 6 5 4 3 2 1

Designed by Simon Sullivan
Printed and bound in Great Britain by Clays, Bungay, Suffolk

The moral right of the author has been asserted.

All rights reserved. Without limiting the rights under copyright reserved
above, no part of this publication may be reproduced, stored or introduced
into a retrieval system, or transmitted, in any form or by any means
(electronic, mechanical, photocopying, recording or otherwise), without the
prior written permission of both the copyright owner and the publisher of
this book.

A CIP catalogue record for this book is available from the British Library.

ISBN 978 1 84668 319 0
eISBN 978 1 84765 427 4

Mixed Sources
Product group from well-managed
forests and other controlled sources
www.fsc.org Cert no. TT-COC-002227
© 1996 Forest Stewardship Council
FSC

The paper this book is printed on is certified by the © 1996
Forest Stewardship Council A.C. (FSC). It is ancient-forest
friendly. The printer holds FSC chain of custody SGS-COC-2061

CONTENTS

The European World of Bernard Délicieux

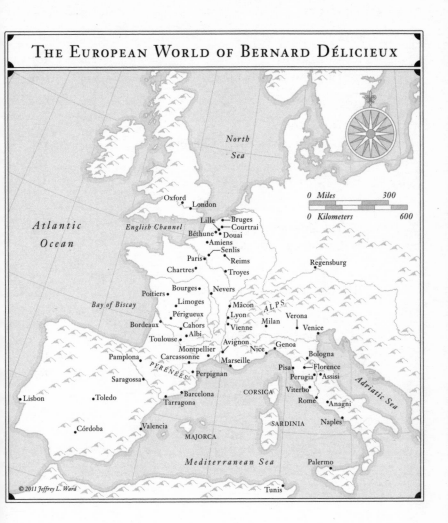

North Sea

Atlantic Ocean

English Channel

Bay of Biscay

PYRÉNÉES

ALPS

Mediterranean Sea

Adriatic Sea

0 Miles 300
0 Kilometers 600

Oxford • London
Lille • Bruges
Béthune • Courtrai
Douai
Amiens
Senlis
Paris • Reims
Chartres • Troyes
Bourges • Nevers
Poitiers
Limoges
Périgueux • Mâcon
Bordeaux • Lyon
Cahors • Vienne
Toulouse • Albi
Montpellier • Avignon
Carcassonne • Nice
Pamplona • Marseille
Perpignan
Saragossa
Barcelona
Lisbon • Toledo • Tarragona
Córdoba • Valencia
MAJORCA
Regensburg
Milan • Verona
Venice
Genoa
Bologna
Pisa • Florence
Perugia • Assisi
Viterbo
Rome • Anagni
Naples
CORSICA
SARDINIA
Palermo
Tunis

© 2011 Jeffrey L. Ward

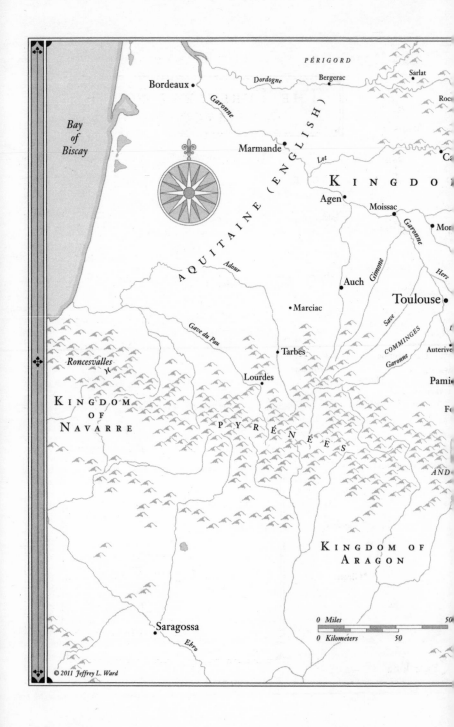

PÉRIGORD

Bordeaux •

Sarlat

Dordogne

Bergerac

Roc

Garonne

Bay
of
Biscay

Marmande •

Lot

Ca

K I N G D O

Agen •

Moissac

Mor

Garonne

AQUITAINE (ENGLISH)

Adour

Auch •

Hers

Gimone

Toulouse •

• Marciac

Save

L

Gave du Pau

COMMINGES

Auteriv

• Tarbes

Garonne

Roncesvalles

Lourdes •

Pamie

KINGDOM
OF
NAVARRE

P Y R É N É E S

Fo

AND

KINGDOM OF
ARAGON

0 Miles   50

0 Kilometers   50

Saragossa •

Ebro

© 2011 Jeffrey L. Ward

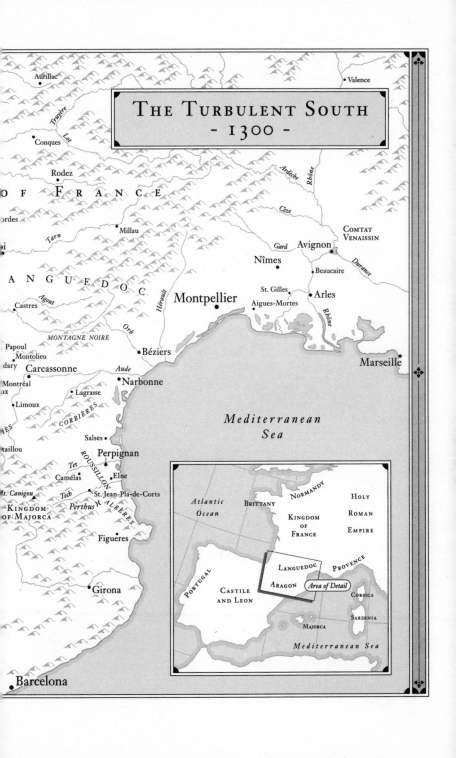

THE TURBULENT SOUTH
- 1300 -

Aurillac

Valence

Trayère

Lot

Conques

Rodez

Ardèche

Rhône

O F   F R A N C E

ordes

Tarn

Millau

Cèze

COMTAT
VENAISSIN

Gard   Avignon

Nîmes

i

A N G U E D O C

Hérault

Durance

Beaucaire

St. Gilles   Arles

Montpellier

Castres

Agout

Aigues-Mortes

Rhône

Orb

MONTAGNE NOIRE

Béziers

Marseille

Papoul
Montoliou

Carcassonne

Aude

dary

Narbonne

Montréal

Lagrasse

ux

Limoux

CORBIÈRES

Mediterranean
Sea

ÈS

Salses

taillou

Perpignan

Tet

Camélas   Elne

t. Canigou

Tech

Perthus   St.·Jean-Pla-de-Corts

ALBÈRES

ROUSSILLON

KINGDOM
OF MAJORCA

Figueres

Atlantic
Ocean

BRITTANY

NORMANDY

HOLY

KINGDOM
OF
FRANCE

ROMAN

EMPIRE

PORTUGAL

LANGUEDOC   PROVENCE

ARAGON   Area of Detail

CASTILE
AND LEON

CORSICA

SARDINIA

MAJORCA

Mediterranean Sea

Girona

Barcelona

USAGE

READERS FAMILIAR WITH THE PERIOD will note immediately that the word *inquisition* appears throughout uncapitalized. The use of the upper-case *Inquisition*, common until recently even in scholarly studies, leaves the impression that there was a well-oiled, centralized bureaucracy supporting the inquisitors, whereas in the early centuries of inquisition this was not the case. The inquisition as an institution did not exist, only inquisitors in limited jurisdictions for limited time periods. However, the idea of an institution certainly existed and its ephemeral manifestation in these years was often referred to as the Holy Office, an uppercase usage retained in the text.

As for the vexed problem of names, I have made the usual stab at exception-riddled standardization that, I know from experience, falls short of being universally pleasing. As is customary, the names of monarchs and popes have been given in English. The exception is the king of Majorca, whose Catalan identity I wished to stress; thus Jaume, not James. The same stress on identity has led me to retain the Occitan names for the men of the south. The tension between the Occitan-speaking southerners of Languedoc and the French-speaking northerners of the Kingdom of France is central to the story. Using a historical figure's Occitan name locates his background and his allegiances. Thus, for example, Peire Autier, not Pierre Authier. However, for those southerners already widely known by their Gallicized names—Bernard Saisset, Pierre Jean Olivi, and Guillaume de Nogaret, for example—I have retained the French so that readers who know something of these figures will not think they are reading about someone else.

Complicating matters is the problem that much of my research involved French-language material, whose authors almost always use French names for everyone in history. Where an obscure Occitan figure appears only in French, I have not attempted the foolhardy task of reconstituting his name in his mother tongue. But I hope enough of the Occitan-French divide is left standing to shape the reader's view of Bernard Délicieux's Languedoc.

As for the names themselves, I am acutely aware of their unfamiliarity and sheer number. Having been chided for a phone-book-like embarrassment of names in a previous work, I have tried to trim as many distracting names from the narrative as possible. Thus, unimportant figures who crop up but once or twice in the narrative are identified by name in the notes, not in the main text.

A friend, after having finished reading my earlier work on the Cathars, *The Perfect Heresy*, exclaimed to me: "I get it! Everyone in the first half of the book is called Raymond, and everyone in the second half is called Bernard!" As this present work deals with the latter half of the Cathar story, there are indeed a lot of Bernards. I have taken special care to keep them from bumping into each other, but the reader will have to be the judge of whether I succeeded.

THE COMBATANTS

Figures of exceptional importance in the story of Bernard Délicieux are marked with an asterisk.

ANGELO CLARENO (1247–1337). Franciscan. Leader of the Spirituals. Exiled at various times to Armenia, Greece, and remote Italian provinces. Argued for the Spirituals at the Council of Vienne (1311–12). Witness to Bernard Délicieux's arrest in Avignon in 1317.

*****ARNAUD GARSIE**. Wealthy lawyer. Consul of Albi in 1302 and 1303. Of a heretical family. Ally of Bernard Délicieux. Attended audience at Senlis in 1301, disputation at Toulouse in 1304. Testified against Délicieux in 1319. Imprisoned in 1319, bought his freedom from the Wall in 1325.

ARNAUD DE VILANOVA (1235–1311). Prominent Catalan physician, alchemist, oenologist, scientist, and Arabist. Translator of Avicenna and Galen. Friend of Bernard Délicieux. Supporter of the Spiritual Franciscans. Suspected, along with Délicieux, of using black magic to kill Pope Benedict XI in 1304.

*****BENEDICT XI**. Pope. Born Niccolò Boccasini in Treviso in 1240. Pontificate 1303–4. Dominican scholar. Called for arrest of Bernard Délicieux. Pressured by Nogaret to annul anti-French bulls of his predecessor (Boniface VIII). Imprisoned Arnaud de Vilanova. Sudden death a source of suspicion.

*****BERNARD DE CASTANET**. Bishop of Albi from 1276 to 1308 (d. 1317). Fearless autocrat. Sponsor of inquisition. Builder of the Cathedral of Ste. Cécile. As cardinal at the Avignon curia, drew up charges against Bernard Délicieux in 1317.

*BERNARD DÉLICIEUX (circa 1265–1320). Franciscan. The Friar of Carcassonne.

*BERNARD GUI (1261–1331). Dominican. Prolific memoirist of the unrest in Languedoc. Inquisitor at Toulouse from 1307 to 1324. Author of influential inquisitor's manual. Drew up the second, more exhaustive list of charges against Bernard Délicieux for the trial of 1319 in Carcassonne. Strong advocate for the canonization of Thomas Aquinas, which came to pass in 1324.

*BERNARD SAISSET. Bishop of Pamiers from 1295 to his death in 1314. Arrested in 1301 for sedition by royal agents Jean de Picquigny and Richard Leneveu. Temporary incarceration led to royal-papal dispute culminating in the Outrage of Anagni. Found shelter in Rome, then reassigned to Pamiers.

*BONIFACE VIII. Pope. Born Benedetto Caetani in Anagni circa 1235. Pontificate 1294–1303. Imperious pope of the Jubilee. Acceded to the papacy after counseling his predecessor (Celestine) to abdicate and then imprisoning him. Hated for this reason by the Spiritual Franciscans. Abrasive, brilliant believer in a maximalist monarchical papacy. Engaged in furious fight with Philip the Fair over jurisdiction that culminated in the Outrage of Anagni in 1303. Vilified by Guillaume de Nogaret, who called for him to be posthumously tried.

*CASTEL FABRE (d. 1278). Wealthy burgher of Carcassonne, treasurer of the royal seneschal, cause célèbre. Attempt to convict him posthumously of heresy in 1300 thwarted by Bernard Délicieux. Eventually convicted, disinterred, and burned in 1319, amid accusations by the Dominicans that the Franciscans deliberately jumbled his bones with those of others.

CELESTINE V. Pope. Born Pietro del Morrone in Molise circa 1210. Pontificate July–December 1294. Ascetic holy hermit whose followers (later called Celestines) had links to the Spiritual Franciscans. Viewed as "angel pope" in subsequent Spiritual apocalyptic prophecy. Abdicated papacy after proving too unworldly for the position. Died imprisoned by his successor, Boniface VIII. Canonized by Clement V in 1313.

*CLEMENT V. Pope. Born Bertrand de Got in Villandraut, Gironde, circa 1260. Pontificate 1305–14. Moved the papacy to Avignon. Succumbed to humiliating French pressure to approve the dissolution and trial of the Templars at the Council of Vienne (1311–12). Equitable in his approach to inquisition and the Spiritual Franciscans. Supporter of missionary work, founded chairs of Oriental languages at Paris, Oxford, Bologna, and Salamanca. Notorious for his lavish nepotism.

DOMINGO DE GUZMÁN (1170–1221). St. Dominic. Founder of the Order of Friars Preachers, the Dominicans.

DURAND DE CHAMPAGNE. Franciscan. Confessor of Queen Joan of France. Influential ally of Bernard Délicieux. Author of a widely read "courtesy" book for princesses, *Speculum dominarum* (French *Le miroir des dames*).

*FERRAN OF MAJORCA (1278–1316). Third son of King Jaume II of Majorca. Warrior. Intended monarch of a new Kingdom of Languedoc. Later Lord of Catania (Sicily). Died in battle trying to secure control of the Principality of Achaea (the Peloponnese).

*FOULQUES DE SAINT-GEORGES. Dominican. Inquisitor at Carcassonne and at Toulouse. Ambushed at the Franciscan convent in the Bourg in 1299. Accused of abuse and depravity at Senlis in 1301. Forced out of office the following year by an angry Philip the Fair.

FREDERICK II (1194–1250). *Stupor Mundi*. Germanic emperor, ruled from his multicultural court in Palermo. Important figure whose fame reverberated well down into Bernard's day. Enemy of the papacy, prophetic figure in Joachite and Spiritual literature, in his lifetime often called the Antichrist.

*GEOFFROY D'ABLIS. Dominican. Inquisitor at Carcassonne from 1303 until his death in 1316. Attempt in 1303 to quell unrest at Carcassonne backfired and led to rioting. Discovered and prosecuted the Autier revival of Catharism.

GILLES AYCELIN. Archbishop of Narbonne from 1290 to 1311 (d. 1318). Of the influential Aycelin de Montaigu family of the Auvergne. As king's prelate, arbitrated in favor of Jean de Picquigny over Foulques de

Saint-Georges in Senlis and held Bernard Saisset in custody on behalf of the king in 1301; in 1303, favored bringing Pope Boniface to Paris for trial; in 1304, laid out the king's position to Bernard Délicieux at the disputation of Toulouse. Later archbishop of Rouen and investigator of the Templars for Pope Clement V.

*GIOVANNI FRANCESCO DI BERNARDONE (1181–1226). St. Francis of Assisi. Founder of the Order of Friars Minor, the Franciscans.

GREGORY IX. Pope. Born Ugolino di Segni in Anagni circa 1155. Pontificate 1227–41. Religious and energetic, favored the development of the mendicants. Canonized Francis in 1228, Dominic in 1234. Founded the papal inquisition, conferring it on the Dominicans. Set up the university in Toulouse, 1233. Pontificate marked by sharp conflict with Frederick II (*Stupor Mundi*).

GUI SICRE. Prominent consul of Carcassonne in the 1290s. Signatory to the accord of 1299, which he subsequently kept hidden until 1303. Raced to Toulouse in 1303 to alert the inquisitor of Bernard Délicieux's incendiary sermon. Testified against Délicieux in 1319.

*GUILLAUME DE NOGARET (1260–1313). Succeeded Pierre Flote as the principal councillor of King Philip the Fair. Present at the Outrage of Anagni in 1303, for which he was excommunicated. Excommunication lifted in 1311 in exchange for resolving his campaign of vilification against the late Pope Boniface VIII. Mastermind of the suppression of the Knights Templar and other brutal royal policies.

*HÉLIE PATRICE (d. 1305). Shadowy figure. Effective leader of the Bourg of Carcassonne 1303–5, powerful ally of Bernard Délicieux. Hanged for high treason.

INNOCENT III. Pope. Born Lotario dei Conti di Segni at Anagni circa 1160. Pontificate 1198–1216. Made pope at age thirty-seven, a brilliant, capable ruler, arguably the greatest pope of the Middle Ages. Preached the Fourth Crusade of 1204. Set in motion the Albigensian Crusade in 1209. Presided over the important Fourth Lateran Council in 1215. Tireless legislator. Far-seeing, gave his approval to the mendicant initiatives of Dominic and Francis.

INNOCENT IV. Pope. Born Sinibaldo Fieschi in Genoa circa 1195. Pontificate 1243–54. Authorized torture in inquisition. Papacy almost entirely taken up by quarrel with Frederick II (*Stupor Mundi*) and his Hohenstaufen succession. Preached St. Louis's Seventh Crusade. Sent several emissaries to the Mongols in hope of alliance against Islam.

JACQUES DE CHÂTILLON (d. 1302). Philip the Fair's haughty viceroy in Flanders. Unsuccessful in quelling rebellion in Bruges. Died at the Battle of the Golden Spurs.

***JACQUES FOURNIER.** Bishop of Pamiers from 1317 to 1326. Gifted and relentless inquisitor. Judge at trial of Bernard Délicieux in 1319. Captured Guillaume Bélibaste, last Cathar Good Man of Languedoc in 1321. Became the third Avignon pope, Benedict XII (pontificate: 1334–42). Began the building of the Palais des Papes.

JAUME II. Lord of Montpellier and king of Majorca, his capital Perpignan. Born 1243, reigned 1276–1311. Uncovered the plot to attach Languedoc to his kingdom. Created the irrigation systems to make the Roussillon a fertile cornucopia. Opened consulates in Muslim world. Ally of France. Cousin to kings of Aragon.

JEAN D'AUNAY. Royal seneschal of Carcassonne from 1305 to 1309. Uncovered the plot to switch southern allegiance from the Capetians of France to Prince Ferran of Majorca. Tortured, tried, and hanged the lay conspirators. Dismissed in 1309 on charges of corruption and venality.

***JEAN DE PICQUIGNY** (d. 1304). Noble of Amiens, experienced courtier. Royal *réformateur-enquêteur* (viceroy-investigator) of Languedoc. Arrested Bishop Bernard Saisset in 1301; subsequently became a strong supporter of Bernard Délicieux and freed the prisoners from the Wall in 1303. Died an excommunicate in Perugia.

JEAN GALAND. Dominican. Inquisitor at Carcassonne from 1278 to 1286. Compiler of controversial inquisition registers, which, he claimed, heretical citizens had plotted to steal. Active at Albi (1286) with Bishop de Castanet and the Dominican Guillaume de Saint-Seine, who succeeded him as inquisitor at Carcassonne (1286–1293).

*JOAN OF NAVARRE. Joan I, queen of France; b. 1273, r. 1285–1305. Wife of Philip the Fair. Sympathetic to the cause of Bernard Délicieux. Mother of three kings of France, Louis X ("the Stubborn"), r. 1314–16, Philip V ("the Tall"), r. 1316–22, and Charles IV ("the Fair"), r. 1322–28, and of one queen of England, Isabella ("the She-Wolf of France"), wife of Edward II, r. 1308–30, d. 1358.

*JOHN XXII. Pope. Born Jacques Duèse in Cahors circa 1245. Pontificate 1316–34. Second Avignon pope. Able administrator and organizer. Had Bernard Délicieux arrested in 1317 and tried in 1319. Declared Spiritual Franciscans heretics. Attacked Conventual Franciscan poverty as well, creating a powerful opposition that included William of Occam and Marsilius of Padua. Spiritual Franciscan Pietro Rainalducci crowned ephemeral antipope Nicholas V (1328) in opposition to John's tumultuous pontificate.

LOUIS IX. "Saint Louis." King of France; b. 1214, r. 1226–70. Grandfather of Philip the Fair. Able administrator, dogged crusader (Seventh and Eighth Crusades), pious monarch, canonized 1297 by Boniface VIII. Built the Wall at Carcassonne. Patron of the arts in France's glittering thirteenth century; had the Sainte-Chapelle constructed in Paris.

MONETA OF CREMONA (circa 1180–1238). Dominican. Philosophy professor at Bologna turned influential friar in the fight against heresy. Author of five-volume treatise, *Adversus catharos et valdenses*. In other works, a vehement proponent of a Christianity of fear and the virtues of persecution.

*NICOLAS D'ABBEVILLE. Dominican. Inquisitor at Carcassonne from mid-1290s until 1303. Negotiated the accord of 1299 with the consuls of the Bourg. Prosecutor of the controversial inquisition at Albi in 1300 with Bishop de Castanet. Outwitted by Bernard Délicieux in the Castel Fabre affair.

NICOLAS DE FRÉAUVILLE (1250–1323). Dominican. Confessor of King Philip the Fair. Refused admission to the king's presence following Bernard Délicieux's presentation at Senlis in 1301. Accused at the 1304 disputation in Toulouse of spying for the Flemish. Principal inquisitor in the trials of the Templars. Subsequently powerful cardinal, nearly elected to succeed Clement V as pope.

PEIRE AUTIER (circa 1245–1310). Notary of Ax in the Pyrenees turned Cathar Good Man late in life. Voyaged to Italy in the late 1290s to receive instruction and the *consolamentum*. Returned to Languedoc in 1300, recruited a dozen other Good Men to lead the last revival of Catharism there. Burned at the stake in Toulouse, April 10, 1310.

*PEIRE PROS. Prominent citizen of Castres. Royal judge. Of possible heretical background, a ringleader of the anti-inquisitorial movement directed by Bernard Délicieux. Present at Senlis in 1301, during the king's visit to Languedoc in 1304, and as a hostile witness to Délicieux at the trial of 1319. Eventually bought his freedom from the Wall in 1325.

PHILIP III ("THE BOLD"). King of France; b. 1245, r. 1270–85. Father of Philip the Fair. Died in Perpignan at age forty following a disastrous war on the other side of the Pyrenees against the Kingdom of Aragon.

*PHILIP IV ("THE FAIR"). King of France; b. 1268, r. 1285–1314. Ruthless, powerful monarch, one of the great Capetians. Expanded the royal domain, despoiled many of his subjects to meet his ever-expanding need for revenue. Quarreled famously with Pope Boniface VIII, warred with England's Edward I, fought rebellion in Flanders, brutally suppressed the Templars. Won over by Bernard Délicieux's eloquence in 1301 at Senlis; appalled by his impudence in 1304 at Toulouse.

PIERRE FLOTE (d. 1302). Lawyer, educated at Montpellier. Most powerful courtier of Philip the Fair at mid-reign. First non-ecclesiastic to be chancellor of France. Organizer and principal participant of the Estates-General in 1302. Stomped to death at the Battle of the Golden Spurs.

PIERRE JEAN OLIVI (1248–1298) Franciscan. Theorist of the Spiritual Franciscans. Author of influential scholarly treatises on poverty and apocalyptic speculation. Many of his works subsequently condemned by the Church. Revered as an uncanonized saint by the Spirituals and Beguins of Languedoc.

PIETER DE CONINCK (d. 1332). Flemish weaver and rebel. Led the Bruges Matins of 1302. Associated with Jan Breydel, a baker of Bruges, as a co-conspirator, though Coninck's role is on surer historical ground.

Statues of both men adorn the marketplace in Bruges. The city's football stadium is named after Breydel.

RAIMOND COSTA. Bishop of Elne, beginning in 1290. Lawyer educated at Bologna in late 1260s. Agitator against inquisition in Carcassonne in 1280s. House in Carcassonne used as meeting place for anti-inquisitorial party.

RAIMOND DE MOSTUÉJOULS. Bishop of St. Papoul. Intimate of Pope John XXII. Judge at trial of Bernard Délicieux in 1319. Made a cardinal in 1327.

RAMON LLULL (1232–1315). Majorcan polyglot scholar, artist, botanist, political theorist. Friend of Bernard Délicieux. Frequent traveler to the lands of Islam. Author of first major works in Catalan, including first European novel, *Blaquerna*. Pioneered the autobiography. Lay member of the Franciscan Third Order.

*****RICHARD LENEVEU** (d. 1309). A bishop of Normandy, appointed with Jean de Picquigny to investigate Bishop Bernard Saisset of Pamiers. Subsequent ally of Bernard Délicieux. Died a leper in Béziers.

BROTHER BERNARD

O N THE CRIMSON WALL of a gallery of nineteenth-century art in the Musée des Augustins in Toulouse, one painting stands out from its fellows. Amidst old-fashioned works depicting deeds of the great and poses of the idealized, a study of a medieval court-room drama beckons the beholder to linger.

It is the autumn of 1319. A Franciscan friar stands in a cold chamber facing a group of five dignitaries seated on a lofty stone bench. They are wrapped in fur and brocade; three wear the miters of episcopal author-ity. Their faces are closed, as stony as their surroundings. Between these petrified postures of hostility and the lone Franciscan is a low desk strewn with parchment rolls and open books. An official enrobed in ermine sits at it, glowering at the upright figure. His companions at the desk are two black-cowled and faceless scribes, one poring over what is undoubtedly a register of past condemnations, the other hunched over at his task, his quill scratching away, transcribing every damning word of the friar's speech.

For the Franciscan is indeed damning himself. His listeners are his judges, who have accused him of interfering with the inquisition in its quest to extirpate "heretical depravity" in the south of France. Yet in the painting they are the accused: the brave friar has his right arm stretched out in front of him, pointing an unwavering index finger directly at his judges. A great, broadening shaft of sun streams through a barred win-dow high up in a corner of the room, but its light illuminates neither the accuser nor the accused. It spills on the floor uselessly. The people portrayed remain in the murk of the Middle Ages.

The painting, executed in 1887, is entitled *L'Agitateur du Languedoc*. Its creator, Jean-Paul Laurens, was in his day a renowned master of the grand genre, or history painting. This academic tradition, popular in the nineteenth century, had ardent partisans in Toulouse, a city of pink brick that seems an unlikely setting for a past of uncommon truculence. As historians of Laurens' time unearthed episodes from that turbulent local past, the demand for paintings in the grand genre, many of them celebrations of the region's cantankerous relations with king in Paris and pope in Rome, became a clamor. Laurens, a native son of Languedoc, obliged, and his work now hangs in many places in the city and its hinterland. Those who commissioned him sought to bolster local pride and regional identity, and to instruct and edify.

Laurens painted other tableaux concerning the inquisition—a long-vanished nightmare in Languedoc by his time, but a nightmare none-theless. Liberals like him were then battling a reactionary Catholic Church, at the same time as they were resisting the centralizing bull-dozer of the French Third Republic. With the *Agitateur*, an episode of history plucked from obscurity in 1877 by a historian of talent, the painter tapped into this dual struggle. For there had, indeed, been a great agitator in Languedoc, a figure who fought a powerful Church at home and a pitiless king in Paris—and who had paid for that fight with his life. That man was Brother Bernard Délicieux.

In Laurens' time, the remarkable career of Bernard Délicieux was five and a half centuries in the past; it is now seven centuries distant. Why we of the present day should remember his story, even those of us who live far from Languedoc, will become apparent.

Bernard Délicieux was a troublemaker of the first order, in the mold of Martin Luther, John Brown, and Mahatma Gandhi. A man of the Church, he challenged the Church; a subject of the king of France, he plotted against France. From his rise out of obscurity in 1299 to his death from the exactions of torture and imprisonment some twenty years later, Délicieux attracted supporters of all stripes and collected a formidable array of enemies. He opposed the misuse of power, the se-duction of wealth, and the recourse to violent coercion. He attacked the inquisition head-on, effectively shutting it down for several years in Languedoc. He enlisted royal support in his campaign—from one of the most dangerous kings ever to sit on the French throne—and did not shrink from fomenting revolt when that support was withdrawn.

Aside from the likeness sprung whole from the imagination of Laurens, no image of him has come down to us. We can assume that he must have possessed a strong voice capable of conveying the force of his arguments. It may have even been mellifluous, given his repeated success in persuasion. Even his many enemies recognized his outstanding gifts in oratory. No doubt he had a commanding physical stature, to stand not only before king and bishop but also before crowds of townspeople whose anger at the inquisition he so effectively channeled into action.

Details of his early life are precious but few. Born between 1260 and 1270 into the petty nobility of Montpellier, Bernard entered the Franciscan brotherhood in 1284. His abundant talents were quickly recognized, and he rose through the ranks, representing the head of the Franciscan Order in dealing with royal authorities in Paris and becoming the prior of the Franciscan convent in Carcassonne just before the turn of the century. His interests were varied, from politics to apocalyptic speculations, and his circle of friendship impressive. He knew some of the great minds of his time. Ramon Llull, the polyglot Majorcan poet, philosopher, and tireless champion of the conversion of the Muslims, counted Bernard as one of his friends. An independent scholar whose prodigious output and fearless travels to the lands of Islam make him something of a patron saint of intrepid freelancers, Llull seems to have respected Délicieux, having given the Franciscan one of his volumes as a gift. Llull is also credited with publishing the first major works in the Catalan language, in which the friar would have been versed. Holding Bernard in similarly high esteem was another Catalan, Arnaud de Vilanova, physician to popes, astrologer to kings, and prominent alchemist. This friendship extended into a shared interest in necromancy and the dark arts, a mark of Bernard's restless intellect. Another admirer, just as unconventional as Llull and Vilanova, was Angelo Clareno, an Italian leader of an exalted faction of the Franciscan brotherhood, who saw in Délicieux a champion of the virtues of poverty and simplicity.

These acquaintances suggest a man of curiosity and, perhaps, inwardness, satisfied with the life of an interesting mind. Yet those facets of his personality did not earn him his place in history. He was also a man of the world, adept at the behind-the-scenes maneuvering necessary to further schemes and scuttle opponents. To the circle of friendship that counted individuals of uncommon genius must be added noblemen and cardinals, who would protect him in his time of need, as well as the Franciscan confessor to the queen of France—and indeed the queen herself. He was no stranger to the society of the great, as comfortable in a palace of the powerful as in a cell of a poor friar.

Délicieux's complex nature has been the subject of scholarly debate. In addition to a raft of articles written by specialists of the period, his three major biographers—Jean-Barthélemy Hauréau in the nineteenth century, Michel de Dmitrewski in the twentieth, Alan Friedlander in the twenty-first—have all held the man up to close scrutiny, in an attempt to divine his motivations. What emerges from these studies is a composite picture of a firebrand, imbued with profound spirituality and possessed of exceptional intelligence, at odds with the persecuting reflex of his time and the cruelty and spiritual corruption of inquisition.

In essence, Bernard believed there are some things that a society must not do. He believed that the two guides in the conduct of his life, Francis of Assisi and Jesus of Nazareth, would have condemned many of the activities and certainties of the Church of his day. In condoning the rack and the stake, the Church had betrayed its origins, its principles. This was an extraordinarily brave position in an era when the use of terror and torture had become the norm in dealing with dissidence. In a larger sense, Bernard's true confraternity is the community of courageous men and women throughout history who have resisted the slide into barbarism. Faced as he was by inquisition, Délicieux's struggle concerned secret proceedings, unlawful detention, and the abuse of power. To him inhumane incarceration and judicial violence were not consonant with civilization.

That he acted on this belief attests to his courage; that he was able to do so, to the particular historical moment in which he lived. If the twelfth century was the one in which the books were opened and the cathedrals begun, the thirteenth may be said to be the one where the books were catalogued and the prisons built. Experimentation gave way to codification. Not only the Church was engaged in this—other, competing structures of power and control had emerged to undertake the same task.

Délicieux, who lived at the dawn of the fourteenth century, looked to Paris, not to Rome, for authority. The invigorated French monarchy, its law courts, officers, and tax collectors mushrooming throughout the thirteenth century so as to consolidate secular power, stood squarely in the way of the Church by Bernard's day. It might be just as cruel and oppressive, but it was separate. If he could not fight the Church from within, he felt he could fight it from without. Brother Bernard understood his times—he seized the cudgel of the monarchy to beat back the brutality of the inquisition.

Aided by the king's men and by a citizenry whipped into a frenzy by his preaching, Bernard put his convictions into practice in a very public way. In Carcassonne at the turn of the century, Bernard comprehensively sabotaged the inquisition, which he believed not only oppressive but also rotten to the core. At the same time, he stymied the powerful bishop of a neighboring town, Albi, who had used the threat of prosecution to extort money from his rich parishioners. Bernard's greatest triumph came in 1303, when he convinced the royal constabulary to storm the jail of the inquisition in Carcassonne and remove its long-suffering prisoners. Truly a singular moment in the Middle Ages, the freeing of the men from the Wall, as the prison was known, fired once again the imagination of Jean-Paul Laurens, whose rendering of the event now hangs in the city hall of Carcassonne. For these activities, Bernard won the adulation of townsfolk fed up with living in fear—and incurred the white-hot wrath of the Dominicans, the other great brotherhood of friars, whose members staffed the inquisition in Languedoc. In the days of Bernard's supremacy, these same friars were openly mocked in the streets of Carcassonne, as townspeople smashed in the windows of their church and made the raucous cawing sound of the crow on seeing them approach.

But the French monarchy, for reasons of state, eventually turned against the Franciscan; Bernard lost his cudgel. Amazingly, he attempted to find another one—by engaging in a seditious attempt to detach Languedoc from France and attach it to another kingdom. Miraculously escaping with his life in this unsuccessful venture, he then became a leader of the Spiritual Franciscans, a party of the brotherhood intent on hewing to the dictates of poverty preached by Francis of Assisi—even if that meant disobeying the papacy. The pope, not just the king, became angry with Bernard, and his purist Franciscan allies were declared heretics.

This last twist in his story contains an irony, for against all of Bernard's high-risk activities looms the ghostly presence of the Cathars, heretics par excellence. A pacific but heterodox Christian credo, Catharism had been mercilessly crushed by the forces of codifying orthodoxy in the thirteenth century, although courageous sympathizers of the creed still trod the byways of Languedoc in Bernard's day. Indeed, as the flamboyant Franciscan had driven the Dominican inquisitors literally to distraction, the Cathars were able to regroup stealthily in Languedoc for one final flowering of their faith.

A personal itinerary this perilous usually ends badly. The story of Bernard Délicieux is, sadly, no exception. Arrested in Avignon on the pope's order in 1317, he was tried in Carcassonne two years later. With so many enemies made, it is hardly surprising that there were more than one hundred counts listed in the docket of charges brought against him. These can be grouped together in four specific areas: obstructing the inquisition, high treason, adherence to heretical notions of poverty, and the murder of a pope through black magic. Délicieux was interrogated, cross-examined, tortured, broken; dozens of witnesses testified against him; and he was sentenced to a harsh solitary confinement that he did not long survive. The inquisition ground on, untrammeled henceforth by any man of his caliber.

To chronicle the life of Bernard Délicieux poses something of a challenge. The years before and after the period of his anti-inquisitorial activity at the turn of the century remain shrouded in darkness. The brief biographical sketch of his early life given above contains just about all that we know of him from the 1260s through the 1290s. The last part of his life, 1305–1320, is not as meager in detail as the first, yet it pales into near-nothingness in comparison to the six-year period at his midlife, from 1299 to 1304. Those years streak across the historical record like a Roman candle, incandescent in detail.

The reason for this spotlight is the trial held in 1319, the subject of Laurens' *Agitateur*. Scores of witnesses were called and much of their invaluable testimony has come down to us in transcripts of the proceedings. His judges, by no means priestly hacks intent on revenge, labored to make sense of what had happened in Languedoc fifteen years earlier. The trial was a torment for him, a gift for us. In 1996, an American historian undertook the task of collating, transcribing, and publishing the charges, depositions, interrogations, cross-examinations, and judgments of the trial. Five years after that, Cathar specialist Jean Duvernoy rendered the Latin of the original into a modern vernacular, French, allowing for wider scrutiny of this astonishing collection of documents. They open wide a window onto a campaign for freedom that occurred seven hundred years ago. In them, the voices of the historical actors, the conflicting memories, the evasions and confessions of the accused, and the tenacity of the investigating judges mingle with such a wealth of everyday detail that the usual inferences necessary for the writing of narrative history can be kept to a minimum.

However rich this source, it cannot do justice to the dangerous complexity of the era in which Bernard lived—and which must first be understood to make sense of his story. A time riven by dispute between a ruthless king and an imperious pope, enlivened by plots of mass arrest and murder, and rich in discontent, rivalry, and riot, the opening of the fourteenth century presents a vivid, almost frightening tapestry against which the revolt led by the Franciscan must be set. Bernard's world was profligate in incident, interconnected and consequential. The actions of the great on the larger stage of western Europe buffeted his Languedoc, as did, just as importantly, the steady growth of the repressive apparatus in Carcassonne and Toulouse and the resistance to it. When, at last, the storms had abated by the second decade of the century and repression resumed unchallenged, Bernard paid the price. He, along with Catharism and Spiritual Franciscanism, met a violent end, the gentler Christianities represented by both the friars and the heretics crushed by a vengeful orthodoxy. Only the memory of Brother Bernard Délicieux—and his example—remained.

Part I

The World of Bernard Délicieux

CHAPTER ONE
THE BRIDGE AT ROME

IN THE *Inferno*, Dante Alighieri has the pimps and whores in Hell troop past each other on a bridge. Miserable but meek, they are whipped into order by a diabolical traffic cop, each single file of people keeping to its side of the passage. The image is odd, for the thought of a medieval mob does not usually suggest pedestrian discipline. Such behavior seems more modern, more conformist, more housebroken: T. S. Eliot, a student of Dante, has the drudges of his *Wasteland* trudging across London Bridge, as forlorn in their twentieth-century funk as the Florentine's damned of the fourteenth.

Yet the original models for these dark rivers of humanity were of this world, and fully medieval, for they lived in the year 1300. Their bridge spanned the Tiber and was unimaginably old even then, having been built by the emperor Hadrian to give access to the hulking mausoleum he constructed for himself on the right bank of the river. By Bernard Délicieux's time, eleven and a half centuries later, that mausoleum had become the Castel St. Angelo, and its bridge the Ponte St. Angelo. The reason for its heavy foot and equestrian traffic in the year 1300 was a great celebration. Dante commanded his underworld denizens to do as the Romans do:

> *As when the Romans, because of the multitude*
>
> *Gathered for the Jubilee, had pilgrims cross*
> *The bridge with one side kept for all those bound*
> *Toward St. Peter's, facing the Castle, while those*

> *Headed toward the Mount were all assigned*
> *The other side.*

Not only Romans were on the bridge. Pilgrims came from all over Europe, having heard that their sins would be forgiven in exchange for going through a few devotional motions and loosing liberally the strings of their purses. The year 1300 had been declared a Jubilee, the first in Christendom, and all believers were summoned to Rome to celebrate. To gain remission of all their sins, pilgrims were enjoined to visit the four papal basilicas of the city several times during their stay. Hordes descended on St. John Lateran, St. Peter's, Santa Maria Maggiore, and St. Paul's Outside the Walls. Of the last a traveler wrote: "Day and night two priests stood at the altar of St. Paul's holding rakes in their hands, raking in infinite money."

With hundreds of thousands streaming through the city, the sheer size of the event gave pause. A gentleman of Florence, Giovanni Villani, was so struck by the sight of so many people that he was moved to undertake his *Nuova Cronica*, a valuable chronicle of his native city and the Italian peninsula in the first half of the fourteenth century. And Dante, Villani's brilliant compatriot, chose to set his *Divina Commedia* amidst the crush and chaos of Holy Week in Rome in 1300.

The great gathering served up an ample sampler of medieval society, as matron, maiden, and wench jostled for elbow room on the bridge with graybeard, squire, and gallant. Noble mingled with peasant, bumpkin with bishop, merchant with purse-snatcher, sinners all, hoping to guarantee themselves a secure berth in the afterlife. Whether, under this heightened expectation, the bridge over the Tiber took on the jolly allure of a Breughel painting or the madness of a Bosch is something we shall never know, but eyewitnesses attested to a crazed enthusiasm in the air.

The impresario behind this lucrative giddiness was an old Roman nobleman, Benedetto Caetani, known to history as Pope Boniface VIII. A brilliant scholar of canon law and an equally accomplished actuary of church accounts, Boniface was the very model of a medieval papal monarch, curling a lip at the ludicrous pretensions of secular princelings when he alone, as pope, held dominion over all of humanity in this world and the next: "We declare, we proclaim, we define," reads the famous foghorn of a sentence concluding his bull *Unam Sanctam*, "that it is absolutely necessary for salvation that every human creature be subject to the Roman Pontiff."

Boniface may be said to be the medieval pope who most resembled his Renaissance successors in excessive self-regard. Taking his cue from Hadrian and his mausoleum, by the Jubilee he had had his workmen put the finishing touches on his massive marble tomb at the Vatican, complete with a fresco showing the keys of spiritual power in the grip of Boniface, and not St. Peter, who is depicted as some sort of apostolic deputy. The expansive pope had called the Jubilee to celebrate the commonwealth of Christendom, of which he believed himself to be the undisputed leader. The religion of Jesus had been out in the open in Rome for nearly a millennium, which was reason enough to celebrate.*

Pope Boniface looked out over the multitudes with satisfaction. He had taken care to have his likeness adorn several monuments of the city, as visible manifestation that Rome, and by extension all of Christendom, had its monarch. Despite the majesty surrounding his person, Benedetto Caetani's transformation into Boniface VIII had not passed without unseemly incident. His predecessor, Celestine V, an octagenarian hermit, had been pulled from his limestone cave and made pontiff in 1294 when squabbling clans of aristocrats could not come up with a compromise candidate from among their numbers. Far too holy to discharge the duties of the office, within months a despairing Pope Celestine, who wanted nothing so much as to return to his mountain fastness, repeatedly sought advice about abdication from experienced cardinals, who sagely counseled that he could, indeed, resign his office. One of those cardinals happened to have been Benedetto Caetani— who then acquired the papal tiara for himself, but not before adding a second tier, signifying temporal power, to the crown. After this bit of legerdemain, he then reneged on a promise to let Celestine return to his hermitage, ordering him kept under lock and key until the old man dutifully died.

Boniface demonstrated his legitimacy and his position at the pinnacle

---

* By the Edict of Milan in 313, Emperor Constantine granted its legitimacy.

of Christendom through the great numbers of the faithful eager to acclaim their *papa*. At his apartments at the Lateran, a new loggia had been completed, from which he could greet his flock in person from a balcony, or failing that, have his image, as immortalized in a newly completed fresco, bless any of his eager children who turned their adoring gaze upward.* This outpouring of affection was a testament to success, proof that the dream of the medieval papacy, from the great popes Gregory VII through Innocent III to himself, had finally been realized. The Vicar of Christ had at last been recognized as the unrivaled leader of Europe and, soon, the world.

On the strength of the adulatory acclaim in his city, Boniface may have fancied himself the unchallenged paladin of Christian civilization; more likely, as an intelligent politician, he may just have made noises to that effect to mask the weaknesses he had discerned in his position. For the hard truth of the matter was that the presumptions of the medieval papacy were dangerously close to unraveling definitively. The papacy in the Jubilee year brings to mind a heroine of a nineteenth-century novel, always at her loveliest, eyes aglimmer, complexion aglow—just prior to expiring. So too with the monarchical medieval pontificate in 1300, so stately, so mesmerizing and magnificent, but just as doomed to disappearance. The pilgrims crowding the bridge over the Tiber were devout, but not devoted; they would witness, indeed usher in, challenges to the old order during the first decades of the fourteenth century as resentments grew and circumstances changed. Through these roiling waters men such as Bernard Délicieux navigated, their acts of courage and defiance observed, perhaps applauded, by those watching from the bridge. The supreme pontiff, or *pontifex maximus*, a title borrowed from ancient Rome signifying he who builds the bridge and guides the souls across it, would in a very short time be nothing more than a toll collector on that bridge, and, as such, a sitting duck for his Reformation critics in the not-too-distant future. And within a few years following the Jubilee, to pay that collector one would cross not the Ponte St. Angelo but the Pont d'Avignon. Not only did the papacy's move to its seventy-year exile in Avignon shatter Boniface's dream and profoundly alter the Church, it also brought the great machinery of

* The fresco may have been executed by Giotto.

papal power uncomfortably close to Languedoc and its agitator, Bernard Délicieux.

Many crowding the Roman bridge in the year 1300 did not have counterparts in 1200 or 1100, as their place in society was of recent creation. Without these newcomers, the career of the friar of Carcassonne would not have been possible. Among them were men in white robes draped with a black scapular, many of their tonsured pates housing a fevered, fanatical intellect. These were the Dominicans, the brothers of the Order of the Friars Preachers. They had not existed a century earlier, yet by 1300 they had hundreds of houses and convents throughout the length and breadth of Europe. Shock troops, scholars, administrators, inquisitors, and eventually popes, the Dominicans were, above all else, the *domini canes*—the hounds of the Lord.

Matching them in numbers marched a legion of similarly soulful men, in simple brown or gray robes: the Franciscans, or the Order of the Friars Minor. Coevals of the Dominicans (both Orders date from the early 1200s), the Franciscans rivaled the men in black and white in their explosive expansion during the course of the thirteenth century. However, the fierceness of their piety came to be directed at divisions within their own ranks. Bernard Délicieux partook fully of this Franciscan infighting.

Together these two brotherhoods (and other smaller religious groupings), known collectively as the mendicant friars, had arisen from the longings awakened by revival. In the eleventh and twelfth centuries a once-drowsy Europe had founded new towns, revivified old ones, launched crusades, cracked the books, begun the construction of soaring cathedrals, and taken to trade routes choked by the weeds of millennium-long neglect. This burst of activity engendered a new outlook and an impatience with the haughty prelates, hidebound monks, and illiterate parish priests who were conspicuously failing to give spiritual succor in a time of change.

Into the breach stepped men more attuned to their day. At first came charismatic outliers—lone itinerant preachers—then informally organized groupings of laymen interpreting clandestine, vernacular versions of the Bible. All were dedicated to pointing out the correct heading to townspeople left rudderless in a new world of grasping guild and showy burgher. Wealth, the filthy lucre that would damn one to Hell, was accruing; the Church itself, its great reformers of the early medieval period having successfully urged it to engage with the world, had evolved into a multinational machinery of the here and now, enacting laws, deposing dynasties, starting wars, imposing taxes, endowing benefices, anathematizing, excommunicating, imposing interdicts—in short, behaving as an overweening institutional technocracy. As for the holy men and women of the Church, they were locked in monasteries, quietly living out exemplary lives of piety in the wilderness, their backs turned to the laity, their concerns otherworldly.

As a reaction to both the bedevilment of wealth and the spiritual remoteness of the institutional Church, the idea of apostolic poverty, living a penniless life in the imitation of Christ, rapidly gained ground. More important, this imitation of Jesus' humanity—itself a novel thing for the Christian to think about—carried with it the obligation to do as the Nazarene had done and preach to the people. Holy beggars stripped to the waist, fakirs at fairgrounds and in meadows, became part of the medieval civic fabric, their message about penance as prelude to personal salvation issuing forth from their heaving, emaciated chests, as their listeners, man and woman alike, swooned ecstatically in the dust and the straw. Worse yet, for a Church adamantly opposed to an increasingly literate laity giving its own reading of scripture, came those who not only viewed the meaning of this scripture differently from that of the dominant orthodoxy, but went so far as to say that the insitutional pyramid with Rome at its apex was the edifice of the devil. Of this latter group, the Cathars, or Albigensian heretics, were the most successful, winning large followings in Languedoc in southern France and Lombardy in northern Italy. To them the Church was the enemy, the impostor, the creature of the evil God that had created the world; their God, the good God announced by Jesus, could be reached only by living a life of apostolic poverty.

In the first decade of the thirteenth century, a hundred years before the Jubilee crowded the bridge, the founder of the Dominicans, a Castilian priest named Domingo de Guzmán, or Dominic, met the Cathars in Languedoc. His beloved Church was woefully unacquainted with the zeitgeist of destitution. It had excommunicated orthodox proponents of poverty and was now attempting to overawe the heterodox Cathars through revivalist preaching tours conducted by papal emissaries decked out in opulent finery.* It was difficult to convince an ascetic of one's spiritual bona fides, Dominic realized, while wrapped in an acre of silk.

Dominic ordered the pope's men to doff the fancy dress and adopt at least a simulacrum of apostolic poverty. The zealous Spaniard then sought out the Cathars and invited them to debate. The heretics believed all of the sacraments of the Church, including marriage, to be illegitimate practices; the cross, a symbol of imperial Roman torture and nothing more; the creator God of the Old Testament, the equivalent of the devil; the notion of Hell, an absurd fabrication; the fate of all men and women as creatures of matter, a repeated return to this vale of tears; and the entire edifice of hierarchy and grandeur ruled from Rome, a monstrously demonic fraud hoisted on Christians of goodwill by a cabal of ruthless voluptuaries enslaved to the pleasures of the flesh and the appetite for gain.

Given the heat these debates between Catholic and Cathar must have generated, Dominican lore soon produced the Miracle of Fire. During one of them, in Fanjeaux, a town south of Carcassonne, some nefarious Cathars supposedly threw Dominic's debating notes, or his breviary, into the fireplace, but the document refused to burn, drifting up and up and up until, at last, it scorched a ceiling beam (still on display at the Dominican church there). However fireproof his notes, Dominic did not win many Cathars back to orthodoxy—but his steadfast selflessness attracted a large following of like-minded men, and soon the Dominican order, begun in Toulouse, awaited papal approval as a confraternity of mendicant friars.

The Cathars, pyromanes or not, were then mercilessly persecuted by the Albigensian Crusade, a twenty-year, papally sponsored series of atrocities begun in 1209 that aimed to eliminate them from the face of the earth. The scorched-earth wars of the Crusade effectively ended the independence of Languedoc, which would in a few generations become a part of France, but it failed to extirpate the heresy. From the 1230s on, the Cathar survivors of the years of ferocity had to face a permanent, Dominican-dominated innovation: inquisition. Involved in the genesis of Dominican austerity and, later, in the spread

---

*Among those excommunicated were, notably, the Poor Men of Lyon, or the Waldenses.

of Dominican inquisitorial activity aimed at rooting out every last one of them, the Cathars would also be a bone of contention in the Order's conflict with Bernard Délicieux, the standard-bearer of the Franciscans in Languedoc.*

The Franciscans differed from their Dominican brethren in several respects. Their founder, Giovanni Francesco di Bernadone, or Francis of Assisi, was a layman. The son of a well-to-do textile merchant, Francis threw off the trappings of wealth and spontaneously embraced a life of indigence and inspiration. Soon he was joined in this revolt against comfort by other sons of affluent traders—but not by the sons of the peasantry, as poverty held no romance for those born into it. Together Francis and his followers took to the roads of Umbria, sleeping rough, refusing to touch money or women, begging for food and preaching the need for repentance.

Hagiographical embellishments aside, Francis of Assisi must have been stupendously charismatic, a superstar of spirituality. To find a pious personage of equal power, a holy man in the right place at the right time, one would have to go back six centuries to the Prophet Muhammad. When Francis famously preached to the birds, he undermined the heretical belief, prevalent in the nurseries of heterodoxy in neighboring Lombardy, that nature and creation were evil. When he traveled on crusade and set out across the Nile delta alone to seek and gain an audience with the Ayyubid sultan, Malik al-Kamil, a nephew of the great Saladin, Francis displayed both missionary panache and a willingness to engage in dialogue.† And when he—dirty, scruffy, and serene—dared go to Rome and confront the greatest medieval pope, Innocent III, the man who lit the bonfires of the Albigensian Crusade and whom Boniface VIII, the pope of the Jubilee, vainly tried to imitate, Francis showed a fearlessness bred of unshakable conviction. The times were on his side. The saint's first biographer had Innocent imperiously dismissing the beggar, then dreaming of him that night, seeing Francis, Atlas-like, shouldering the massive load of the Church of St. John Lateran, then the mothership of Christendom.

Innocent decided to channel the spiritual athleticism of this motley

---

* It would be too great a leap to say that Dominic consciously copied the Cathar clergy.
† This was during the Fifth Crusade, in 1219.

crew of ragtag beggars into reinvigorating the Church. In the decades to follow, that daring decision to accept rather than to anathematize the mendicant friars proved resoundingly right. Within a few generations, after jettisoning some of the more impractical dictates of destitution, the Dominicans and Franciscans had stormed the nascent institutions of the thirteenth century. The fledgling universities—at such centers as Bologna, Paris, and Oxford—became hotbeds of recruitment and brotherly achievement. Even a partial roll call of friars of genius from their first century—Roger Bacon, Albertus Magnus, Thomas Aquinas, Robert Grosseteste, Bonaventure, John Duns Scotus—gives an idea of how influential the brothers were in shaping the Western intellectual tradition. Even the fellow usually credited with slicing scholasticism to pieces with his logical razor, William of Occam, was a Franciscan.

But their reach extended far beyond the universities. Proselytizing missions were dispatched to the Muslim world (often with friars actively seeking martyrdom by insulting the Prophet in their harangues) and to places farther afield, as in the Franciscan 1294 embassy to the Mongol khan in China.* At home, hospitals were set up, convents established and churches built. The Franciscans gradually went from a lay confraternity to a clerical one, dispensing sacraments, hearing confessions, and celebrating mass. As for the Dominicans, who had been disciplined and clerical from the outset (Dominic had a knack for organization sorely lacking in the dreamy Francis), they took to the pastoral task as well.

Not that the friars were all living embodiments of some unblemished Christian ideal. With expansion and the normalization of the orders came a watering down of their initial purity: the supposedly gentler Franciscans became inquisitors in some parts of Europe, most notably in Provence and Tuscany—although they were discharged from their duties in the latter province by Boniface because of their venality. The Friars Preachers and the Friars Minors competed fiercely over real estate—who would get the best building site in any given town—and over wealthy benefactors. Landing a rich corpse, with the requisite burial bequests, helped put a lot of food on their communal table, so unseemly squabbles over dead grandees could break out. Few things were

---

* Beijing got its first Catholic church in 1299.

exempt in this quarrel of the mendicants: the evangelization of Bosnia, for example, was held up for several years as Franciscans and Dominicans fought bitterly over who would have the honor of going there first. And the two Orders did not just have each other as brotherly enemies. Very early on they had earned the hostility of ordinary priests and bishops for diverting the faithful—and their funds—away from them. The newcomers were seen as poachers, and their runaway success as the thirteenth century progressed created suspicions that behind their convent walls might lie a very nonapostolic opulence.

Yet, overall, the fat indolent brother of folklore lay in the future, for the dynamic men of the first blossoming of the mendicants were by no means cut from the same cloth as Friar Tuck. To the contrary, the best of these men were engaged in what their literature calls metanoia, a heartfelt conversion in the struggle to get closer to God. Had they lived on another shore of the Mediterranean, they would have called their journey "the greater jihad."

As they crossed the Ponte St. Angelo, to celebrate the Jubilee with their papal protector, they had reason to look back on the past century with a great deal of satisfaction. They had reshaped the Church and Europe.

The friars were at their apogee. Others on the bridge were, unwittingly, nearing their vanishing point. They were men in white cloaks embroidered with a red cross. Influential and incalculably rich, these were the Knights Templar.

The Temple was one of the two great orders of warrior monks—the other was the Hospital—to have waged war against the Muslims and protected pilgrims to Outremer, the crusader states of the Levant. In 1300, however, Outremer was no more. The last toehold had been relinquished just nine years earlier, when St. Jean d'Acre had been lost to the armies of the Mameluke sultan.* The Templars and Hospitallers had put up a heroic fight, but they were eventually thrown back into the sea, a Muslim ambition since the crusaders had first arrived in Palestine at the close of the eleventh century.

The Hospitallers stayed on in the region by moving to Rhodes. Not

---

* St. Jean d'Acre is present-day Akko, Israel.

so the Templars. They had been content to retire to their commanderies and castles in Europe. They might have lost their *raison d'être* but they most definitely still had their *avoir*. Two centuries of moneylending by the Templars—issuing letters of credit in exchange for deposits at home—and the constant acquisition of new properties and receipt of new bequests had left them immensely wealthy. Such wealth excited jealousy, but they were untouchable. Like the friars, they too answered only to the pope. Barons and kings might fume, but whenever they needed money it was to the Templars that many turned. No matter that they were crusaders in a lost cause, the Templars believed themselves to be indispensable, a belief that was to prove horribly wrongheaded within a decade of their traveling to Rome for the Jubilee.

But doubtless the largest contingent shuffling across the Ponte St. Angelo was the laity, the ordinary people immortalized later in the fourteenth century by Chaucer and Boccaccio. Some would have been prosperous artisans in colorful tunics and hose, their womenfolk adorned with extravagances that a scandalized Church tried to curb through the encouragement of sumptuary laws. Western Europe had seen two hundred years of growth, what historians call the Commercial Revolution, and the thirteenth century had been devoid of invasion and major war. These pilgrims, then, were the products of that expansion, living at a time when the medieval period shone with a vigor that is even now underestimated. The humanists of the Renaissance did a good hatchet job on their predecessors—labeling their architecture barbarian, or "gothic"; relegating their era to intermediate "middle" ages that a dullard humanity had to endure between the glories of Antiquity and the Renaissance. Given that legacy, it is difficult to appreciate their achievements.

In Brother Bernard's day international trade was several orders of magnitude greater than it ever had been in the most cosmopolitan period of the Roman Empire. The medieval merchant and mariner were intrepid, their manufacturing counterparts prolific. Wind and water had been harnessed throughout western Europe, and from such booming textile centers as Bruges and Ghent great bolts of woolen cloth were ferried regularly down to the fairs of Champagne, where the Italians, laden with their own products and those originating in the East, would be awaiting them. Trade had exploded, capital had multiplied exponentially.

And while the Crusades may have been a disaster for the West's image in the lands of Islam, they nonetheless opened the eyes of Venetian, Pisan, and Genoan merchants to the bounties of places such as Aleppo and Damascus, way stations on the Silk Road from the far East. Even an event as abjectly unredeeming as the atrocity that kicked off the thirteenth century—the vicious Crusader sack of Constantinople in 1204—did not come without benefits: for sixty years or so, Latin westerners ruled Greek Constantinople, and soon the Black and Aegean seas of its great hinterland saw the sails of Venetian and Genoan traders.

If the emergence of the friars signaled spiritual vitality, then the activities of these merchants and townsmen showed remarkable creativity. Throughout western Europe the commune with its consuls—town governance by an association of all the wealthy traders of a city—became the norm, its participants truculent defenders of their rights, as set down in hard-won charters in the face of clerical and noble opposition. Banking was more or less invented in the years preceding the Jubilee. Medieval Italians pioneered accounting methods recognizable to a modern, and long-distance lending of capital soon became commonplace. The precious number zero, borrowed from the Arabs, who had borrowed it from the Indians, was embraced by the northern Italians of Lombardy, who set up shop in most major capitals. Almost every important European city still has its Lombard Street.*

Bernard Délicieux's world was not one of toothless oafs shivering in the shadow of their lord's castle keep. Many of the mobile energetic masses on the bridge of the Jubilee, thanks to the exigencies of trade and commerce, were literate, no longer dependent on the priestly class to make sense of the world for them. Many were bankers, traders, skilled craftsmen, and lawyers—for the medieval era was as litigious as our own. While a wrenching century lay in wait for them, with its Hundred Years' War, recurrent famines, and Black Death, the men and women of the year 1300 still had the wind in their sails.

---

* Boccaccio, according to tradition, was born in the rue des Lombards in Paris.

CHAPTER TWO

THE KING'S MEN AT THE DOOR

A T DAYBREAK THERE CAME A CRASHING at the door. In some places, a weighty metal door knocker thundered down again and again; in others, the wood splintered under the hammer blows of a great mace; in yet others, the portal swung open soundlessly, guided from within by a betrayer's hand. All over France, in Paris, Troyes, Reims, Toulouse, Tours, Poitiers, and many isolated manors in the countryside, the king's men at arms rushed through thresholds and rounded up startled knights. It was dawn on Friday, October 13, 1307, the day of reckoning for the Knights Templar.

In subsequent months, the once-proud members of the Order were taken whimpering from their dark dungeons and viciously tortured. The rack, the leg screw, the hot iron—nothing was too inhumane to wring confessions from them. The charges? Spitting on the cross. Idolatory of the goat Baphomet. Assassination of a pope. Sodomy. The obscene kiss. Heresy. Blasphemy. Usury. Lack of charity. And many more. The cascade of lurid accusation was meant to distract from the purpose of the whole operation: to destroy a competing center of power and comprehensively loot its fabulous treasury.

Given the sordidness of the affair, the trial of the Templars, which dragged on for years, remained the subject of speculation long after their leaders were burned alive on an island in the Seine. Whether they were guilty of at least some of these charges or wholly innocent has enlivened centuries of historical and esoteric debate. Certainly they were no saints—"drink like a Templar" ran the conversational commonplace in medieval France—yet the grotesque tapestry of accusation hints at outright fantasy. Only very recently has a scholar found in the archives of the Vatican proof that the Church, for its part, did not find the Templars guilty of anything.

But there was, indubitably, a guilty party: the men who engineered the mass arrest. Like the pedestrian discipline on the Ponte St. Angelo, the event can be viewed as distinctly unmedieval, combining as it did careful planning, covert deployment, and simultaneous execution on a grand scale. For an era that saw mounted knight and wild-eyed mercenary regularly make sordid messes out of pennant-snapping battle orders, the arrest of the Templars stands out as a superbly coordinated act. To find its rival in the sudden, ferocious choreography of state terror, one would have to travel forward to the sixteenth century and the St. Bartholomew's Day Massacre, or to the twentieth, with its Kristallnacht. The event was truly abominable, the act of very dangerous operatives. These were the king's men.

The king whose operatives took down the Templars was Philip IV of France, usually called Philip the Fair—for his tall, handsome bearing, not his character.* France had been fortunate in the thirteenth century to have had three outstanding, long-lived monarchs in the Capetian line: Philip Augustus (Philip II), Saint Louis (Louis IX), and Philip the Fair. The French star was on the rise. "France" may have consisted of a congeries of competing duchies, independent communes, and episcopal jurisdictions, but the royal domain nonetheless was growing and being consolidated. Brother Bernard's Languedoc, for example, had come into the French fold only recently. On the death of the last Count of Toulouse in 1249, the land was held in what was called appanage, a sort of lifetime lease, by a member of the Capetian family. On his death, in 1271, Languedoc became incorporated into the kingdom, and France, improbably, now touched the Mediterranean. Not that the speakers of the *langue d'oc* felt fully French overnight; to the contrary, Bernard's actions would have been impossible without widespread resentment of the new northern masters.

The inexorable growth of the kingdom governed from Paris would change the course of medieval history. Prior to France's rise, all eyes

---

* French Philippe le Bel avoids any such misunderstanding.

had been riveted on the Germanic emperors and their jockeying for power and land with the papacy in Italy and beyond. The greatest of them, Frederick II, had shaken up the first half of the thirteenth century by doing a credible imitation of the Antichrist: consorting with Muslims, warring with popes, adopting Eastern manners, engaging in philosophical speculation, indulging in oriental despotism, and just generally being an out-of-time genius of intrigue, learning, curiosity, vanity, and ruthlessness. His awed contemporaries, when not calling him the Antichrist, referred to him as *Stupor Mundi*, the Marvel of the World; on his passing at midcentury, the papacy wasted no time in crushing his descendants, its fierce and unprincipled determination to exterminate a great royal family ultimately debasing its claims to divinely guided leadership. Just as important, the 1268 beheading in the market square in Naples of sixteen-year-old Conradin, the last in Frederick's line, constituted a pivotal event in ensuring that Germany would remain a patchwork of statelets unable to stride the world properly until long into the future.

France was headed in another direction. Hitherto considered a fairly obedient child of the Church—"the Church's eldest daughter," went the customary piety—and the major source of manpower and money for crusades to Outremer, France had begun to flex its sinews and prepare itself to occupy center stage in European affairs, a position it would not relinquish for many centuries. The Commercial Revolution had been good to more than the thriving merchant republics of the Italian peninsula. France—or what was to consolidate as the unified country of that name—was a beneficiary of the boom, too, and, as Europe's largest and most populous territory, it constituted a power to be reckoned with.*

Its king was respected and feared, but not loved. Philip the Fair had been raised motherless, in a court filled with rumors of lethal scheming on the part of his stepmother and in the absence of his oft-warring father, Philip the Bold (Philip III). His biographers claim the career of his sainted grandfather, Louis IX, exercised a great influence on his lonely, suspicion-filled boyhood and came to serve him as an exemplar of Christian devotion and steady stewardship. Upon the death of his older brother, Philip became first in line for the throne and eventually

---

* Estimates range up to twenty million inhabitants.

ascended to it in 1285 at age seventeen. Surrounded by courtiers and the functionaries of the nascent Capetian state, the young king appeared from the outset a taciturn and difficult leader. He matured into a rather unpleasant man; in the words of one historian, "a captious, sternly moralistic, literalistically scrupulous, humourless, stubborn, aggressive, and vindictive individual, who feared the eternal consequences of his temporal deeds."

He was not entirely to blame. Kingship a hundred years earlier had principally involved trotting out on hawking parties trailed by one's itinerant entourage—a few priests, noble advisors, bedmates, servants, jongleurs, and fools—with occasional stops in courtyard and castle to render judgment, rein in minor vassals, or ride in tournaments. Indeed, prior to the reign of Philip Augustus in the late twelfth century, the French king's holdings in what we now call France were dwarfed by the French lands of his two greatest vassals, the king of England and the duke of Burgundy. By Philip the Fair's day in the late thirteenth century, the kingdom had multiplied in size, and the business of managing it was much more complex. Not only did the monarch act as the God-appointed feudal supremo, he had also to govern.

To meet the needs of this economic and political expansion, the great Capetians of the thirteenth century presided over the gradual building of a state ruled from the top. New law courts came into being, to rival those of the Church, and new taxes were levied to finance crusades and wars. The days of relying solely on a group of baronial vassals to scrounge up men at arms were coming to a close. Money was also needed for the ever-growing establishments of royal officials—tax collectors, judges, inspectors, soldiers—in Paris and the provinces. All this institutional novelty signaled a significant shift in outlook and functioning, one that would culminate, in the French experience, in royal absolutism and the divine right of kings.

The newly fledged universities of France, particularly the Sorbonne (named for Robert de Sorbon, Louis IX's confessor), were not, as is sometimes remarked, concerned with placing angels on pinheads. A fresh batch of Aristotle, much of it from the Islamic world via the translators of Spain, had landed on the desks of the schoolmen in the thirteenth century, with revolutionary consequences. Aristotle was mined not only for philosophical insight, in the delicate enterprise of reconciling Reason and Revelation, but also for his solid empiricism. Aristotle's notion of natural law and of politics dovetailed with the new realities. The mendicant friars studied the philosopher and looked toward God, but many others did the same and looked toward the King. Political thinking—dangerous, secular, national—began to develop. In a very influential manual of such thought, *De regimine principum* (On the Government of Princes), penned by Giles of Rome for Philip the Fair in 1286, the blueprint for royal rule according to the dictates of reason and natural law was laid out. The just king bent his knee to no one, not even the pope. And within a couple of generations of Giles' manual, another political thinker, Marsilius of Padua, baldly stated that the papacy's possession of lands was inimical to the idea of Christian kingship and to the Church's place in society.*

Such sedition toward the older medieval order was not just the stuff of undergraduate shouting matches in the taverns of the Left Bank. It formed a necessary corrective to Pope Boniface's failing dream of a continent-wide commonwealth. Men had to be found who were ready and willing to break with the past and venture into new territory. Fortunately, for the royal cause, the same schools that produced the theorists also produced the practitioners. This new class of educated laymen was suited to the challenge. Although not necessarily anticlerical, they used their elbows in getting rid of their literate priestly rivals in the growing administrations of law and the royal exchequer. Nor were they friends to the nobility, whose place at the king's side they sought to supplant. As for the low station of the great unwashed, from which some of them had escaped, these clerks felt no *nostalgie de la boue*. To the contrary, disdain was their dominant feeling toward the illiterate peasantry, as in this prayer recited half in jest by the medieval bureaucrats: "O God, who has sown discord between clergy and peasant, permit us by thy grace to live from their work, enjoy their wives, cohabit with their daughters, and delight in their death."

What also marked them, beside this dubious sense of humor, was their loyalty to the monarch. There was a simple reason for this: their

---

* It was only a matter of time before later humanists exposed the Donation of Constantine, an imperial decree of Constantine's granting the pope lands in Italy, as a medieval forgery concocted by a revenue-hungry curia.

fate was yoked to the king's. When fortune smiled on him, she smiled on them. When the king suffered setback, they felt it, too. If competing powers in the medieval free-for-all over jurisidiction—bishops, barons, burghers—gained the upper hand and encroached on the monarchy, the king's men saw their power and their purview shrink. Thus it was in their personal interest—quite apart from the theory behind the new dispensation—for the king to succeed, to trounce his enemies at home and abroad, and to acquire the wherewithal to lavish largesse on his devoted functionaries.

In such an airless atmosphere of ambition and risk, there was little oxygen for scruples to thrive. In the case of Philip the Fair, the men on whom he relied—the men behind the Templar operation and the men whom Bernard Délicieux would have to win over—stopped at nothing in reaching their goals. Historians have argued whether the king was their pawn or he their puppeteer, but what is indisputable is that their record impresses through its brutal exercise of power.

In the latter part of Philip's reign, the most prominent of the king's men was Guillaume de Nogaret. A man of Languedoc born at midcentury, he grew up on a modest manor near St. Félix de Caraman, a notorious locale in the annals of heresy.* In 1167, some one hundred years before Guillaume's lifetime, a well-attended conclave of Cathars had been held in St. Félix, brazenly, out in the open. The event had been unprecedented; indeed, it was never repeated. The conclave, in a strange echo of the conciliar meetings of cardinals and bishops of the Church, welcomed visiting heresiarchs from as far afield as Milan and Constantinople and lasted several days. The event at St. Félix would have been known and remembered a century later. Thus a slight whiff of heresy clung to Guillaume's garments because of his origins; it was even rumored his grandfather had been a Cathar sympathizer. This skeleton in his closet emboldened his enemies to invoke his background when opposing him and, it has been speculated, drove him to new degrees of zeal when wielding charges of heresy and sorcery against whichever of the king's foes he happened to be engaged in demonizing. In the mid-

---

* Its name today is St.-Félix-en-Lauragais.

1290s he moved from his chair in jurisprudence at the university in Montpellier to the halls of Philip's expensive new palace being built alongside St. Louis' Sainte-Chapelle in Paris.

Expensive is the operative word for Philip's reign. Whether waging war, hiring functionaries, endowing institutions, building residences, or living in the grand style befitting the dignity of his office, the king needed money. Guillaume de Nogaret found it. Together they hatched extraordinary schemes. The crown attacked the Lombard bankers, expropriating their assets and expelling them from the kingdom. The Jews of France suffered the same fate, and although bad treatment of the Jews had been something of a Capetian specialty, particularly under the pious Louis IX, Nogaret's outright theft of their property was audaciously bald. Another trick concerned debasing the coinage of the kingdom by reducing the amount of gold and silver it contained (Philip was called, behind his back, *faux-monnayeur*, "counterfeiter"). One such campaign of currency manipulation in 1306 resulted in the merchants of Paris taking to the streets to riot. The king, frightened for his life, found shelter in what was then the safest place in the kingdom: the headquarters of the Knights Templar, a castle just outside the city walls of Paris. He remained there, under their protection, until the unrest died down and the requisite number of rioters were hanged. The following year Nogaret had all of these same Templars arrested and tortured, and he moved much of their treasury out of that castle and to the Louvre. Ingrate, ruthless, Machiavellian *avant la lettre*—such are the traits that spring to mind when speaking of Philip's cadre of trained lawyers. Among the general population, they were hated.

Yet much of this pales when put alongside the king's relations with the pope. The eldest daughter of the Church had turned wanton. Christendom watched aghast, or perhaps amused, as Guillaume de Nogaret and his ilk humiliated the supreme pontiff at almost every turn. There had been prior medieval incidents pitting monarch against pope: the Investiture Contest of the eleventh century, which famously had a penitent Emperor Henry IV barefoot in the snows of Canossa; the extravagant twelfth-century penance meted out to England's Henry II for the slaying of Thomas Becket; and various crises involving excommunications and interdicts, to which the thirteenth-century *Stupor*

Mundi was no stranger. But Philip the Fair and Boniface VIII broke new ground in vituperation.

The conflict began, as ever, over money. Philip needed it for war against England. Like any medieval French monarch worth his salt, combating those known up until the First World War as the *ennemi héréditaire* came naturally. Indeed, fighting the English—or *les goddams*, as they were called more jocularly at the time—could be said to form a part of a French king's job description. One reason for this sturdy antipathy stemmed from familiarity and dynastic squabbling— royal houses and noble clans having cross-Channel ties of kinship. The greater reason, however, arose from the inconvenience of the English king's holding a huge part of what is now southwestern France: Aquitaine, or Guyenne, and much of Gascony. Philip, in the late 1290s, tried unsuccessfully to dislodge his brother-in-law, King Edward I of England, from Aquitaine in a protracted and expensive series of battles, somewhat of a dress rehearsal of the ruinous Hundred Years' War that was to begin four decades later. To finance the hostilities, both kings taxed the Church for revenue, to which Boniface objected strenuously by issuing blistering papal bulls. Such secular rerouting of church monies was not without precedent, but usually the monarch had the decency to ask first. Philip's men blithely decided to impound no less than half the revenues of the French Church every year. In their view, the king was the protector of the French Church; thus it was in fact his Church.

Boniface issued more strident proclamations, which were pointedly ignored. He tried diplomacy of an unusual kind: in 1297 he had Philip's grandfather, Louis IX, canonized as St. Louis. Philip was grateful but nonetheless extended his prohibition on the export of all gold from his kingdom, which cut into the Holy See's annual revenues even more. Boniface howled, wrote ever more insistent and in some instances insulting bulls, one of which Philip's men tossed into the fireplace. Unlike Dominic's notes, it burned. Another bull, *Ausculta Fili* ("Give ear, my son"), was waved dismissively in the spring of 1302 before an assembly of eight hundred clerics, nobles, and burghers—delegates of the three estates—from the altar of Notre Dame in Paris. Pierre Flote, the king's man making the presentation of the pope's latest missive, neglected to mention that the document he held had been edited by royal lawyers to make Boniface appear even more unreasonable than he already was. In

Flote's telling, the pope claimed that the king and his people were sub-servient to Rome in all matters, spiritual and temporal. The assembly—the Estates General—was suitably horrified, and voted to support the king in his struggle with the pope.

Like Flote, Guillaume de Nogaret also excelled at dragging the pope's name through the mud and exciting resentment directed at Rome. Thanks to him, intimations arose that Boniface's predecessor, the hermit Celes-tine, had been murdered or that at the very least Boniface's election had been illegitimate. The pope, Nogaret's whispering campaign added, might even be a heretic.

By the time Nogaret had fully taken the reins of the antipapal cam-paign, the subject of the dispute had changed from money to another medieval predilection, jurisdiction. The conflict deepened dramatically when the king's men took an unprecedented action: in 1301 they ar-rested a bishop, Bernard Saisset of Pamiers, a town near the Pyrenees. The bishop had been heard arguing that Languedoc should secede from the kingdom of France. A colorful and controversial figure, Saisset was to play an important role in the rise of Bernard Délicieux; here, on the stage of king and pope, he served as the spark setting off a conflagration that was waiting to happen.

The king had Saisset charged with high treason, heresy, simony, sorcery, fornication, and blasphemy.* If Philip was angry at the bishop, Boniface was now livid with the king. Like almost every pope of the preceding two hundred years, he was a lawyer, trained in canon law. He and his predecessors had an exacting view of the limits of temporal power over a member of the clergy. The prerogatives of the Church were guarded jealously, ferociously. If some sort of action was to be taken against Saisset, it had to be taken by a Church court. The dispute exem-plified perfectly the tension between a partisan of canon law, Boniface, and an advocate of territorial, secular law, Guillaume de Nogaret. The products of two separate strains of thirteenth-century codification, a priestly lawyer and a royal lawyer, stood toe to toe.

The pope summoned the French clergy to Rome in the autumn of 1302 to discuss their monarch's conduct. Many were brave enough to

---

* Simony is the selling of ecclesiastical offices. The word is derived from Simon Magus, the Samaritan sorcerer who tried to bribe the apostles in Acts 8:9–24.

go, some seeing God's hand in a military catastrophe dealt to Philip a few months earlier in which the powerful Pierre Flote had been slain. In response to this provocative conclave, Guillaume de Nogaret drew up a list of charges against Boniface himself, claiming the pope was a murderer who held office illegitimately, espoused heretical beliefs, and, with the usual medieval accusatory flourish, committed unspeakable and unnatural deeds. The fraudulent pope would be summoned to Paris to stand trial. This proposal represented an extraordinary nadir in the relation between Paris and Rome. But worse was to come.

In the late summer of 1303, an exasperated Boniface readied himself to excommunicate Philip the Fair and place his kingdom under interdict so that no religious services—masses, weddings, baptisms, funerals—could be performed there. Since their monarch would now be an excommunicate, that is, an outcast from the community of the faithful, the people of France would be freed from their allegiance to him. This was the heaviest weapon in the papal arsenal and had to be wielded advisedly. The pope retired to his residence in the hilltop town of his birth, Anagni, in the verdant Latium countryside south of Rome, to prepare the dreadful sentence against the greatest monarch in Christendom. The locale chosen to roll out this awful papal power could hardly have been more fitting: aside from Boniface himself, the town had produced three other thirteenth-century popes, including the indomitable Innocent III.*

On September 7, 1303, there came a crashing at the door. Soldiery could be heard running through the streets of Anagni. There were sounds of looting, fighting, dying. The pope's guards were overrun, his entourage fled. Boniface, now in his eighties, prepared for the worst.

Soon standing before him were the two leaders of the commando. One was Sciarra Colonna, of the family that detested his and whose cardinals had actively tried to undermine the pope in the interests of getting one of their own on the throne of St. Peter. The other was Guillaume de Nogaret.

Faced with the Italian and the Frenchman he hated most, Boniface

---

* The other two were Gregory IX and Alexander IV.

is said to have gestured with his hand and spat out, in the vernacular, *"E le cole, e le cape!"*—"Here is my neck, and here is my head." A source states that Sciarra obliged, slapping the old man hard until restrained by Nogaret. The king's man wanted his quarry alive, to be brought to France in chains for trial.

That was not to be, for three days later the people of Anagni rallied to the defense of their illustrious kinsman and drove the intruders from the town. The pope, severely shaken by the experience and humiliated by the theft of his worldly goods and the sack of his house, returned to Rome. Within a month the broken old man was dead.

The incident, known to history as the Outrage of Anagni, sent shock waves far and wide. That the pope—the Supreme Pontiff—could be manhandled by a band of rowdy mercenaries in the pay of the French king, in effect assassinated by them, was an unholy act worthy of infidels, not a reigning Christian monarch. Dante wrote scathingly of Philip in the *Purgatorio*, calling him "a new Pilate" crucifying Christ anew by attacking his vicar. Sciarra Colonna and Guillaume de Nogaret were the "two thieves" between whom Christ had been crucified. And yet this was the same Dante who despised Boniface for conspiring with his political enemies to banish him from his cherished Florence. He took care elsewhere to ensconce Boniface firmly and definitively in Hell for the crime of simony. That Dante should have felt obliged to come to the defense of the pope's memory in this affair is indicative of the indignation it must have aroused elsewhere.

But Nogaret and Philip did not blink. Nogaret launched a seven-year-long campaign to have Boniface tried posthumously, surely one of the most egregious instances of lawyerly chutzpah in history. His campaign of continued vilification ceased at last when a council of the Church wearily consented to take up the case, only to end up dismissing it. As a sop to the royal party, the churchmen lifted Nogaret's well-deserved excommunication.

In this overheated, tempestuous atmosphere, when a great Jubilee was called, a king denied the Church its income and its dignity, and his minister claimed the pope was a heretical criminal, a delegation arrived in 1301 before King Philip the Fair from far in the south of France. Their distant cities were in open revolt against the servants of Pope Boniface's Church. Many of these churchmen were corrupt, unjust, and, most important, harmful to the interests of the kingdom, declared the leader of the delegation. Philip, one can easily imagine, would have started at the mention of this last offense—he might even have looked searchingly into the eyes of the speaker, a Franciscan friar of unusual oratorical gifts.

As the king's ministers listened intently, Bernard Délicieux proclaimed that his city wanted peace. His companions seconded him. And they proposed a solution: the inquisitors had to be stopped.

CHAPTER THREE

THE HOLY OFFICE

CARCASSONNE RISES ON HIGH GROUND overlooking the tranquil river Aude. Or, rather, the Cité does, the episcopal and royal administrative city, surrounded by tall battlements and a parade of forbidding guard towers. This is the familiar postcard image of medieval Carcassonne, the one that attracts three million sightseers every year. Although it received a fanciful makeover in the nineteenth century at the hands of architect Eugène-Emmanuel Viollet-le-Duc, the Cité still retains a great measure of authenticity—a grandee of the Middle Ages miraculously stopping by to spend time with us. Its mass of old stone and fortification fires the imagination of the susceptible. The motto of the city's tourist board is "Carcassonne, un rêve qui se visite"—Carcassonne, a dream you can visit. Few places in Languedoc inspire such intimacy with people long gone.

There is another Carcassonne. The lower town, called the Bourg, is a rather raffish mix of the modern and historic that stretches out in the flats on the left bank of the Aude, to the west of the Cité. It is laid out in a grid, having been built explicitly for defensive purposes, normally to fend off the marauding English. The grid was constructed this way, and named the Bastide St. Louis, after England's Black Prince had destroyed the older medieval Bourg in the mid-fourteenth century. Much of the martial heritage still lives on—the modern city houses a marine infantry parachute regiment—as does the lively and long-standing commercialism in the crisscrossing of narrow streets. Although much of what he saw is now gone, Bernard Délicieux's Bourg was Carcassonne's beating heart, where merchant allies and other townspeople listened to his fiery sermons and took action against the hated Dominican inquisitors. Theirs, too, was a lively, raffish Bourg, and it was this part of Carcassonne, not the stately Cité standing aloof on a hilltop, that brought the authorities such grief.

To reach the Bourg from the Cité one must naturally descend. Once past the fortress of the royal governor and then the bishop's palace and the towers that held the offices and torture chambers of the inquisition, one emerges through a western gate onto a steep grassy slope. The path downward, called Trivalle, gradually becomes lined with houses, as it may have been seven hundred years ago. The warm domestic scene at that time then suddenly gave way to the cold fist of fear.

Nearer the river, off to the left of the Trivalle, rose the hulking prison of the inquisition, constructed in the reign of Louis IX and known thereafter as the Wall. Today, it must be conjured up in the mind's eye only, as it was long ago torn down. In Bernard's day, however, it loomed unmissable, halfway between the royal and priestly power of the Cité and the merchant and commercial ambition of the Bourg. In its dark stone cells rotted those convicted by secret trial and anonymous accusation. Built by a saint, maintained by the king, and staffed by black-robed friars, the Wall served as a daily reminder of the authority of Crown and Church. If they stood together, the people stood no chance. To break the hold of the inquisition, to shatter the climate of fear and betrayal, the Wall had to be attacked. Prior to the rise of Bernard Délicieux, no dissident of Carcassonne had realized that—even though its baleful presence could be seen every day from the upper stories of the Bourg's half-timbered houses and the western gates to the town. Its presence constituted a threat; in the view of a gifted rabble-rouser, it rose as a challenge.

Aside from the town mill at the riverside and the usual huddle of huts, the no-man's-land surrounding the Wall at the foot of the Cité contained no other structures of note.* There were, however, wells in this part of the city, which is why the hard men of the Albigensian Crusade attacked here in the hot summer of 1209, in the hope, soon realized, of making the panicked, overcrowded Cité surrender out of thirst. This, then, was the place that sealed the doom of Languedoc's

---

* The mill, known as the King's Mill, was an important source of royal revenue.

independence. The Wall, constructed a half century later, only empha-
sized this mournful reality.

Spanning the river is a fine medieval bridge, the Pont Vieux, which
was being built during the lifetime of Brother Bernard. The tendrils of
graceful willows reach down from the riverbanks to touch the gently
flowing water. Ahead is the Bourg proper, on the left bank, a noisier,
more populous settlement than the Cité, with its church spires and
market buildings. The first great square reached—indeed, the city's
largest—stretches out barren and rectangular, its smooth granite slabs
left unadorned. Its only notable vertical feature, a glass booth that reveals itself to be the top of an elevator shaft, betrays the unseen, underground parking lot below. At ground level, the flat slab of this Square
Gambetta looks like an immense tabula rasa, waiting to be inscribed.
On this spot there stood the Franciscan convent overseen by its prior,
Bernard Délicieux.

Rabies Carcassonensis, la rage carcassonnaise, Carcassonne rabies, or, better still, Carcassonne madness. Such was the term to describe the febrile
discontent in the Bourg as the year 1300 approached. Worse yet for the
Church, the madness was to spread virulently through the placid woad
fields of medieval Languedoc to the important city of Albi, infamous
for lending its name to the Albigensian heresy, or Catharism, 150 years
earlier.

The root of the anger was a long-standing irritant in the cities and
towns of the south: inquisitors. They had plagued Languedoc for seven
decades. The year 1229 saw the end of the Albigensian Crusade, a
twenty-year-long pageant of atrocity aimed at extirpating Catharism
and breaking the backbone of a fiercely independent region. The Church
realized that, while Languedocian independence was fatally injured, to
the future benefit of the French crown, the feared heresy still had many
adherents, even after the Crusade's years of savage repression and devas-
tation. In just one instance from the campaign that beggars the imagination, at the town of Lavaur midway between Toulouse and Albi, on a
spring afternoon in 1211, some four hundred people were burned alive
just outside its shattered battlements, as churchmen joyfully sang hymns
and northern nobles looked on. Earlier in the day, these same nobles

had torn the lady of Lavaur from her castle, thrown her down a well, and then hurled rocks on her as she lay dying in the dark. Then they hanged her brother. Given this behavior, and Lavaur was no exception, the madness in thirteenth-century Languedoc had not been confined to Carcassonne—or to the Church's enemies.

But Catharism, wounded and much reduced, nonetheless remained. Prior to the Crusade, the faith had been practiced openly; afterward, it went underground. The most important of the Languedoc nobles, the defeated count of Toulouse, Raymond VII, had by the terms of the peace treaty of 1229 pledged to continue the fight against the heresy. But his family, most notably his late father, had been notoriously loath to inflict punishment upon the people of Languedoc for crimes of conscience. Indeed, the competing power centers in medieval society, the rich town consuls, the merchants—even some of the local Catholic clergy—had family or friends of a heretical bent, or were themselves so. All of this was known only too well in Rome, so Pope Gregory IX forced Count Raymond to fund a university in Toulouse with the express purpose of defending the faith and training Dominican brothers. Dominic had founded his order in that city; it was only fitting to aid its expansion there. But Gregory had other, greater plans. These friars would go on to become inquisitors, answerable not to a bishop or a Dominican provincial, but to the pope alone. With the letter *Ille humani generis* in 1231 to a Dominican prior in Regensburg, he took the historic step of creating a papal inquisition, thereby ensuring himself a posterity of dubious distinction.* Two years later Gregory would write to the Dominicans in Languedoc instructing them to appoint inquisitors.

Much has been imagined about inquisitorial practice as a sort of malevolent and centralized medieval Department of Homeland Security. In reality, there was no unified inquisition, just individual appointments in certain jurisdictions for varying periods of time. The phantasmagoric uppercase "Inquisition" owes much of its existence to nineteenth-century liberal historians whose ideological repugnance toward the

* Regensburg is a Bavarian city on the Danube near Munich. The current pope, Benedict XVI, taught theology at the University of Regensburg from 1969 to 1977.

practice also informed the work of history painter Jean-Paul Laurens. That inquisition subsequently leached memorably into popular culture—for example, as buffoonish broad comedy (*Monty Python*) or literary villainy (*The Name of the Rose*)—only makes clarification more necessary.

At the outset, the rise of heresies in the eleventh and twelfth centuries—or, rather, the detection and definition of these heresies—put the men of the Church in a quandary as to how to handle a laity forming its own opinion about man's relation to the divine. When persuasion proved ineffective in bringing people back to orthodoxy, which itself was constantly undergoing modification and renovation, Rome looked back to old Rome, to the empire and institutions of which the Catholic Church came to feel itself the inheritor. Perusal of this authoritarian past focused on the *inquisitio*, a procedure by which the empire's legists hunted down those who were thought treasonous, disloyal, or guilty of some form of classical lèse-majesté. The investigator in old imperial Rome—the inquisitor—searched for evidence, collected testimony, extracted (or didn't) confession, passed judgment, and in some cases carried out the sentence. He was detective, prosecutor, jury, and judge all rolled into one. There were no adversarial proceedings, no real opportunity for mounting an effective defense or bringing down a prosecutorial argument. In effect, the plaintiff was the imperial state—and now, a millennium later, it would be the imperial Church. A streamlined, rationalized method of repression heretofore foreign to the medieval mind, an inquisition, or the Holy Office as it came to be called by its supporters, held out many attractions in the changed circumstances of the late twelfth century.

The times called for the lawyerly, given the explosive growth of different and competing bureaucracies and courts in the High Middle Ages. States and institutions were aborning, needing to define themselves and their place in the world. The sheer number of heretics had become a major problem, a threat to a worldview of a Christian commonwealth ruled from Rome. And the times were turning toward persecution, not only by the Church but also by agents of kings and their barons. This "formation of a persecuting society" was a deliberate, conscious choice driven by social change and the entry of new actors, particularly literate lay bureaucrats, into the arena of power. The

Church was far from immune to these currents of thought. A "Christianity of fear" pervaded the period. As one example, the notion of Purgatory, perfected in the thirteenth century, changed from a sort of benign cotton-cloudy waiting room for souls still sullied by minor sin to a place of unspeakable physical and spiritual torment rivaled only by Hell itself. As a French historian writes: "Burdened with the weight of oriental apocalyptic literature, a literature full of fires, tortures, sound and fury; defined by Augustine as the site of punishments more painful than any earthly pain; and given its finishing touches by a Church that dispensed salvation but only in fear and trembling, Purgatory had already veered in the direction of Hell." The thought experiment of Hell itself had been heightened during the same period into a horror show so vivid and terrifying as to stand as impressive testament to the demons resident in the human psyche. A Dominican scholar of the thirteenth century, Humbert of Romans, whose biography of Dominic became the officially sanctioned life story of the saint, also penned a work in praise of the utility of Hell, entitled *On the Gift of Fear*.

Thus the time was propitious for inquisition, which is not at all to say that papal fiat could make it arise full-blown. A late twelfth-century pope issued a bull enjoining bishops to become inquisitors, but many lacked the expertise, willingness, revenue, or stomach to launch open-throated campaigns of heretic elimination. Further, the idea was a novelty, so it could hardly be expected that these episcopal inquisitions could suddenly Christianize what was a practice from antiquity. Time was needed to make the adjustment, to lay the sacerdotal groundwork, to find the necessary rationalizations.

Some of these last arose from the belief in the pope's firm hand on the tiller of Christendom. In the first fifteen years of the thirteenth century, with the pontificate of Innocent III, a brilliant man imbued with a sense of papal supremacy and capable of organization on a grand scale—as shown in the legislative overdrive of the Fourth Lateran Council of 1215—heresy at first proved resistant to argument. The Church's second rejoinder came as a brutal recourse to arms, as the unfortunates of Lavaur and other Languedoc towns were to learn to their sorrow. Innocent approved of the innovative founders of the mendicant orders: he dreamed Francis would rejuvenate the Church, and he appointed Dominic to debate the Cathars prior to launching the

Albigensian Crusade. While the latter's mission bore little fruit in the short term, the long-term bequest of Dominic's actions provided the Church, and future popes, with a cadre of Dominican friars ideally suited to undertake the third, and final, response to heresy: systematic, painstaking inquisition. It was from the Dominicans rather than the Franciscans that the greater number of inquisitors came. Through them and their police work the Church would prevail. The word had been tried first, then the sword—it was now the turn of the law.

The Dominican mendicant friars, unlike earlier monastic movements, chose to live in the world, amidst the laity. Thus they were already, in a sense, walking the beat. And while the impulse to live among the people might at first blush seem laudable, there was a flip side to the notion: by shunning the unworldly, isolated monastery of the past, the Dominicans had decided to make the world their monastery. The laity became members of that monastery, with their consequential obligations and obediences clearly delineated. This view of spiritual discipline dovetailed nicely with the job of hunting heretics. While other churchmen might cite scripture about heretics being "foxes in the vineyard of the Lord," claim heresy to be lèse-majesté toward the pope, or put forward any other of a number of arguments to justify persecuting dissident Christians, the Dominicans could see heresy as an affront and a danger to their monastic community, which englobed all men and women and stretched into the afterlife. And as the Dominican order itself, in the narrower sense, practiced robust corporal punishment and incarceration of backsliding friars—most convents had a jail—importing such tactics into the *inquisitio hereticae pravitatis*, inquisition of heretical depravity, was but a small step to take.

The Dominicans were the Order of Friars Preachers, and they melded that vocation into their new assignment as inquisitors. At the outset of an *inquisitio generalis* (or fact-finding inquisition) in the early days after Gregory IX's letter, the inquisitor and his scribes, notaries, and servants would leave the Cité of Carcassonne and descend on a village they had targeted. First a sermon would be delivered to the assembled populace, in which the inquisitor took care to explain through the use of *exempla*—parables about animals were a medieval favorite—why Cathars were wolves in sheep's clothing, why heresy was the worst crime of all, and how tolerating heretics of any description, whether

Cathars or Waldenses, in the midst of a community endangered everyone's eternal soul. For the problem, explicitly recognized in Dominican
literature, lay precisely in perception. The people of Languedoc, whether
orthodox or not, could plainly perceive that the Cathar clergy, the ascetic,
gentle, pacific Good Men and Good Women (or perfected heretics—
the Perfect, as they were termed by their enemies) had all the trappings
of holiness. The preacher/inquisitor faced an uphill battle in what
amounted to convincing people *not* to believe what they could see with
their own eyes. He had to establish the idea of a counterfeit holiness,
condemning all who tolerated it to the fire and brimstone that often
came as the stem-winding finale of his initial sermon.

The villagers were informed that they enjoyed a grace period of a few
days before a formal summons to appear before the inquisitor might be
served upon them. If, before that time, they came of their own accord
and owned up to their depravity, a certain measure of clemency would
be shown. They had to tell the inquisitor if they or any of their neighbors, kinsmen, or other acquaintances had ever given material or spiritual support of any kind whatsoever to the Good Men and Women. It
was a crime to withhold any information germane to the eradication of
heresy. And if they, or any people they knew, were Cathar believers,
they had to recant their heresy and endure a penance before being welcomed back in the bosom of the Church. Depositions were taken
confidentially—no one but the inquisitor ever knew who said what
about whom. Further, should the inquisitor receive at least two credible
depositions about someone believing in, supporting, or giving comfort
to the Good Men and Women, charges could be laid. That created the
mala fama, the infamy necessary for investigation. Derived from old
Rome, the notion held that a person's own reputation (*fama*) func-
tioned as his accuser, exempting him from normal legal protection. A
powerful and pliable tool of coercion, inquisitors came to use just general public notoriety, rather than denunciations or confessions, to start
a proceeding against someone. In all cases, the accused never knew who
his accusers were.

One can imagine how the sermon's listeners felt on returning home
for whispered discussions over whether to cooperate. Would they be
denounced, and by whom? By one of their enemies, with whom they
had had a land or livestock dispute years back? If innocent, would they

be falsely accused? Should they settle old scores by accusing someone falsely before he accused them? Did they really have to squeal on heretical neighbors and kin whom they liked? The inquisitor's sermon, in short, contained a recipe for tearing village life apart, the customary friction of antipathy and affinity within a living community giving way to a deadening, dread-filled atmosphere of revenge and betrayal. This indeed was a Christianity of fear, in practice as well as in theory.

The inquisitor, for his part, gauged if the town was going to be a tough nut to crack. The first collaborators might arrive quickly, perhaps under cover of night to avoid neighborly scrutiny; or they might not—some brave villages observed an *omertà* that took years to grind down. Further on in the thirteenth century, the inquisitor was able to examine records of past inquisitions held in the locality. These were carefully guarded in bound registers, containing scores of transcripts of interrogations and sentences handed down. Fairly uncharacteristically for document-keeping practices of the era, the registers were systematically organized, cross-referencing individuals and allowing archival retrieval of damning detail that might otherwise have been lost or forgotten. They were, in essence, a collective database designed for a sole user—many a time an inquisitor confounded individuals with contradictory testimony they had given years earlier. Not unsurprisingly, an inquisition register first brought *la rage carcassonnaise* to a boil.

Further reading for the visiting Dominican investigator were materials concerning heresy itself. At the Council of Tarragona in 1242, the assembled prelates spelled out an entire taxonomy of dissent, yet another testament to psychology, this time to the mind's capability to create neat hierarchical mountains out of complex human molehills. One can almost see the lips of the novice inquisitor mouthing the different categories as he rehearsed the Tarragona checklist: "heretics," "believers," "suspects"—acting "simply," "vehemently," or "most vehemently"—along with "concealers," "hiders," "receivers," "defenders," and "favorers."

The Dominican likely also would have possessed an example of a supremely peculiar self-help genre, the inquisitor's manual. The first was written in Carcassonne in 1248. These manuals compiled admonitions, tip sheets, descriptions of different forms of heresy, and tactics of interrogation. Years of questioning people with something to hide had given the authors of these manuals insights into the dodging and weaving tactics developed by heretics and their sympathizers. Nicolas Eymerich, a Dominican of the fourteenth century, listed ten different techniques of evasiveness that the exasperated inquisitor should be on the lookout for when questioning heretics. They ranged from artful casuistry to blatant excuse-making:

> The third way of evading a question or misleading a questioner is through redirecting the question. For example, if it is asked: "Do you believe that the Holy Spirit proceeds from the Father and the Son?" he replies, "And what do you believe?" And when he is told, "We believe that the Holy Spirit proceeds from the Father and the Son," he replies, "Thus I believe," meaning, "I believe that you believe this, but I do not." . . .
>
> The eighth way of evading a question is through feigned illness. For example, if someone is interrogated concerning his faith, and the questions having multiplied to the point that he perceives he cannot avoid being caught out in his heresy and error, he says: "I am very weak in the head, and I cannot endure any more. In the name of God, please let me go now." Or he says, "Pain has overcome me. Please, for the sake of God, let me lie down." And going to his bed, he lies down. And thus he escapes questioning for a time, and meanwhile thinks over how he will reply, and how craftily he will conduct himself. Thus they conduct themselves with respect to other feigned illnesses. They frequently use this mode of conduct when they see that they are to be tortured, saying that they are sick, and that they will die if they are tortured, and women frequently say that they are suffering from their female troubles, so that they can escape torture for a time.

There were heretical Christians, particularly the Waldenses, who believed that capital punishment was prohibited under any circumstance, no matter what the claim of legitimacy might be. Any qualms that Dominican inquisitors, as followers of Jesus Christ, might feel in condemning people to death were countered in Dominican literature. The Order's saintly founder, Dominic, came to be seen above all else as an inquisitor, even though he died a full decade before Gregory IX declared judicial war on heresy.

Many saints, particularly those who founded orders, were subject to what might be termed sedimentary hagiography—layers of successive biographies ascribing miracles or modes of exemplary conduct to the subject long after his or her death. These were often added with a specific agenda in mind. The technique was by no means confined to Christianity: for instance, the hadith, or tales of Muhammad's life appearing nowhere in the Qur'an, have guided and shaped Islamic piety and practice for centuries. The astute Dominic is reputed to have said on his deathbed that he would be far more useful to the brothers dead than alive.

Dominic's transformation from compassionate preacher to merciless inquisitor was effected within a few generations of his death in 1221. The Miracle of Fire at Fanjeaux became in later biographies a judicial proceeding in a neighboring town called Montréal, and, in this telling, the document that refused to burn was in all probability an inquisition register. The humane and flawed holy man that Dominic must have been in reality (his first biographer had him admitting to preferring the conversation of younger women to that of older ones) became idealized as a persecutor.

At the hands of inquisition apologists, God received the same treatment. In one of the more unusual roles assigned to Jesus Christ by his flock, the protean preacher of peace in the New Testament came garbed in the robes of an avenger. He had arrived on earth to persecute. Much use was made of the many violent, vengeful passages in the Old Testament, with their far fewer counterparts in the Christian scriptures also deployed for full homiletic effect. And God was not only cruel, he was sadistic. The greatest torment of Hell was not the boundless and eternal physical agony but the sound of God's spiteful mockery and malicious cackling at the sight of such suffering.

A radical Dominican thinker of the mid-thirteenth century, Moneta of Cremona, went so far as to say that a true way to imitate God was to kill. His logic, based on the behavior of God in the Old Testament, ran something like this: God does not sin, God kills, therefore killing is not a sin. In some ways, this bald reversal of the sixth of the Ten Commandments was nothing new, for churchmen throughout the twelfth and thirteenth centuries—the heyday of the Crusades—had meandered far into sophistry in their attempt to reconcile their savior's message of nonviolence and the notion of holy war. The great twelfth-century Cistercian Bernard of Clairvaux had famously opined that the killing of an infidel was not the killing of a man but the killing of evil. What was new in Moneta's formulation was that God, far from forgiving the regrettably necessary recourse to violence, instead stood cheering on the sidelines, seeing his own image in the torturers and killers. Just as the medieval Hell fantasy speaks volumes about human psychology, so too does the worldview espoused by Moneta of Cremona and his followers, proving that at all times and in all places, sincere people will always find a way to justify whatever action they believe consonant with their duty, no matter how nakedly reprehensible that action is. Moneta's inquisitor differs from Dostoevsky's, whose Grand Inquisitor has no need of—indeed, despises—Jesus Christ; but the Dominican's may be more pernicious in that Jesus is fully in favor of persecution. The poor wretch moldering in the dank cell of an inquisition prison thus had no higher authority to implore for succor. He was utterly alone, damned by a God who was laughing at him.

Thus the inquisitor visiting a village in Languedoc went to work armed with a clear conscience, a good deal of practical advice from his predecessors, and the certitude that he was performing a sacred duty. After days, perhaps weeks, of taking depositions from all and sundry, those fingered as heretics would be haled before him for detailed and robust questioning.

By the middle of the thirteenth century, the use of torture had been papally approved. Torture in its many forms, what today's boosters of the practice call "enhanced interrogation techniques" and what their medieval counterparts called "putting the question," began to play a greater role in eliciting information from those under a cloud of suspicion. Partly thanks to the availability of the torturer's services, the focus of inquisition gradually came to center on obtaining a confession from the accused. Expediency was not the sole explanation for this change: the certainties of older customary law, with the god-given verdict delivered in a trial by ordeal, had been replaced by the nuances of Roman

THE FRIAR OF CARCASSONNE | 47

law, with its apparatus of partial proofs, imperfect witnesses, and, most important, reliance on human rather than divine judgment. The lawyers were hoist on their own petard—only a full confession constituted grounds for absolute certainty. For this reason, it was termed the *regina probationum*, or "queen of proofs."

No longer was establishing guilt on the basis of two or more credible accusations satisfactory. These would kick off the proceedings, but the prisoner had to be forced—tortured—into admitting his errors. If he was smart, he could then recant them and beg forgiveness. For those unable to be tortured—the dead—ghoulish ingenuity came into play: their bodies were dug up, carted through the streets, and burned in the public square. If the corpse had been a heretic, or simply a sometime host of a heretic, his or her dwelling would then be demolished and the resulting vacant lot transformed into a dung pit. As early as 1207, Pope Innocent III had decreed: "The house, however, in which a heretic had been received shall be altogether destroyed, nor shall anyone presume to rebuild it; but let that which was a den of iniquity become a receptacle of filth." For good measure, all of the deceased's worldly goods and wealth were confiscated from his or her heirs, leaving them destitute.

The inquisitor rarely tarried in the locales he was investigating. When he repaired to his headquarters in Carcassonne or Toulouse, more police work was done, summons issued, testimonies compared, conclusions drawn. Those villagers who had given unsatisfactory accounts of their beliefs and activities would accompany the inquisitor back to the city to be thrown in prison. Incarceration was a technique used to focus minds, and it usually did. The Wall in Carcassonne had two types of prisoners: those subjected to the *murus strictus*, or harsh confinement, shackled and manacled in solitary confinement, with little food, light, and air, and those confined in the *murus largus*, a more relaxed imprisonment, perhaps in an expansive collective holding room, or in cells surrounding a courtyard, with rights to roam the grounds and receive visitors. In both instances, prisoners had to pay room and board to the warden. Although that last detail might seem strange, one historian points out that the entire strategy of incarceration was novel: "What the inquisitors had done, and they may have been the first in medieval Europe to have done so, was to create a socially delimited space, in which they could isolate individuals from the outer world and subject them without interruption to an enforced and forcible persuasion. Such a planned and active use of imprisonment for behavior modification was possibly without parallel in medieval Europe."

When, after several months of diligent investigation, the inquisitor had readied his sentences, he would return to the village to mete out punishment. The people were assembled to watch their fellows pay for their spiritual impertinence. The inquisitor took the opportunity to deliver a stern *sermo generalis*, a public homily and sentencing, in which he would attempt to edify the common folk on the nature of divine justice and the perils of straying from the right path, the ceremony serving as a spectacle to nudge the people toward salvation. The *sermo* was the culmination of the entire inquisitorial enterprise: the tares would be separated from the wheat, the wolves from the sheep, the depraved from the decent. It was also the only public moment of the entire proceeding, the trials and questioning having been conducted in secrecy. Thus its importance to the inquisitor's redemptive mission can hardly be overstated.

The inquisitor had considerable leeway in determining the appropriate type of punishment. The most benign was a command to go on a pilgrimage. Those who had admitted and abjured minor heretical activity could be given two large yellow crosses made of cloth, to be sewn on the front and back of their tunics and to be worn at all times for a period that stretched from months to years. However harmless that sounds, it was in fact a badge of obloquy, guaranteeing a substantial loss of livelihood and standing. The cross wearer was henceforth a pariah, or at the very least a dangerous person to be seen with. To sharpen the sting, the convicted individual had to appear in this apparel every Sunday at mass, bearing with him some strong rods, so that the priest could flog him in front of the congregation. The same shameful humiliation awaited him on every important feast day, of which there were many in the medieval calendar, during which he was energetically flogged in religious processions.

A painfully similar fate was assigned to those found guilty of giving false testimony to the inquisition. To their clothes would be attached a red cloth in the shape of a tongue, and frequent public whippings constituted a further penance. Penance had to be public and ongoing, as a continual reminder to the faithful about who was in charge of their relationship with God. Those who had been convicted earlier but had not kept up with their penitential obligations—those who had taken off the crosses or avoided the floggings, for example—were given a more severe punishment this time: imprisonment and confiscation of all material goods.

The Wall at Carcassonne and a similar establishment in Toulouse also housed those deemed unsuitable for further social intercourse with the faithful. The length and harshness of their sentences depended on the temperament of the inquisitor. Many died incarcerated, their disinherited and wholly innocent sons and daughters reduced to begging in the streets or selling themselves in the alehouses. Ruining lives was of no concern to the inquisitor, this collateral damage of heresy's being, in fact, yet another instructive lesson for the Christian to take to heart. The spiritual infraction occasioning the ruin of a family might seem, to less zealous eyes, fairly trivial. Many in the Wall were held because of actions taken decades earlier, when Catharism was out in the open. A common crime was to have performed the *melioramentum*, a ritual show of respect performed when passing a Good Man or Good Woman in the street. It involved a brief genuflection and an utterance asking to be guaranteed of a "good end" to life. In the long-gone Languedoc of coexisting Christianities, this homage was a fairly common courtesy, akin to tipping your fedora in the presence of a lady. To the inquisition, however, it constituted "adoring" a heretic and was punishable by imprisonment and dispossession.

The most serious condemnation the inquisitor could hand down was death, by burning at the stake. It was the marquee attraction of the *sermo generalis*, and little insight is required to imagine the mixed feelings of the onlookers, whether despair at seeing a loved one perish or delight at seeing an enemy or rival get his comeuppance. All, however, bore witness to the blunt power of the Church.

Technically, the inquisition did not do the burning. The prisoner was, as the phrase had it, "relaxed to the secular arm," handed over to the civil authorities to be executed. To claim, as some defensive Catholics have done over the centuries, that this eleventh-hour switch somehow means that the Church had no blood on its hands must be called out for what it is: a lie. To the crowd assembled around the stake, it was clear whose show this was. The inquisitor, delivering his sermon in the company of his chanting fellows, may not have lowered the burning brand to the straw, but all aspects of the ghastly public ceremony had been carefully orchestrated by him, after months of secret interrogation and torture. If an adept of Moneta of Cremona, he would have realized that this killing made him not only an instrument but also an imitation of God. Sincere in his persecutorial and prosecutorial conduct, the good inquisitor might permit himself a flush of pride if high-profile heretics were among those perishing in the flames.

This meant the Good Men and Good Women, if caught up in the inquisitorial dragnet, were almost always sent to the stake, whether or not they abjured their beliefs. Some did, under torture, only to take it back when recovered from the torment. Some adopted the Cathar tactic known as *endura*, a form of hunger strike ending in death. To the inquisitor, such resistance only spurred him to bring the prisoner to the stake before death cheated him of a more public victory. Prominent Cathars, however, were comprehensively tortured before being consigned to the flames, to obtain the names of those who had helped and believed in them over the years.

Some of these believers, called *credentes*, also perished by fire. Either their association to the heresy had been too long or too deep or they stoutly refused to recant, preferring death to disavowal. In cases where their recantation seemed tinged with insincerity, the inquisitor decided whether to imprison or to impose punishing penance. Here is where the wisdom of the Dominican was most tested.

But when he had been demonstrably fooled by a heretic, that is, by one whose recantation had been followed by a return to his original faith, the inquisitor was pitiless. The relapsed heretic was a finger in the inquisitor's eye, as the change in faith called into question his competence as a judge of men. At least the unrepentant Good Men and Good Women were clearly, honestly damnable. The double apostate—Cathar to Catholic to Cathar—represented a rebuke to the rightness of the cause, to the irrefutable, infallible argumentation laid out by the inquisitor in his sermons. The Holy Father had encouraged his servants to construct a system of uncommon ugliness, dependent on deceit, betrayal, secrecy, pain, and punishment—the dirty work of the Holy

Office carried out by the holy men of the brotherhood was proof enough of the seriousness, the sacredness, of the Church's message. The relapsed heretic was thus tied to the stake, his tormentor readying a homely phrase from Proverbs 26:11. The heretic had gone back to his errors, the inquisitor shouted to the villagers over the roar of the fire and the shrieks of the dying, "like a dog returning to his vomit!"

CHAPTER FOUR

THE UNHOLY RESISTANCE

*W*ILY DEPONENTS OR RELAPSED heretics could muddy the spotless dream of the inquisitor, where investigation was scrupulously conducted and culprits unmasked and undone, but he nonetheless operated with an ideal in mind, no matter how warped or worthwhile others might deem it. Some of the rage against the inquisition did indeed lie in opposition to its mission, its ideal. "The development of [the] inquisitorial mentality," a historian notes, "was a heated dialogue, not a monologue." But much of the resistance also arose from its misfires, from the all too human lapses in the functioning of a system whose only blueprint lay in the individual inquisitor's mind, not in any statutory document recognized by all.

A gap existed between the ideal and the real. The inquisitor was dependent on the secular authorities. If they did not provide the funds and the men, and if they were reluctant, in the face of popular pressure, to make the arrests, haul in the suspects, and eventually carry out their sentences, the inquisitor could do nothing except appeal to Rome to intervene. And that intervention was not always forthcoming. As a major political figure, the pope sometimes needed to cement shifting alliances to meet his larger goals. Hence, for a time in the 1240s, the inquisition in Languedoc lay in tatters, checked by a hostile populace and bereft of support from a pope who needed the backing of Christendom's great lords, including the count of Toulouse, in his struggle against *Stupor Mundi*, Emperor Frederick II. After the latter died, in 1250, the Languedoc inquisition eventually got its second wind.

On a less exalted level, there was the problem of the milieu in which the inquisitor worked. An enterprise reliant on delation and treachery did not attract the best elements of society, nor did it bring out the best in people. The informant and the turncoat were morally compromised at the outset. Some went on to work for the inquisition, their interest in long-term employment having less to do with the inquisitor's ideal than with the dictates of self-preservation and the possibilities of self-enrichment. A shady demimonde of abjured heretics grew up around the inquisition, and instances of corruption—blackmail, kickbacks, and the like—occurred not infrequently. Add to that the looseness, the importance of personalities, and the improvisation necessary in developing medieval institutions, traits that tend to be forgotten when talking of the period from the viewpoint of the professionalized present day, and the ample latitude for abuse becomes apparent. At the Wall of Carcassonne, the crown jewel of the repressive apparatus, the warden in the 1280s was found to be spectacularly corrupt, trading favors for cash, in ways diametrically opposed to the penitential and persuasive purpose of incarceration as conceived of by the inquisitor.

Most important was the inquisitor himself. He had to be a man of discerning probity and great integrity, given the power invested in him to ruin lives. Most were honest; a few were not; none was perfect. The belief that an inquisitor acted out of malice or dishonesty, beliefs that gripped Carcassonne in the time of Bernard Délicieux, completely undermined his legitimacy.

This is not to suggest that the enterprise was a fraud, a nest of extortion and spite hiding behind the robes of sanctimony. Inquisitors sometimes scored remarkable successes. In Toulouse in 1240, one Raymond Gros, a prominent Cathar Good Man, defected to the side of orthodoxy, giving up a trove of names that would, through careful police work, eventually eviscerate the remnants of heresy in that city. In Italy, even greater strides were made: two Cathars, Raynier Sacconi and Peter of Verona, not only betrayed their coreligionists but themselves became inquisitors. Peter was murdered for his pains in 1252 (thereby becoming St. Peter Martyr), but not before his and Sacconi's understanding of heretical beliefs strengthened the hand of other inquisitors in the entrapment of suspects.

Peter's assassination, which helped lead a scandalized Pope Innocent IV to authorize torture, underscored the dangers run by inquisitors, especially in the early days. In Languedoc, utter exhaustion, induced by the horrors of the Albigensian Crusade, turned to incredulity when the first inquisitors arrived on the scene, as if adding insult to injury. In Albi, in the spring of 1234, inquisitor Arnaud Cathala escaped within an inch of his life when a mob attacked him as he attempted to disinter and burn a dead heretic. In a war-weary land finally free of violence and the mass bonfires of the type seen at Lavaur, the grotesque spectacle of digging up the dead and burning them violated not only the newfound peace, but also a taboo that had nothing specific to medieval France. In most human societies, whatever the burial or crematory customs that obtain, a modicum of respect is accorded the deceased; this new activity seemed as diabolical and indecent as the so-called heresy the inquisitor so loudly denounced.

In Toulouse of the same year, similar indignities outraged public sensibility. In an infamous incident, an old woman on her deathbed was tricked into admitting her heretical beliefs, inspiring the Dominican bishop of the city to have her lashed to her bed, hauled through town, and thrown on a bonfire. A Dominican chronicler witnessed the event and joyfully claimed it proof of divine intervention, or perhaps the action of the late St. Dominic himself, whose very first feast day was being celebrated on that afternoon of August 8, 1234. The friars, after dispatching the poor woman, returned to table for a hearty lunch, while one of their number was left behind to preach a *sermo generalis* to the dumbfounded crowd, which had just witnessed a harmless old woman at the very end of her natural life subjected to a cruel and inhumane death.

Within a few months these Dominican hounds of the Lord had themselves been hounded out of town. Certainly, many Toulousains had something to hide, but the near unanimity of their opprobrium attests to widespread disgust at inquisitorial activity. Prior to quitting the city, the Dominicans had been, in effect, ostracized—no one showed up at their services, no tradesman supplied them with food or labor, no passerby greeted them in the streets, save to hurl epithets or rocks and refuse. The autumn of 1234 marked a dangerous moment of civic truculence in both Toulouse and Albi. That the Dominicans, albeit with the pope's support, eventually dared return within a few years speaks not only of the disorganized nature of the resistance to them but also of the implacable, sincere determination of the friars to do God's dirty work.

The countryside was even less welcoming. In 1242, in the small settlement of Avignonet, a morning's ride to the west of Carcassonne, two inquisitors and their party were set upon in the middle of the night and massacred. One of the inquisitors was Guillaume Arnaud, a feared Dominican; the other, Etienne de Saint-Thibéry, an unlucky Franciscan who had been appointed alongside Arnaud to allay fears among the populace of Dominican ferocity. Etienne was to be the good cop, but he did not live long enough to perform that function.

The perpetrators, from the Cathar stronghold of Montségur, had believed that by killing the inquisitors they would kill the inquisition. This was to misunderstand the Dominican hydra: within a short time replacements appeared, and the action of the murderers proved, disastrously for them, to be the last straw for the Church. Money and an army were raised to reduce the almost impregnable mountain fortress of Montségur, a citadel of Catharism that previous prelates had quailed at the thought of attacking. The killing at Avignonet had provided the political will, and in March 1244, after a ten-month siege, Montségur surrendered and more than two hundred Good Men and Good Women were consigned en masse to the flames. Those not condemned to the stake were then interviewed by inquisitors.

Languedoc licked its wounds and kept quiet. The Good Men vanished into thin air. The inquisitors, undaunted by their initial reception in the region, busied themselves with investigation, honing technique and expertise. They became sedentary, summoning suspects to headquarters rather than venturing into isolated and dangerous villages. King Louis IX had the Wall at Carcassonne constructed, and its dark chambers slowly filled with prisoners of conscience. Burnings were few, but inquisition registers grew, each passing year yielding a fresh harvest of names to retain and cross-reference. Many unfortunate families were undone, with the "doctors of souls," as the inquisitors came to style themselves, dispensing cruel remedies for salvation in the hereafter, heedless of their consequences in the here and now. An active inquisitor, Jean Galand, conducted thorough investigations in the Cabardès, the rugged hinterland to the north of Carcassonne. Smoldering resentment glowed deep in the dark night.

In the 1280s, three lawyers of Carcassonne appealed to the king to halt the depredations of inquisition in Languedoc. The two laymen in this impudent trio represented the new social order: literate clerks fed up with the Church's disruptive role in civil society. They feared an unsympathetic hearing in Rome, so they turned to their sovereign to set matters to rights. The inquisition, they argued, was harming his subjects, weakening his kingdom, causing unrest. They demanded that the king's agents in Languedoc cease helping the inquisitors undermine the peace and prosperity of his loyal province.

The first two appeals, in 1280 and 1284, fell on deaf ears. The documents themselves have been lost. But by 1286, circumstances had changed. On returning from a losing campaign south of the Pyrenees, in Aragon, the forty-year-old French king, Philip the Bold, contracted dysentery in the autumn of 1285 and died. This calamity occurred in Perpignan, close to the schemers of Languedoc. Perpignan was not then a part of France, a particularity that was to play an important role in the career of Bernard Délicieux.* The king's body was therefore moved from Perpignan to the nearest French city, Narbonne. The lawyers of Carcassonne, or their sympathizers in the nobility, may have seized the opportunity to attend the funeral in Narbonne in order to determine whether the dead king's successor, seventeen-year-old Philip the Fair, could be influenced to look favorably on a renewed appeal.

In 1286, the men of Carcassonne wrote a petition to the hated inquisitor Jean Galand and the young king, identifying the flaws in the inquisitor's ideal vision of what he was doing:

> We feel aggrieved in that you, contrary to the use and custom
> observed by your predecessors in the Inquisition, have made a
> new prison, called the *mur* [Wall]. Truly this could be called
> with good cause a hell. For in it you have constructed little cells
> for the purpose of tormenting and torturing people. Some of
> these cells are dark and airless, so that those lodged there cannot

---

* Perpignan was the capital of the ephemeral Kingdom of Majorca, a Catalan entity that remained independent from 1276 to 1349 and included the Balearic islands, the Roussillon, some regions of the eastern Pyrenees, the city of Montpellier, and a part of the Auvergne.

tell if it is day or night, and they are continuously deprived of air and light. In other cells there are kept miserable wretches laden with shackles, some of wood, some of iron. These cannot move, but defecate and urinate on themselves. Nor can they lie down except on the frigid ground. They have endured torments like these day and night for a long time. In other miserable places in the prison, not only is there no light or air, but the food is rarely distributed, and that only bread and water.

Many prisoners have been put in similar situations, in which several, because of the severity of their tortures, have lost limbs and have been completely incapacitated. Many, because of the unbearable conditions and their great suffering, have died a most cruel death. In these prisons there is constantly heard an immense wailing, weeping, groaning, and gnashing of teeth. What more can one say? For these prisoners life is a torment and death a comfort. And thus coerced they say that what is false is true, choosing to die once rather than to endure more torture. As a result of these false and coerced confessions not only do those making the confessions perish, but so do the innocent people named by them . . .

Whence it has come about that many of those who are newly cited to appear, hearing of the torments and trials of those who are detained in the *mur* and in its dungeons, wishing to save themselves, have fled to the jurisdiction of other kings. Others assert what is false is true; in which assertions they accuse not only themselves but other innocent people, that they may avoid the above mentioned pains, choosing to fall with dishonor into the hands of God rather than into those of perverse men. Those who thus confess afterward reveal to their close friends that those things they said to the inquisitors are not true, but rather false, and that they confessed out of fear of imminent danger . . .

Likewise, and it is a shame to hear, certain vile persons, both defamed for heresy and condemned for false testimony, and, it is reported, guardians of the dungeons, seduced by an evil spirit, say with a diabolical suggestion to the imprisoned: "Wretches, why do you not confess so that you can be set free? Unless you confess, you will never leave this place, nor escape its torments!" To which the prisoners reply: "My lord, what do we say? What should we say?" And the jailers reply, "You should say this and this." And what they suggest is false and evil; and those wretches repeat what they have been told, although it is false, so that they may avoid the continuous torments to which they are subject. Yet in the end they perish, and cause innocent people to perish as well.

The authors of the petition had every interest in painting as bleak a picture as possible of the inquisition at Carcassonne. Yet the document speaks eloquently across the centuries of the indignation felt by educated people at the excesses of fanatical persecution. To brook the power of the inquisitor took courage—and Brother Jean Galand was a formidable figure, having spent more than a decade actively torturing and imprisoning people. Of the trio of lawyers behind these appeals, two would spend years in the Wall. The third, Raimond Costa, possessed survival skills so astonishing that he later became the bishop of Elne, near the Kingdom of Majorca's capital, Perpignan, and thus was beyond the jurisdiction of the inquisitors in France.

In this extraordinary environment of accusation and antipathy, defenders of Galand claimed that the appellants had tried to steal an inquisition register out of fear that they had been named as heretics. Opinion is divided over whether this actually happened, but given the importance the registers would assume in stoking *la rage carcassonnaise* in later years, the story cannot be discounted entirely. Certainly if their names appeared in the register, the would-be thieves had good reason to make it disappear—or at least find out what had been alleged about them. In any event, the theft did not occur. The accusers' story held that when the bribed clerk of the inquisition had let agents of the Carcassonne agitation into Galand's private chambers, they discovered, to their dismay, that the inquisitor, away on business in Toulouse, had shrewdly taken with him the key to the strongbox that contained the register. Even if not true, that friends of the inquisition could credit their foes with such audacity reveals how toxic an atmosphere existed between the citizens of the Bourg and the inquisitors of the Cité.

◆　　◆　　◆

Events in the following decade are as murky as Carcassonne's cri de cœur to the king is clear. The monarch eventually had the citizens' charges investigated and, in 1291, instructed his seneschal (his governor in the south) to have no further truck with the inquisitors. No royal official was to arrest anyone at the inquisitor's behest, except in cases of notorious heretics, such as a Good Man or Good Woman whose spiritual deviancy was common knowledge and established beyond a reasonable doubt. Agents of the king were to judge whether a suspect should be apprehended—the Dominicans were not to be taken at their word. Young Philip, his dramatic conflict with the pope still in the future, no doubt wished to appease his angry subjects. In keeping with the course he charted throughout his reign, he felt no qualms at swatting away buzzing intermediary irritants—in this instance, the Dominicans—that interfered with the direct relation he sought to establish between ruler and ruled. Philip did not want the inquisition halted—heresy had to be stamped out—but neither did he want the Dominicans sowing havoc in his kingdom.

The whip hand now lay in the hands of the king's men in the south, many of whom hailed from the region (although the seneschal was usually from the north). A few came from families tainted with heretical connections, in a much more direct way than the heretical notoriety of their birthplace, as was the case with the powerful Guillaume de Nogaret. Given these dangerous ties of kinship and the king's explicit ordinance, there must have been little incentive to go the extra mile for the inquisitors. When, in 1295, Philip renewed his injunction, the inquisitorial enterprise stuttered further.

Soon events spun out of control. Few details exist, and those that do come largely from an important figure and prolific writer, Bernard Gui, future inquisitor at Toulouse, who was present at Carcassonne in these years, residing as an ordinary friar in the Dominican convent in the Bourg.* Gui coined the term *rabies Carcassonensis* to describe the tumult of recrimination that characterized these shadowy years. The people of the Bourg must have scented blood and moved in to shut the infernal inquisition down. In 1297, as a riposte, the inquisitor Nicolas d'Abbeville excommunicated the entire town, thereby rendering it an outcast in

---

* Gui is also the villain in Umberto Eco's *The Name of the Rose*.

Christendom, to be shunned by trader and wayfarer. One can imagine the consternation at court in the north at this costly upheaval. Philip relented a little; in the following year, he issued an ordinance urging more cooperation with the inquisitors. The Carcassonnais took their case to Rome, to the imperious Boniface VIII. He refused to countenance their complaints—perhaps because the huge bribe promised His Holiness by the townsmen had been withheld, a witness would claim under oath years later.

By 1299, exhaustion had set in and the two sides engaged in protracted negotiations that lasted months. The townspeople wanted the excommunication lifted, their transgressions forgiven. The inquisitor wanted to haul in the more notorious heretical sympathizers who had eluded him for years. Two of the lawyers behind the appeals of the 1280s were eventually handed over, and other prominent burghers were to be arrested once an agreement was reached. The deal was signed on October 5, 1299; its details were kept secret from the people of the town. They were informed only that by the terms of the agreement their sins of the previous few years had been forgiven and that they had been restored to the embrace of the Church. Another proviso obliged them to build a new chapel in the Dominican convent. The inquisitor Nicolas d'Abbeville, they were told, was being generous.

What the inquisitor obtained in return, from the consuls signatory to the document, was a secret list of twelve names, all of them important citizens, who were to be exempt from the amnesty. After years of tribulation and frustration, the inquisitor was ready to make a move against them. He had the accord to back him up. He could now get on with his job.

Part II

The Years of Revolt

1299

CHAPTER FIVE

THE AMBUSH AT CARCASSONNE

OME WEEKS AFTER THE SIGNING of the accord, probably at the same time as the first of the Jubilee crowds headed for its rendezvous on the Ponte St. Angelo, the inquisitor's Dominican deputy, Brother Foulques de Saint-Georges, accompanied by a representative of the king and two dozen of his sergeants at arms, marched out of the inquisition headquarters in the Cité and through a western gate. Below them was the Bourg.

In all probability they took the Trivalle down the slope, with the Wall and the King's Mill rising up on their left. They crossed the Aude and walked smartly through the narrow, congested streets toward the gate of the lower town's fortifications. People would have snatched children out of their way; eyes followed them from open windows, watching, waiting. The armed contingent's destination was the tabula rasa of today, then the Franciscan convent at Carcassonne. Within its walls, the Dominican Brothers Nicolas d'Abbeville and Foulques de Saint-Georges believed, two prominent heretical sympathizers had taken shelter. Their names figured on the list of the doomed dozen that the consuls of the town had given up in the secret agreement. In the inquisitors' view, the freshly signed accord not only provided a chance to clean up the last of the Cathar vipers but also gave the Dominicans a golden opportunity to humiliate the Franciscans. As this was the first initiative taken by Brother Nicolas after the agreement had been reached, its target suggests that the Order of the Friars Minor had been no friend of the inquisitors in the years of sporadic strife leading up to the truce.

The party arrived at the outer portal of the convent, knocked at it repeatedly, and demanded entry. The great door eventually swung open, and they streamed into the courtyard. A second locked door gave entry into the convent proper. The king's representative pounded on the door. The Dominican then read out, loudly, the names of those he sought.

After a silence, a bell began ringing frantically, and torches blazed into life atop the building. The men at arms looked at each other, bewildered at the growing bedlam: the sound of distant shouts, then footfalls, dull thuds, and metal clanks, soft at first, but getting louder and louder.

The soldiers in the courtyard turned to the outer doorway they had just passed through. In the street leading to it an armed mob ran toward them, converging on the convent. The leader of the sergeants bellowed for the outer door to be closed. It was slammed shut and made fast with a great wooden bolt.

Crossbowmen appeared on the roof. A rain of missiles whizzed down into the courtyard. Rocks were thrown from windows in the upper gallery. At one of them, hurling stones and bellowing orders, was the ringleader of the ambush, a friar of Carcassonne named Bernard Délicieux. The trapped men hunched over instinctively to protect themselves.

"Traitors!" Bernard roared, urging the crowds to shout the same. The meaning was clear: those who cooperated with the inquisition betrayed the people of Carcassonne. There could be no better clarion of what the future held. The inquisitors may have signed an agreement with the consuls, but the disgruntled townsmen had at last found a dangerous leader, one who was fearless even before the power of the king—for Philip would soon hear that his agents had been called traitors. Willing to brave his displeasure was an unusual friar, heretofore a shadowy figure, a student in Montpellier, an obedient novice, then an accomplished, devout Franciscan whose talent, learning, and gifts at preaching had been recognized by the superiors of his Order. This exemplary friar clearly reveled in the risk, egging his Franciscan brothers to throw whatever they had at hand down at the soldiery, yelling up to the bowmen to keep up their fire, and, doubtless, cursing liberally at the trapped Dominican. This was the opening salvo of a campaign unlike any other in the history of the inquisition.

The day concluded as memorably as it had begun. Judging the courtyard to be a death trap, a sergeant lifted the bolt and swung open the outer door of the convent. His men formed a wedge of slashing blades to protect the Dominican and the royal officer, hacking and fighting their way through the streets toward the river. As they reached the left bank of the Aude, the affray came to an end. The townsmen lowered their clubs and returned home, sated and no doubt immensely pleased with themselves. The party of the inquisitor, bloodied and battered but nonetheless alive to tell the tale at Bernard's trial twenty years later, crossed the river and staggered up the slope to the embrace of the Cité. Nicolas d'Abbeville's hope that the city had been pacified by his deal-making was shattered.

The next day dawned with the realization that this had been not a rabble led by lawyers of a possible heretical background, as in the past, but rather a riot incited by the Franciscans, the serene brothers of the Dominicans. The rivalry between the Franciscans, the Order of Friars Minor, and the Dominicans, the Order of Friars Preachers, had known verbal extravagance and invidious maneuvering, but physical outrage visited upon a Dominican in the precincts of a Franciscan sanctuary was something far more disturbing. It was akin to a Cathar Good Man swinging a broadsword or landing a haymaker—an act of violence once thought inconceivable.

None doubted who had masterminded the muscular pushback. The Dominican Bernard Gui would write that Délicieux was "the commander and standard-bearer of the army of the forces of evil." Other voices of an appalled orthodoxy would pour on further vitriol, as this new obstacle, all the more terrible since Délicieux came from within the Church itself, had emerged to imperil the Holy Office.

Nicolas d'Abbeville, the inquisitor, pondered his options. The Dominicans were fully invested—professionally and spiritually—in persecution. Even Thomas Aquinas, the greatest of the thirteenth-century friars, believed heresy to be a capital crime. To Brother Nicolas, doubtless, his Franciscan counterparts seemed not to be taking their mission seriously. Whether the Franciscans of Languedoc ran a safe house for targets of the inquisition is difficult to answer conclusively. Brother Bernard's subsequent actions and statements showed that he had no faith in the integrity of the inquisitor and the veracity of his registers, so to him any accusations of heresy were baseless, or at the very least compromised by what he saw as a culture of abuse that had grown up around the inquisition at Carcassonne.

Yet more fundamental and far more important than that objection was his approach to heresy in the first place. He was as dedicated as the Dominicans to its elimination, but the nature of his pastoral mission differed radically. Where the Friars Preachers wielded the heavy club of torture and imprisonment, the Franciscans in Bernard's mold relied on the force of example and good works to change hearts and win souls. Their founder, Francis of Assisi, had garnered a large following among the laity for his kindness to his fellow man and his distinctly un-Cathar-like love of God's creation. Although the brotherhood had grown into a complex, continent-wide apparatus, sometimes participating in inquisitions, most notably in Provence, there were many among the Franciscans who by century's end had revived the purity of Francis's example. These Spirituals, as they came to be called, were numerous in Languedoc, its long history of ostentatiously holy heretics acting as a magnet for like-minded men from the Order. They would show that a Franciscan could be as pure and poor as a Good Man. From Narbonne, in the 1290s, the influential theologian Pierre Jean Olivi dominated Franciscan intellectual circles in Languedoc and elsewhere, his philosophical works on the nature of poverty an overlooked landmark in medieval thought.* On his death, in 1298, he was revered locally as a saint, and though his apostles later came to be considered heretical themselves, a man of such gifts could hardly fail to have shaped the outlook of his fellow Franciscans in the South.

Informed by Francis' example and inspired by Olivi's presence, the Friars Minor preached tirelessly, in an effort to persuade. God's work would be a long process, and if, during that time, those yet unconvinced and unconverted called for help, they would come to their aid, not only out of Christian duty but also in the hope that their actions would demonstrate the rightness of their faith. Given this admirable commitment to patience and piety, the Franciscans of Carcassonne may have sheltered some heretical sympathizers from the wrath of the inquisitor. A present-day specialist nicely characterized Bernard's viewpoint as

---

* He was known as Peire Jean Olieu to the speakers of the *langue d'oc*.

widely at variance with that of the Dominicans: "He did not consider the Cathars as diabolical enemies but as Christians who sought salvation fervently, and whose choices, in the end, were not so different from his own."

Nicolas d'Abbeville did not accept this radical Franciscan line. As an inquisitor wielding real political power, he resolved to strike a blow at the Franciscans in the public arena. Shrewd inquisitors chose their battles carefully, sometimes waiting years before prosecuting, until the time was ripe and the payoff greatest. They had to be sure of their target and their timing. To begin a proceeding and then to have it thwarted, as had happened in the courtyard of the Bourg, diminished the power of inquisition, the Dominicans' redemptive cudgel.

Brother Nicolas would eventually have his revenge—as always, it was a dish best served cold. At some point in the days after the ambush, the Dominican decided to quit Carcassonne for an extended period of time. He could not conduct an inquisition in the venomous atmosphere on the banks of the Aude, so he would conduct one on the shores of the Tarn. D'Abbeville traveled to do God's work in the birthplace of heresy, to demonstrate the sanctity and power of the Holy Office in the town whose very name evoked the vile creed of the Albigensians. He had been summoned by the bishop of Albi to rid the town of its depraved dissidents.

1300

CHAPTER SIX

THE BISHOP OF ALBI

HE BISHOP OF ALBI, Bernard de Castanet, is not remembered fondly, but he is most certainly remembered. Unlike Brother Bernard Délicieux, whose itinerary of revolt lay undiscovered for centuries, the bishop bequeathed an infamous and eloquent legacy: Albi's Cathedral of Ste. Cécile, a redbrick monolith that is the most gloweringly belligerent Gothic church in all of Europe. Attached to it, and even more of a crimson terror, stands his personal residence, a cyclopean mass known as the Palais de la Berbie. Castanet did not live to see his great cathedral completed, but he bled his flock white to finance its construction.*

As Nicolas d'Abbeville traveled north to Albi at the turn of the century to help out his episcopal ally, he could not have realized that the Church's powerful response to heresy—inquisition—would one day seem ephemeral alongside the enduring physical presence of Ste. Cécile. Few now know of the persecuting sanctity of Moneta of Cremona, the vindictive brilliance of Innocent III, or even the sacred penitentiary of the Wall, but no one today can behold Albi's cathedral and not sense the fathomless anger once felt by the Catholic Church toward the Cathars. The bishop did the world a service in immortalizing this fury. Just as the Basilica of St. Peter captures the pharaonic pretensions of Renaissance popes, Ste. Cécile displays in monumental fashion the horror in which the medieval Church held dissidents threatening its

---

* In a long-overdue nod to Castanet's dynamism, Ste. Cécile and the Berbie were selected in 2010 (as was the Cité of Carcassonne in 1997) for inclusion on Unesco's list of World Heritage Sites.

all-encompassing worldview. In a sense, to look at this church is to understand the inquisition.

The man behind the monument was a theocrat. A native of Montpellier who conducted a distinguished career in coercive diplomacy for the papacy in Italy and Germany, Bernard de Castanet was awarded the see of Albi in 1276. At that time it had been vacant for five years, and previous bishops had seen their rights and privileges whittled away by the king and the town. Albi was, by long-standing custom and law, ruled by its bishop: he was the lord of the region, with all the temporal revenue and obligations that such a position entailed. Lax churchmen had let the once-splendid bishopric slip into the moribund margins of power; even the inquisition, after the rowdy reception given it in the 1230s, had not been active there.

Castanet spent his entire tenure clawing back the money and temporal power that he believed was rightfully his. As for pastoral care of the souls in his diocese, one historian has drily termed his approach as "terrorist." The bishop's prison at Albi was renowned for its harshness— many inmates died quickly after incarceration there, an occurrence unusual in medieval jails. In some instances, the families of the deceased, left in the dark on the fate of their kin, continued to bring food and other comforts to the prison for years, all of which would be quietly confiscated by the bishop's minions. Castanet declared war on usury, meting out capital punishment to its practitioners. He was known to intervene frequently in the courts, usually stiffening sentences—death, on one occasion, for a woman who had stolen a loaf of bread. In his drive to regain lands and tithes, he showed particular ferocity. He refused Christian burial in consecrated ground to those who had died on lands withheld from him, decreeing instead that the corpses should be hung from trees (*funera per arbores*) and left to rot for public edification. Even sex fell within his punitive purview. Invoking the specter of his prison, Castanet ordained that sexual congress had to be heterosexual, that only the missionary and sidewise face-to-face positions were permitted, and that ejaculation must occur in the vagina of one's wife and nowhere else. Such attention to detail in these matters was rare in medieval France, but behind his zeal for prosecuting usury and regulating sex lay his targets: the rich men of the town who were skilled at making money through high-interest loans and adept at keeping inheritances large and families small through the usual methods of birth control. They sought to get out from under his thumb and find shelter with the king.

A supremely political man, the bishop seemed concerned less with heresy, even though the Cathars were called Albigensians for good reason, than with power. Castanet's first foray into inquisition occurred in the 1280s, when the beleaguered inquisitor Jean Galand arrived from Carcassonne, then thick with appeals to the king, denunciations of his methods and, he claimed, plots to steal inquisition registers.* Together, Galand and Castanet cherry-picked their way through the bountiful ranks of wealthy Cathar sympathizers in Albi and its surrounding countryside. Only a handful were convicted, but Castanet got what he really wanted: accusations against many of his foes, several dozen names in all. This was a bludgeon to use in his struggle for control of the town, another threat he could deploy to get his hands on more power and money.

The unkinder among the townsmen called it extortion. Factions arose within Albi opposed to the bishop's overweening authority. In this, they were aided by royal officers, to whom the townsmen turned for protection. Prisoners being led to Castanet's jail yelled out to the royal officers in the streets—in several instances, they were then physically wrested from the bishop's control and transferred to the more humane custody of the king's justice. In Albi and nearby towns such as Cordes, many of the king's servants, men of the region, were openly sympathetic or had ties to heresy.

As the century dawned, Castanet made a new year's resolution: his papal patron may have been calling a Jubilee, but he would organize a purge. He would also be doing a favor for the inquisitor at Carcassonne. By coming to Albi, Nicolas D'Abbeville, like Jean Galand before him, was escaping serious embarrassment. D'Abbeville had been woefully, perhaps naively, inept in taking on the Franciscans immediately after the signing of the accord of 1299. From the coordination and discipline exhibited by the mob in repulsing his envoys, his opponents were clearly well organized—and had no doubt been taking orders

---

* Galand was accompanied by his subordinates: Dominican inquisitors Guillaume de Saint-Seine and Jean Vigouroux.

from Bernard Délicieux long before the Franciscan cropped up in the historical record. The inquisitor would learn from the experienced bishop the wisdom of laying the political groundwork before taking any action.

Castanet provided the equivalent of a master class in politics, for the two men were able to proceed with remarkable alacrity, taking just weeks to dispatch one after another of the heretical sympathizers. Normally trials could last months, but the Albi inquisition kept up a breakneck tempo in dispensing holy justice, as the bishop's torturers busied themselves. The pace was so fast that dread had no time to take hold, only sudden terror. Dozens were haled before the inquisitor and the bishop, torn from their homes and wives and livelihoods by a soldiery galvanized by the threat of excommunication and imprisonment. Ste. Cécile might have been still a work in progress, but its uncompromising message was delivered in that terrible winter and spring of 1300.

The Franciscans of the Albi region, aware of the individual tragedies occasioned by this repressive whirlwind, sent the sad tidings to their brethren in Carcassonne, where the absence of the inquisitor was being savored. The more farsighted of the Carcassonnais, including Bernard Délicieux, might have feared a similar recrudescence of inquisitorial activity in their own city, especially on learning the scope of the final verdict. In the end twenty-five men of Albi were sentenced to life imprisonment in the Wall of Carcassonne. Their property was confiscated, their lives ruined. Almost all of those convicted for some sort of tenuous association with the Cathars—none was a Good Man—were prominent, wealthy burghers, the leaders of the town, precisely the class that Castanet wanted to crush under his episcopal heel. Brother Nicolas' *sermo generalis* at the mass sentencing must have been triumphant, given the display of inquisitorial power shown in bringing a rebellious city to its knees.*

Nicolas d'Abbeville returned to Carcassonne in the late spring of 1300 with his haul of rich men to lodge in the Wall. His exalted position, so badly battered by the ambush of 1299, had been restored. His prisoners were his trophies.

---

* A witness from Albi at Bernard's trial, Peire Pros, claimed that the rich men convicted could not possibly have been heretics who secretly met at night and shared meals—they all hated each other too much!

Their families left behind in Albi could only wring their hands in despair. They had no champion to defend them, no advocate to take a stand against the iniquity of their dispossession. As Carcassonne stared agog at the long line of manacled wretches, once the high and mighty of its sister city on the Tarn, stumbling past the fortifications to the torments of the Wall, Brother Bernard Délicieux decided to make their cause his own. The spectacle over, the twin settlements on the Aude— the Bourg and the Cité—settled into nervous anticipation as spring turned to summer.

THE DEAD MAN OF CARCASSONNE

NICOLAS D'ABBEVILLE AND Foulques de Saint-Georges pored carefully over the registers bequeathed to them by their predecessors. The momentum won at Albi would not be allowed to slow, leaving the depraved of Carcassonne untouched by divine punishment.

By late June they had their man. The faces of the Dominicans must have lit up as they made their decision, so perfectly did their intended victim meet their need for justice and revenge. The registers revealed that one Castel Fabre, a rich burgher of Carcassonne, had had intimate contact with the heretics. His was a high-profile name, his family one of the city's most prominent. Fabre had been the royal seneschal's treasurer in Carcassonne; his son Aimeri was a prominent trader and probably a heretical sympathizer as well. Punishing a Fabre would have the added benefit of sending a clear message to the consuls and the merchant class that the inquisitor had not been intimidated by recent events.

According to the registers, Fabre had received the Cathar sacrament, the *consolamentum*, from two Good Men, Bernard Costa and Guilhem Pagès, on his deathbed in 1278. The ceremony involved the laying on of hands by a Good Man, the recital of the Lord's Prayer, and the promise to live an unblemished life of exemplary asceticism. Thus "hereticated," in the Church's lexicon, the person in receipt of the sacrament became a Good Man or a Good Woman.

This ritual was commonly administered as a last rite to Cathar believers. To expire in the state of holiness conferred by the *consolamentum* meant that the individual could at last escape the cycle of return to the world's garden of evil and be joined forever with the good God in the hereafter. Once Catharism was forced underground, the sacrament had to be be performed surreptitiously, away from the eyes of the inquisitor's informers. Naturally, then, vigils at deathbeds were watched with interest in Languedoc—when dying, especially, a person showed his hand.

The grave of Castel Fabre was in the grounds of the Franciscan convent. To strike two blows at once, Nicolas d'Abbeville planned to disinter and burn his remains—and punish anyone connected to his depravity.

In July 1300, the Dominicans announced from the pulpits of the Bourg that an *inquisitio* concerning the late Castel Fabre had confirmed his suspected involvement with vehement heretical depravity. The import of the proclamation would have escaped only the dim-witted. Fabre had entrusted his mortal remains to the Franciscans, no doubt in the hope that he would be spared posthumous indignity were the Dominicans ever to accuse him of heresy, on either real or trumped-up charges. He had given a large bequest to the Franciscan convent. If the friars proved powerless to protect him, the Dominicans knew, other burghers of Carcassonne would hesitate before entrusting themselves to the Franciscans, for fear that they too could be molested, their families ruined, their remains incinerated, never to be resurrected on Judgment Day. They would decide that the charity strategically dispensed at death's doorstep was best directed elsewhere.

Worse, if the Friars Minor were shown to have sheltered a heretic, they too were guilty of abetting heresy, and thus contact with them endangered one's immortal soul. Fabre had been watched by six praying friars for weeks as he lay dying: had they just stood aside when the Good Men Bernard Costa and Guilhem Pagès paid a visit to hereticate him? D'Abbeville's accusation called into question the spiritual respectability of all Franciscans.

News of the inquisitor's announcement rocketed up the Franciscan hierarchy. Alarmed provincial leaders huddled in meetings, trying to decide what action to take. The accusation was as serious as could be made: the convent at Carcassonne stood charged, implicitly for the moment, with encouraging heresy. According to the taxonomy established at Tarragona sixty years earlier, the brothers were favorers, perhaps even supporters, of Catharism. They could be locked up in the Wall. No doubt the Dominican leadership was rubbing its hands in glee at the discomfiture into which the Franciscans had been thrown.

Time was of the essence. The Franciscan hierarchy decided to appeal directly to the inquisitor, however unusual or unprecedented that might be. When the inquisitor, as an administrator of God's justice, delivered his sentence, it was taken as a matter of faith to be just and deserved. Appeals were rare (partly because defending a heretic cast a cloud of suspicion on the defender), but an appeal to Nicolas d'Abbeville and his colleague Foulques de Saint-Georges had to be made; some face-saving compromise had to be reached, to avert the grievous harm the Friars Minor faced. Two men were designated by the Franciscan leadership to engage with the Dominicans. From Carcassonne word then came from the brothers that a third man was needed—the prior of the convent, Bernard Délicieux.

On July 4, 1300, the three Franciscans crossed the Aude and made their way up the Trivalle and through the gate of the Cité to the house of the inquisitor. They came unannounced but not unprepared—Bernard had seen to that. They were eventually ushered inside, a tactical error by the Dominicans. The inquisitors were under no obligation to receive the Franciscans, either cordially or frostily, but once they were confronted with Délicieux and his confrères, an official proceeding can be said to have begun. Certainly that was the light in which Bernard chose to cast it. Thus on the basis of this meeting, an appeal, a transcript of the discussion and further explanations in writing, could be required.

Bernard began to lay out his case. Foulques must have strained to keep his cool in the presence of the man who had jeered at him the previous winter. Bernard likely reasoned that to arrive at a conviction of Castel Fabre his beloved Dominican brethren had used Registers X and XI, compiled some years earlier by Jean Galand, inquisitor at Carcassonne. If Délicieux did mention these documents in the discussion, the color would have drained from the faces of his Dominican listeners, for much of the agitation of the past fifteen years had cited the registers as a cause of grievance.

Nicolas d'Abbeville cut him off and told the Franciscans they were not welcome and that they had no business being there. He quit the room abruptly, leaving the friars to be evicted from the premises by Foulques. This rudeness was, significantly, grounds for appeal—the irregular termination of the meeting needed to be explained, the proprieties of procedure respected.

The Franciscans returned to their convent and conferred with their fellow friars. No doubt sympathetic lawyers were summoned from the Bourg for advice. Some time toward day's end, Bernard and his companions left the lower town and made their way back up to the Cité. They knocked on the door of the Holy Office. It swung open and Foulques de Saint-Georges stood before them. They asked him for a transcript of their interview with the inquisitors earlier in the day. Foulques informed them that no such document would be drawn up and that they would not be allowed inside again. He shut the door in their faces.

The next step required the writing of a formal, notarized appeal regarding the inquisitor's actions at the meeting and the charges against Castel Fabre. A duly empowered notary was fetched from another town. No such official in Carcassonne had sufficient backbone to brave the ire of the inquisitor. Bernard dictated, scribes transcribed, the notary awaited with his seal. Copies were made for distribution.

Bernard Délicieux stated what had been whispered for years: Registers X and XI contained outright fabrications. The registers, the appeal argued, had been used and abused thoroughly, to cow the poor people of Carcassonne and its countryside into submission and to imprison and torment the innocent. Even for one as headstrong as Bernard, this was a stunning accusation to make in public, given the aura of menace surrounding the Holy Office.

In the case of the late Castel Fabre, the appeal maintained that the two men alleged to have hereticated him, Bernard Costa and Guilhem Pagès, never existed. They were men without a past, a trade, a residence, having left no trace of their passage. They had been invented by the inquisition to bring down Christian men and women with concocted tales of mysterious Good Men moving wraith-like through the vineyards to spread the sickness of heresy. If they had ever, or still, existed, Bernard demanded the inquisitors show proof.

At his trial two decades later, Bernard repeated the charges to the closed faces of the judges in front of him. Two former supporters, called as hostile witnesses, remembered Bernard saying at the time of the Castel Fabre incident that the inquisition always found those who adored the heretics and never the heretics who had been adored. Clearly, the Franciscan believed that the registers contained a mountain of lies.

The appeal was completed after a few days of work, and Bernard and his entourage trooped back up to the Cité and knocked on the inquisitors' door. This time there was no answer. That had been foreseen, for a hammer was produced and Bernard Délicieux, like Martin Luther two centuries later, nailed his appeal to the door. He then addressed the crowd that had gathered, at last using his tremendous gifts of oratory in the service of a wider cause. The problem, Bernard told his listeners, was no longer just the scandalous prosecution of Castel Fabre, but the scandalous abuse of power by the Dominicans of Carcassonne.

The inquisitor's masterstroke had turned out to be a blunder. Now everyone in the Cité and the Bourg, from the seneschal on down, had reason to suspect the inquisition. Bravery of the type displayed by Délicieux was unlikely to have been spurred by insincerity or frivolous gamesmanship, and it would resonate as far as Paris and Rome.

The Franciscans returned to their residence in the Bourg, leaving their appeal to flutter in the hot summer wind. There was a reason no one had answered the door—the inquisitors had fled town and taken the registers with them, suggesting that Brother Bernard was not alone in doubting the veracity of their leather-bound compilation of accusation. The case of Castel Fabre was dropped.

1301

CHAPTER EIGHT

THE BISHOP OF PAMIERS

HE NEW YEAR DAWNED QUIET in the south of France. In Albi, Bishop Bernard de Castanet reaped the rich harvest of property from those he had so speedily condemned to life imprisonment. Having returned to Carcassonne some time after the Castel Fabre debacle, the inquisitors kept a low profile. They absented themselves frequently, no doubt consulting with their enviably untroubled colleagues in Toulouse and, according to Bernard at his trial, laboriously recopying and "fixing" the registers that had cast a pall of suspicion over them.

They could not very well excommunicate the town again, for two reasons. The first arose from the accord of 1299. The leadership of the Bourg had lived up to the letter, if not the spirit, of its conditions: the new Dominican chapel had been built and the consuls, as promised, had not stood in the way of the arrest of the prominent citizens mentioned in the document. Bernard Délicieux had stood in the way, but that was not the fault of the consuls—and nowhere in the agreement did it say they had to help make these arrests. Second, at this delicate juncture the Dominicans charged with the inquisition at Carcassonne could not invite further attention to their procedures. Taking the drastic measure of excommunicating the town would have occasioned investigations and outside interference in the workings of the inquisition.

For the moment, the Holy Office at Carcassonne was toothless, unable to do much. The city could breathe again. However welcome the lull, Bernard Délicieux was not satisfied. He had only to leave the confines of his convent and look east over the Aude. The Wall still stood. The wretches within still suffered, including the twenty-five unfortunates of

Albi. And at any moment, given shifting winds of royal or papal favor, the Dominican machinery could start up again, unleashing the dread repression so at variance with his view of a Christian society. He had stalled the inquisition, not stopped it. For that he would need allies far more powerful than the people of the Bourg.

The diocese of Pamiers, close to the towering Pyrenees, had been carved out of the diocese of Toulouse in 1295. That administrative change and consequent loss of revenue to his see would have angered Toulouse's bishop, who may have had a hand in spreading rumors about the new diocese's first bishop, Bernard Saisset. Whatever their provenance, the stories about Saisset provoked consternation and, in some quarters, hilarity. Famously, Bishop Bernard is reputed to have said that while King Philip the Fair was "more handsome than any man in the world . . . [he] knew nothing, except to stare at men like an owl, which, though beautiful to look at, is an otherwise useless bird." In addition to delivering this memorable put-down, which implied that the king was a pretty boy exploited by his corrupt ministers, the bishop also characterized the monarch as a bastard, a counterfeiter, and a statue.

All of this, however wounding, might have been taken as the harmless raillery of an old crank in his cups had not the bishop also ventured into political critique. As a scion of a proud Languedoc family, Bernard Saisset clearly resented the presence of the French in his homeland and volubly shared his low opinion of them with others. Of his enemy the bishop of Toulouse, a Parisian and thus automatically the target for withering scorn, Saisset said that he was "useless to the Church and to the country, because he was of a language that was always an enemy to that of our ancestors, and that the people of the country hate him because of that language."

While inflammatory, such words were not that unusual in Languedoc, even well into the twentieth century. Where Saisset departed from the norm was in openly hectoring the local lords of his region to ally with the Kingdom of Aragon and secede from France. This was treason. Many of the other customary medieval accusations of moral turpitude—

heresy, simony, sorcery, fornication, and blasphemy—came to be leveled at Saisset, but there can be no doubt that his talk of secession was what first caused the king to sit up and take note.

In 1301, Philip ordered two of his loyal servants, Jean de Picquigny and Richard Leneveu, to go to the south and investigate the matter. They were appointed as *enquêteurs-réformateurs*, posts that gave them authority greater than the seneschal's. Leneveu was an important prelate of Normandy; Picquigny, a nobleman and experienced royal magistrate (*vidame*) from the great Picard center of Amiens. These men, viceroys in a sense, were precisely the type of grandee Bernard Délicieux had to meet in order to amplify his campaign against the inquisition. Bernard Saisset's troublemaking had given the mischief-maker of Carcassonne the opening he needed.

The post held by Picquigny and Leneveu was a Capetian innovation, having originated during the reign of the saintly and punctilious Louis IX. The first *enquêteurs* had been Franciscan friars. They had shaped the office and its duties—making sure the prerogatives of the king remained free from encroachment, seeking the cause of complaints from his subjects and working to redress them, and ensuring that the king's agents in the provinces were fulfilling their duties in an appropriate manner. Given such sweeping powers, the opportunity for all kinds of personal treasure hunting was boundless; fortunately for Philip, and for the people of the south, the pair he sent to Languedoc in 1301 seems to have been irreproachable.

By the middle of that year, Picquigny and Leneveu had found ample grounds to charge Saisset with high treason. They ordered him arrested and, in exercising secular authority over a man of the Church, set off the tremendous struggle between king and pope that culminated in the Outrage of Anagni. While adding further piquancy to the relation between Crown and Church that forms a backdrop to Délicieux's agitation, the fate of Saisset matters less than the acquaintances made by the men sent to investigate him. For Leneveu and Picquigny took up with dangerous company.

Leneveu, the Norman priest, hovered in the wings of the drama told two decades later at Délicieux's trial, whereas Picquigny played a role front and center. Multiple testimonies speak with one voice: the great magistrate from Amiens fell under the spell of the friar of Carcassonne. Starting in the summer of 1301, Picquigny sought Bernard's counsel on all of his major decisions. As he was a man of the world accustomed to wielding authority, his allegiance to the friar bespeaks the force of character Bernard Délicieux possessed. To have won over such a great man, the friar had to have been a formidable presence, and not just when he mounted the pulpit. His was a personality that impressed the great and the small alike and inspired affection and admiration, as is abundantly clear from the course of his career.

Picquigny's principal character trait seems to have been loyalty. He would stick with Délicieux throughout the turbulent years to come, but, above all else, he was a truly faithful courtier of King Philip's, keenly interested in keeping Languedoc equally faithful to their monarch. Men of the south, he had seen in the matter of Bernard Saisset, harbored no great love for the men of the north. To keep the kingdom united, prosperous, and loyal, the people of the Midi had to know that the king's justice was impartial and fair.

This was an echo of the argument Bernard Délicieux would advance repeatedly to Picquigny against the Dominican inquisitors: they were untrustworthy, they abused their power, they had to be replaced—but, most important, they were endangering the Kingdom of France. The people of the south, Bernard argued, were deeply unhappy, primed for revolt at any moment, because of the depredations of the inquisition and the king's acquiescence in its excesses. Whether Bernard cared a whit about the Kingdom of France is highly doubtful, given his subsequent actions, but he recognized in this argument a cogent and persuasive tool to shift the great power of the north to his side.

He first traveled to meet Picquigny and Leneveu in Toulouse some time in early 1301, accompanied by the wives of the men of Albi who had recently been condemned to the Wall. Bernard would have other occasions to bring these lonely women along with him, in an effort to soften hearts and appeal, perhaps, to the dying embers of chivalry. The women, for their part, shared the enthusiasm of their kinfolk on the arrival of this providential man. His success at knocking the inquisitors off stride in Carcassonne had been noticed by aggrieved parties throughout Languedoc. The people of Albi and such towns as Cordes and Castres raised money for Bernard to keep up the fight and to agitate on their behalf. Neither the riot at the convent nor his deft defusing of the Castel Fabre bombshell would have inspired distant burghers to open their purses for him. Rather, they took heart in hearing that the inquisitors at Carcassonne had been intimidated into making themselves scarce and, more important, that Bernard Délicieux had the ear of the most important royal officials in Languedoc.

After their initial meeting, Délicieux consulted frequently with Picquigny and Leneveu in Carcassonne, in a townhouse of the Bourg. The dwelling still belonged to Raimond Costa, the agitator of the 1280s who had escaped imprisonment and set himself up as the untouchable bishop of Elne, in the Kingdom of Majorca. Thus, from across the Corbières mountains, then the frontier of Capetian France, this rather peculiar bishop continued to lend a hand to the foes of the inquisition.

The persuasive Bernard laid out his case forcefully to his two powerful auditors from the north. The prisoners from Albi deserved justice from their king. They had been left to rot in the Wall, just as their deceased kinsmen had been left to rot in the trees of the lands that they had refused to hand over to an avaricious tormentor. Bishop Castanet was a wicked, amoral prelate, his lordship of Albi inimical to the interests of the king, his brazen conflict with the royal agents there a vivid reminder to the townsmen that their true lord lived impossibly far away, in Paris, unaware of their troubles. Bernard would not have complained, however, of Castanet's liberal recourse to torture, as the men seated in front of him had no qualms about its use. In the investigation of the Saisset matter, Picquigny and Leveneu had given free rein to the torturer—one of their recalcitrant witnesses emerged from the dungeon to testify with both arms irredeemably broken.

In Carcassonne, Bernard argued, matters were no better than at Albi. Thanks to years of merciless persecution, a sullen cloud of suspicion lowered over the town like a thunderhead ready to unleash its fury. People feared each other; factions thrived; the townsmen were at each other's throats. All knew that, guilty or not, they could one day be taken from their families and immured in the prison. Though no one had seen the infamous registers, many knew some of their contents, having heard family, friends, and neighbors tell of their testimony before the inquisitors. Then, at the well and the washhouse, in the fields and taverns, there was gossip, always gossip, all the more urgent and contagious since life and livelihood might depend on it.

Bernard would have detailed the objections he had nailed to the inquisitors' door. Their registers overflowed with falsehoods, for heretics did not betray each other—they betrayed the innocent. On leaving the Wall, destitute and penniless, they were repaid for their false testimony by the heretical people they had shielded. Unscrupulous people got even with their enemies. Merchants named competitors. As for Registers X and XI, they were works of the imagination dreamed up by two inquisition clerks in the interest of enriching themselves through extortion. They had come up with two make-believe Good Men to bolster their shameful lies. No one had seen Bernard Costa and Guilhem Pagès; no one could say anything substantial about them. Their names were so common in the Languedoc as to be meaningless. Indeed, Délicieux, Picquigny, and Leneveu were meeting in the house of one Raimond Costa.

By early autumn, Picquigny was convinced. If not a co-conspirator, he was an active fellow traveler in the camp of the Carcassonnais and the Albigeois. To his mind, taking on the inquisitors and Bishop Castanet was not an act of rebellion against the established order—it was an action necessary to remedy a deplorable state of affairs, the sworn responsibility of a royal plenipotentiary charged with redressing the grievances of Philip's subjects.

Although powerful, he did not have enough power to set things aright on his own. For that he needed the approval of the highest authority in the land. Picquigny thus planned to go north to meet with the king, haul Bishop Bernard Saisset in front of him, and relate in detail the investigation that he and Richard Leneveu had conducted. The moment would be propitious for broaching the question of inquisitorial abuse in Languedoc, when Philip's attention was turned toward the south of his kingdom and its Church. Hearing of his intention to meet with the king, the consuls of Albi and Carcassonne selected delegations, laid out the necessary funds—and approved Bernard Délicieux as their leader.

In late September 1301 the men of the south made the journey north. On arrival, Picquigny immediately petitioned the king to accord them the privilege of a private audience. The request was granted. Some time in October—we are not sure of the precise day—Brother Bernard Délicieux of the Order of Friars Minor stood before King Philip IV of France. The momentous meeting occurred not in Paris but in a small town called Senlis.

CHAPTER NINE

THE KING AT SENLIS

T HE TOWN OF SENLIS NESTLES IN THE PAST, alive with birdsong, its old houses and stone steeples a lovely medieval surprise just past the northernmost edge of the grimy suburban sprawl of modern Paris. Nowhere in the town is the pink of Toulouse and Albi or the russet brown of Carcassonne, just the gentle gray of northern France. Senlis has somehow retained its verdant character—all around stretch leafy forests harking back to the time when a sea of green covered the Île de France. The woods around Senlis were part of the royal domain, a place for huntsmen in the service of their great lord to maintain with plentiful supplies of game and to protect from the desperate poachers who straggled through the trees in times of famine. For Philip the Fair, the place was a respite from the intrigues of the Louvre, but, as in his other residences scattered throughout his lands, he could never really escape the turmoil of his kingdom. Many of his courtiers came with him when he removed to his hunting quarters, always ready to petition favor for their various clients.

In the heart of the old quarter stands a quiet park with gravel drives that lead to several buildings standing in evocative Gothic ruin. They are called the Palais Royal. One building houses the king's quarters; the other, the queen's. The most impressive ensemble, however, is an empty shell, the stained glass long gone from its graceful embrasures and the sky alone supported by its ogive arches. This was the grand hall in which the king granted his audiences, and where Bernard Délicieux and Jean de Picquigny stood in October 1301.

They had been accompanied to Senlis by several consuls of Albi and Carcassonne, who flanked Bernard as he spoke to the king. Just outside the hall a gaggle of worried Dominicans paced and prayed. This delegation included the inquisitor Foulques de Saint-Georges, smarting that the pestiferous Délicieux had been granted the privilege of a private audience. With Foulques outside the door was a fellow Dominican, Nicolas de Fréauville, the king's confessor and, as such, enormously influential at court. That even he had not been admitted to the audience augured well for the men of Languedoc.

The king already had an inkling of many of the complaints of his subjects. Comprehensive dossiers had been assembled by the disgruntled citizens of Carcassonne and Albi. The latter's damning litany of grievance toward Bernard de Castanet verged on the encyclopedic. The Albigeois sought a royal ordinance to put an end to his extortion, his unlawful and inhumane incarceration practices, his abuse of inquisitorial procedure, and his arrogation of the king's rightful authority. In later complaints about Castanet, which may also have spiced up the presentation at Senlis, the bishop's enemies added a series of accusations concerning his sexual proclivities, eye-popping even by medieval standards. His residence, the Palais de la Berbie, was nightly the scene of shameless debauch, the loose ladies and unclad lads invited there to pleasure him appearing brazenly at the windows for all to see.* Darker still, the burghers alleged, his depravity ran so deep as to include molesting young girls; one had vanished into the Berbie, later to be found headless, floating in the river Tarn below the bishop's palace of sin.

Carcassonne's grievances, while not quite as lurid as Albi's, also painted a picture of a town on the verge of despair. The corruption of the inquisitors had so corroded the attachment of the people to their monarch that the potential for revolt was great if the king's justice was denied them. The falsity of Registers X and XI had to be brought to the monarch's attention, the abuse of power revealed, the prisoners freed immediately. Last, the moral disgrace of Foulques de Saint-Georges, similar in nature if not in degree to that of Albi's evil bishop, merited a full airing.

The problem for Bernard Délicieux, as spokesman and lobbyist in Senlis, lay in how to present these arguments to Philip in a way that

---

* In the type of palimpsest at which France excels, the Berbie now houses a gallery of similar ladies painted by Albi's most famous son, Henri de Toulouse-Lautrec.

would win him over. The king's advisors no doubt warned Philip that he was soon to be at loggerheads with the pope over the Bernard Saisset affair; thus he might be inclined to court the support of members of the French Church, including the French Dominicans, to shore up his position. The king was no longer the mystery boy attending his father's funeral in Narbonne. The mature Philip the Fair was now known—and feared—for keeping a poker face in front of petitioners, announcing his decision after letting slip no "tell" about his intentions. Less anachronistic French tradition styles him *le roi de marbre* and *le roi de fer* (the marble king, the iron king), each sobriquet indicating a different aspect of his character, respectively, impassiveness and implacability.

But Bernard possessed a trump, in the person of Jean de Picquigny. The magistrate was no stranger to the king's humors and caprices, having dealt with Philip many times during his career. The king's man and the friar could not have failed to confer extensively on how to handle this meeting, for the stakes were too high. Although few disputed Bernard's abundant abilities as preacher, orator, and persuader—the last conclusively proved by Picquigny's allegiance to the Franciscan's cause— the gifted friar had to avoid rubbing the king the wrong way, or giving the impression of issuing threats or dispensing advice. He had to rein in his commanding personality, on conspicuous display in the tumultuous two years leading up to this crucial interview, and learn the devious ways of the courtier. If one considers Bernard's own recollections in 1319 of the push-me-pull-you beginning to his presentation in 1301, it seems likely that the two men had hit upon a strategy worthy of a courtroom drama, an elaborate choreography of deception.

Picquigny, Délicieux, and the men of Albi and Carcassonne entered the great hall in Senlis and made the customary obeisances to their lord. Doubtless Philip greeted his faithful servant Picquigny with some familiarity. Then he looked at the man about whom he had heard so many clamorous rumors, and bade Bernard Délicieux speak.

The friar began hesitatingly, saying that he would not have been in his majesty's presence had not his magistrate, Jean de Picquigny, ordered him to come. Picquigny would have nodded on cue. The king inquired as to what had brought the men of Carcassonne and Albi to Senlis. Bernard replied that it was too awful to relate, too disturbing . . . he did not want to upset the king with such horrible tales.

At one moment Picquigny commanded the Franciscan to speak. Bernard refused, again saying he could not. He was too afraid. Other Franciscans had tried to tell the king's loyal servants in the south of the evil being done to the kingdom, but they had been dismissed as tale-tellers intent on diminishing the Dominicans. Laymen over the years had tried as well, lawyers of Carcassonne, but they ended up in the Wall, falsely accused of heresy. He feared that if he spoke out, then he too would feel the pain of Dominican fury.

Whether Bernard then gestured to the door, on the other side of which chafed the angry Dominicans, is unknown, but the temptation to do so for someone as histrionic as Délicieux must have been consid-erable. Neither do we know how long this pantomime of reluctance continued, only that it came to a rather dramatic end.

Stony-faced, the king pondered the men before him. They had trav-eled at great expense up to the north, encouraged in their suit by one of his most trusted *enquêteurs*, then obtained an audience with him—yet they dared not speak. Philip rose from his chair and crossed the short distance separating him from Bernard Délicieux. He placed his right hand on the friar's tonsured head. The king swore that no harm would come to him no matter what he said or whom he accused. He gave his word, the king's word—a royal guarantee of safety—and commanded Délicieux to speak.

The moment had come, and the friar of Carcassonne seized it. He launched into his arguments, doubtless using all of the rhetorical and predicatory weapons at his disposal. The king was told that the inquisi-tion thwarted his subjects at every turn. Whenever they defended the king's prerogatives, acted in the king's interests, tried to fulfill their duties and obligations to the king, they were attacked by the inquisi-tors and the bishop of Albi. These men actively undermined the King-dom of France and, by their actions, led Philip's subjects to the extremities of dangerous despair. An inquisitor had even preached that heresy had spread through the malevolence of the king of France.

It was a curious way to frame the complaints of a Languedoc still indignant at the deprivation of its independence, but Bernard had crafted his presentation for an audience of one. After having established what was at stake for Philip and his realm, he moved on to the particulars of the case: the iniquitous registers, invented Good Men, scandalous prosecutions, unconscionable extortions, unjust incarcerations, inhuman torments, the reign of terror. Given what contemporaries said of Bernard's powers, the king must have opened wide his eyes—like an owl, perhaps.

No detail was spared. The men of Albi chimed in with their condemnation of Bishop Castanet. Bernard cited the swath cut by Foulques de Saint-Georges through the honest womanhood of Languedoc, who submitted to his lust for fear of his power. The inquisitor showed a keen interest in torture, rolling up the sleeves of his cassock to take an active part in inflicting pain and then, if the victim was female, lifting up his skirts to rape. Foulques, this so-called man of God, had fathered several children, and a woman, Navenias, who had borne him a daughter, had traveled with them to Senlis and was willing to expose her shame before the king if he doubted what they said. Foulques de Saint-Georges, the inquisition's opponents consistently maintained throughout these years, was a far more objectionable and unsavory fellow than even Nicolas d'Abbeville, who had done such harm to Albi.

The spell Bernard had cast on Jean de Picquigny and Richard Leneveu now enveloped the divinely appointed sovereign of France. Through the force of his personality he had won the king over, planting the idea in Philip's mind that corrupt inquisitors consituted a grave danger to his realm. The message had been driven home with mesmerizing conviction.

The men of Languedoc left the Palais Royal, passing on their way out the agitated Dominicans eager to make their case before the king. Shaken by what Brother Bernard had told him, the king did not consent to receive the Dominicans until five days after the friar's speech; Délicieux testified that when they had tried to enter the hall earlier, the king shooed them away with an angry gesture.

When at last the Dominicans did get to see their agitated monarch, they launched into a full-scale attack not on Délicieux but on Picquigny. This was a mistake, as the latter had the full confidence of the king. Summoned to defend himself, Picquigny protested his inno-

cence, proclaimed his integrity, and repeated the charges against Foulques de Saint-Georges. Judiciously, Philip set up an ad hoc committee
of two to look into the character assassination proffered by each side.
The constable of France and the archbishop of Narbonne, Gilles Aycelin, a high-placed prelate always ready to do the king's bidding, were
charged with the investigation.

It took but a few days. The constable and the archbishop found in
favor of Picquigny. The king then acted accordingly. Brother Bernard
had made it rain.

Fr. Foulques, of the Order of Friars Preachers, who pretends to
be the inquisitor of heresy in the region of Toulouse, trying
rather to sow (than to uproot) those errors and vices it was his
duty to destroy, who under the pretext of the law violates the
laws, who under the semblance of piety commits impious,
utterly inhuman acts, and under the guise of defending the
Catholic faith commits evil deeds abhorrent to the human
mind . . . through his trials and inquisitions, by capture and
tortures of the utmost refinement, has extorted confession
from helpless people whom he declares, according to his whim,
to be stained by the crime of heresy . . . (and convicts) through
the power and the fear of torture and the suborning of false
witnesses . . . Whence throughout those regions scandal plainly
has arisen as has the fear of an uprising of the people, unless
steps are taken swiftly to correct the situation.

The words came not from Délicieux but from King Philip. The monarch had become an ally of the friar. Never before and never again would
the inquisition face such overt wrath from a king of France. The angry
letter cited above, sent in December 1301, was occasioned by the foot-
dragging of the Dominican Order in dismissing Foulques de Saint-
Georges. He had been moved from Carcassonne to Toulouse, but he had
not been removed from the office of inquisitor. Given the subsequent
behavior of the king and Guillaume de Nogaret in the affair of the
Templars, Philip could hardly shriek like an outraged virgin at the

specter of torture and injustice, yet the indignation of his letter be-
spoke a monarch determined to justify his actions: he singled out one
friar, but intended to punish the Dominicans.

In a flurry of royal ordinances issued at about the same time as his
heated missive, Philip stipulated that henceforth his agents would proceed with no arrests on suspicion of heresy until the inquisitor had
cleared his request with the local hierarchy—the bishop and senior secular officials. In case of dispute, the matter would then be referred to
the leaders of the Dominican convent in Carcassonne and their Franciscan counterparts. The leadership of the Friars Minor could include, of
course, Brother Bernard Délicieux. This was a stinging slap in the face
of the inquisitors. Overseen by its greatest foe, the inquisition at Carcassonne was now hamstrung.

That did not mean that the office of inquisitor had been abolished,
as Délicieux was only too aware. Philip would not go that far—even if
Guillaume de Nogaret could willingly have found his master some
flimsy pretext for stepping on the pope's toes so egregiously. The king
wanted a harmless inquisition, at least for the moment, so that the sul-
fur of revolt hanging over his southernmost province would dissipate.
His interlocutor at Senlis had impressed on him the dangers of unrest.
Civic peace became the king's goal.

1302

ISHOP BERNARD DE CASTANET SPENT much of the winter in Toulouse, complaining to his fellow churchmen. Following the masterly presentation by Délicieux at Senlis, the king had been especially harsh with Castanet. In addition to having levied a fine in the staggering amount of 20,000 livres, Philip had taken the temporal offices away from the bishop, arrogating them and their revenues to himself. Now the bishop was just the bishop, not the lord, of Albi, his treasury looted by the royal ordinances. Philip may well have wanted to have the man arrested as well, but Bernard Saisset, already in custody, was giving him headaches enough with Pope Boniface.* Two detained bishops would undoubtedly trigger an instant excommunication. More important for the people who had embraced Délicieux as their spokesman, the king's displeasure with their bishop was so great as to render any further inquisition in Albi unlikely.

Castanet, although diminished and embattled, was determined to fight the royal decrees, appeal to the pope, and, in the meantime, reinforce his authority over his troubled see. In February, he made the decision to leave Toulouse and return to Albi. Fearless but not foolhardy, he took with him a contingent of armed bodyguards for his entry into the city. His flock awaited him in the square before the construction site of Ste. Cécile. The mood was ugly, sullen. Truncheons in hand, the townspeople blocked the way to the bishop's palace.

Castanet's men ordered the mob to disperse. No one moved. The

---

* Saisset was not held in the royal prisons. Gilles Aycelin, the archbishop of Narbonne, kept him under house arrest for the king.

standoff grew tenser, as shouts of "Death!" echoed louder through the square. Clubs were raised, the mob advanced. The bishop's men at arms, greatly outnumbered, unsheathed their swords, ready to wade into the townspeople. Then, at a sharp word from their master, Castanet's men lowered their weapons. Another order, and the phalanx of bodyguards parted. The mob now had a clear path to the bishop. He waited for death, his face a mask, daring them to come and kill him, a bishop of the Holy Church.

The moment passed. Resolution began to falter. No one had the courage to strike the first blow. The crowd eventually melted away and the bishop regained the Palais de la Berbie.

The Dominicans of Albi did not receive such a gift of faintheartedness. From overhead the outer doorway of their convent, the portraits of St. Dominic and St. Peter Martyr were torn down by a mob, to be replaced by likenesses of the architects of the friars' humiliation: the king's envoys, Jean de Picquigny and Richard Leneveu, and the consuls from Albi and Castres, Arnaud Garsie and Peire Pros, who had traveled north for the momentous audience in Senlis.

The change in portraiture hardly constituted the only insult, for the period following the decision at Senlis passed as an unrelieved calvary for the Dominicans of Albi—the prolific memoirist Bernard Gui recorded their tribulations for posterity. Their convent became an eyesore, its herb and vegetable gardens uprooted and destroyed. Windows were smashed in the night. The friars scarcely dared venture out of the convent's protective confines, so enthusiastically were they manhandled, pushed, shoved, and taunted in the narrow streets of Albi. Whenever their prior summoned the king's officers to view the latest outrage, they did nothing, except perhaps suppress a smile. The Order of the Friars Preachers became, effectively, a prisoner in the pink city on the Tarn.

Following Brother Bernard's triumphant return to Languedoc from Senlis, the Order of the Friars Minor appointed him to a convent in Narbonne. If the transfer of the famous friar was meant as a diplomatic sop thrown to the Dominicans, it was entirely unconvincing. Bernard enjoyed a freedom of movement that could be granted only by the

Franciscan leadership in Languedoc. Not content to rest on his laurels, he set about increasing his renown as the scourge of the inquisitors by going on extensive preaching tours to the smaller centers of Languedoc and Périgord. His public excoriation of the inquisition, now done with complete impunity, appalled the Dominicans and their allies, who heaped abuse on him from their pulpits.

Despite this renewed activity, Délicieux's campaign had, in fact, stalled. No amount of stirring oratory could hide the simple reality that the inquisition had survived to fight another day. It was hobbled, not eliminated. Men and women still suffered in the Wall. Cruel and punitive Christianity, of the kind promoted by the Dominican Moneta of Cremona, still overshadowed Bernard's vision of the Franciscan ideal. He needed still more help, and that, he knew, could happen only if he could convince Philip to take more drastic action.

Accordingly, in the early spring of 1302, Brother Bernard made the arduous journey north once again, picking his way up the Rhône Valley, then through the downs of Burgundy to the forests of the Île de France. With him rode the consuls of Carcassonne, Albi, and Castres, who had accompanied him the previous year to Senlis, and a delegation of women of Albi, the lonely wives of the men wasting away in the Wall. Such a voyage was a costly proposition—clearly the townspeople who raised the money to pay its expenses thought that King Philip had not gone far enough in punishing the inquisitors of Carcassonne and the bishop of Albi. Bernard had intended to bring along Jean Fresquet, a jailer of Albi willing to bear witness to the crimes of Bishop Castanet, but the man had died suddenly that spring under circumstances that were never fully elucidated. The people of Albi, however, had no doubt that Fresquet had been murdered on Castanet's order, yet another black mark on the soul of their bishop.

His embassy weakened by the absence of a valuable witness, Bernard deployed his other strength. Once settled near the royal court, Brother Bernard took the women of Albi to meet with Joan of Navarre, queen of France.* Her confessor, Durand de Champagne, was a Franciscan friar

---

* As usual, Philip kept on the move to enjoy the hunt. In 1302, Bernard and his delegation caught up with the court in either Pierrefonds or Compiègne, the king's royal residences in Picardy, both a long day's ride to the northeast of Paris.

sympathetic to the cause of Délicieux and doubtless the instigator of the audience. Queen Joan comforted her visitors from Albi, listened as they evoked their conjugal plight, then sent them away with a sizeable cash gift, 1,000 livres. Bernard implored the queen to intervene with her husband, insisting that Bishop Castanet be punished more forcefully and removed entirely from the see of Albi, that the prisoners caught up in the shamefully hasty inquisition of 1300 be freed, that the Wall itself be shut down. At the very least, the Dominicans had to be deprived of the inquisition. Joan heard the friar out and, given his gifts of persuasion, must have been moved to compassion for her subjects in the south and a clear understanding of their grievances. Yet she alone could do nothing. At some point—the details are unclear—Bernard, the consuls, and the women of Albi were allowed into the king's presence, but the meeting proved inconclusive, save for a further cash gift to the women and a modest increase of the fine on Castanet. Nothing more would be done, as the king was preoccupied with other matters of great moment.

Bernard sent his disappointed allies home. He would see King Philip again, but at a distance, on the high altar of Notre Dame de Paris. Bernard had been delegated to attend the Estates General in place of the Franciscan provincial of Languedoc, a sign that his star was ascendant in the Order. In April, the friar sat in silence in the great nave as the assembly took up the matter of the king's row with Boniface and listened to the royal chancellor, Pierre Flote, hurl outlandish charges at the pope. The concerns of Languedoc had never seemed more irrelevant. A man of the south, Bernard Saisset, may have sparked the fracas, but it had moved far beyond the confines of regional or even national conflict. Guillaume de Nogaret hovered in the background, ready to launch his final, historic offensive against the pope, while Saisset himself was eventually forgotten and allowed to go to the safety of Rome, where a forgiving hierarchy awaited him. Even if on this occasion Délicieux did meet the king's ministers, which is more than likely given that news of his bravura performance at Senlis six months earlier had reached their keen ears, they would have told him the time was not right to take up the matter of the inquisition. The king had made enough enemies in the Church.

Brother Bernard embarked on the long journey back to the south, probably some time in late April 1302. He no doubt was discouraged by the failure of his ambitious delegation in the halls of power and his own fruitless stay in Paris for the Estates General. Crippling the inquisition without freeing its victims did not solve the problem, Bernard and his allies knew, and allowing persecution to continue guaranteed future strife. The king had to be brought around to seeing things their way, to be coaxed along a path to action that then seemed strewn with impassable obstacles. A few weeks later, the road ahead came clearly marked from the other extremity of Philip's turbulent realm.

CHAPTER ELEVEN

THE WEAVER OF BRUGES

IETER DE CONINCK, A WEAVER, lived in Bruges, an immensely wealthy town reliant on a steady supply of English wool to transform into Flemish cloth. Bruges, Ghent, and Ypres were the foremost weaving centers of Flanders, their blue dyes provided by the woad merchants of Languedoc, their bolts sold to the Italians in the fairs of Champagne.

Philip the Fair had laid his heavy hand on Flanders in 1297, after its count had had the temerity to plump for the English forces in the French king's struggle against them. The count's decision seemed reasonable enough, given the firm economic ties binding England and Flanders together, but for Philip and his court, English political influence had to be diminished, as rich Flanders was a milch cow that could do wonders for the Capetian treasury. The barrier of language mattered little—Philip's expanding kingdom encompassed a babel of peoples, as the remarks of Bernard Saisset about the Parisian bishop of Toulouse made clear. As well, a large contingent of speakers of the *langue d'oïl* (French) in Flanders welcomed the protection of Paris and, not incidentally, formed the wealthiest class of merchant burghers in the towns. They also wanted to curb direct English trade with the weavers, preferring to keep their privileged and lucrative positions as middlemen.

Philip had annexed the region outright in the Jubilee year of 1300. When he took Queen Joan for a state visit to Flanders the following year, so sumptuously attired were the merchant wives and maidens watching the royal procession from the balconies of their magnificent gabled houses that Joan is said to have complained, "I thought that I alone was Queen, but here in this place I have six hundred rivals." As it was the first visit of a monarch to his new province, medieval etiquette held it as a Joyeuse Entrée—but here the joy was to be remarkably short-lived.

The atmosphere in the cities of Flanders was so explosive that the royal visit sparked off acrimony over who was going to get stuck with the costs of the festivities. The Flemings resented the traders and patricians not just for fawning over a foreign potentate but also for keeping their stranglehold on the communal governments of the towns. In the closing decades of the thirteenth century, the guildsmen of Flanders had risen regularly in revolt against the upper classes. The men ruling the towns, the men whose womenfolk caused the queen of France to marvel at their wealth, ignored the great changes that decades of broadening prosperity had brought. De Coninck and his ilk, for their part, demanded a say in their destiny; instead they were excluded from the public square, saddled with onerous taxes, and forced to watch the distasteful spectacle of conspicuous wealth being flaunted by a small, condescending elite.

Like Bernard's Languedoc, De Coninck's Flanders had not been immune to the spiritual ferment of the twelfth and thirteenth centuries. The mendicant friars had thrived there, imparting a sense that personal salvation was a matter that had to be attended to by the newly awakened sense of the individual. The guildsmen were not ants to be trod upon by their betters, or those who styled themselves as such. Many disagreed with even that: one itinerant preacher of Antwerp, echoing what must have been a popular sentiment, stated that the rich man, even if he be virtuous, was no better than a whore.

In unconscious imitation of the strife besetting their Italian trading partners, the cities of Flanders of the first decade of the fourteenth century saw the birth of organized, bitter civic factions given to brawling and mayhem, the patrician Leliaert, or "Lilies" (so named for the fleur-de-lis of France), and the guild-friendly Clauwerts, or "Claws" (after the paws of the heraldic Flemish lion). In the spring of 1302, in the midst of upheavals between Lilies and Claws in many Flemish cities, a distinctly obstreperous Claw magistracy seized power in Bruges. Jacques de

Châtillon, a Flemish nobleman who served as King Philip's viceroy, raised a force of some one thousand men to occupy and punish the defiant town. He was, in the judgment of an eminent historian, "a violent and haughty man, a true representative of feudalism, harsh and disdainful toward the people, incapable of understanding the interests, aspirations and the power of the great cities subject to his government." The French entered Bruges on May 17, 1302; De Coninck fled, knowing the fearsome Châtillon capable of terrible reprisal.

Fatally, the French did nothing on that first day. Tradition holds that they passed a long evening in well-irrigated revelry, content to put off their repressive chores until the morrow. De Coninck took advantage of the lull to steal back to the city in the dead of night, at the head of a troop of Claws primed for murder. The signal was given just before dawn on the eighteenth, and the Flemings stormed the houses in which the French were sleeping it off. The morning turned into a full-scale slaughter, known to history as the Bruges Matins.* Very few of the soldiers sent out to chasten the city survived.

The Bruges Matins were only a prelude. An alarmed King Philip raised a feudal host to teach the lowly Flemings a lesson, calling on the greatest of his vassals to gather their men and ride north. The finest flower of French chivalry, as the doom-laden catchphrase has it, met the foe near the city of Courtrai (Kortrijk in Flemish) on July 11, 1302. The greatest nobles of Artois, Picardy, and Normandy, caparisoned in splendor, trotted out into the clearing before their ranks then broke into a deafening charge of heavily mailed rider and warhorse. They bore down on the the motley infantry of the Flemish towns, then faltered. In the Flanders fields muddied by rains and overflowing streams, destrier and knight flailed and fell, the thick muck riddled with waterlogged traps set by the Flemish. The French riders pulled from their floundering mounts were beaten and hacked to death. As in the First World War, the mud of Flanders had won.

Hundreds, if not thousands, of French perished, many of them great lords—including the aloof Jacques de Châtillon and Pierre Flote, the king's chancellor, who was trampled to death. The Flemish had de-

---

* Evoking the monastic hours, the name given the Bruges revolt echoed a similarly termed massacre of the French twenty years previously in Palermo, the Sicilian Vespers.

cided to dispense with the medieval custom of sparing the great in the hope of a large ransom. The grisly event came to be known as the Battle of the Golden Spurs, so called for the five hundred of these items retrieved from the fallen noblemen. The prizes, far from being melted down and transformed into yet more adornment for the ample bosoms of the Flemish burghers' wives, were instead hung in a church of Courtrai as a sign of thanksgiving. At his home in Anagni, Pope Boniface VIII ordered all the town bells to peal in joyful cacophony. His mighty enemy had been mightily humiliated.

The tidings from Flanders sent shock waves through the Kingdom of France. Rumors flew fast, far, and wide—the most fantastic of them holding that the terrifying Pieter de Coninck, his patronym the Dutch word for "king," was now King Peter of Flanders. Less fanciful but no less astounding was the realization that the Capetian juggernaut had been tripped up by a rabble of commoners. A rich acquisition was slipping through the fingers of the most powerful French monarch since St. Louis, and Philip the Fair seemed unable to salvage the situation. Although he personally and courageously led the fight two years later, winning a tactical victory near the Flemish town of Mons-en-Pévèle, he eventually had to let Flanders go, holding on to only the prizes of Lille, Béthune, and Douai. Much of the north had, in effect, resisted incorporation into Philip's kingdom.

For the agitators of Languedoc, lessons lay in abundance on the sodden ground of Flanders. However different the circumstances in the north and south, the Flemings had demonstrated that the kingdom of France was not an adamantine entity, immune to division and schism. And although no Lilies and Claws clashed in the alleyways of Toulouse and Carcassonne, there were similarities between the two extremes of Capetian territorial ambition. Like the Flemings, the southerners, too, had links to England—neighboring Guyenne was an English possession and trade ties were strong. The south also bordered the power of Aragon, just beyond the Pyrenees; talk of enlisting its aid to regain independence was not idle jabber. In addition, the people in the south, like the northerners, had a linguistic bone to pick with their overlords, for they spoke not the *langue d'oïl* of France but the *langue d'oc* of the Midi.

Philip was shaken by the reversal in Flanders, knowing it to be a set-back of an unusual magnitude. Important lessons could be drawn from the episode, the foremost of which was the folly of siding with the Lily oligarchs in their struggle with the Flemish guildsmen and laborers. He realized he could not neglect local grievance and factional friction in the distant reaches of his kingdom.

With Pierre Flote dead on the battlefield of the Golden Spurs, the mantle of power passed to Guillaume de Nogaret, a man of the south. Nogaret, soon to become wholly occupied as the king's attack dog in the conflict with Boniface VIII, no doubt counseled his master to tread cautiously. The king could, and would, organize a military campaign to try to repair the damage in Flanders, but his advisor urged him to remember that sedition thrived elsewhere. He need only repeat the vile words of Bishop Bernard Saisset. Nogaret had grown up among such people and understood the deep unhappiness in the south exacerbated by the inquisitors. It may be an overreach to assume that Nogaret, his family's Cathar baggage his biggest liability, advised the king to go even easier on heresy to keep the south calm, but that was the de facto result of the Bruges Matins. The king was willing to let the remaining Cathars remain unmolested in return for a precious few months of stability.

If Nogaret had indeed met with and taken the measure of Bernard Délicieux in Paris just prior to the Bruges Matins, he could not have been surprised by the subsequent developments in the south, for the astute friar had taken away several important insights of his own from the uprising in Flanders. Like others in his camp, he would have viewed the event as a mixed blessing: on one hand, it distracted attention from the cause of Languedoc even more, but on the other, it focused the king's mind on the frightening reality of revolt. But the most important element imparted by the weaver of Bruges would not have eluded a student of politics as gifted as Délicieux. The Flemish guildsmen had attacked French and Flemish supporters of the merchants; the ordinary men of the town had struck a blow against the interests of the consuls, the governing elite. In the end, the riot had been sparked by class resentment, the type of civic hostility rife in the elbow-rubbing familiarity of the medieval city. After two centuries of rapidly increasing trade and wealth, there were now many conflicting, important interests in the life of any city. De Coninck knew how to exploit such divisions in his native Bruges. Brother Bernard would prove to be equally expert in stirring the resentments lying dormant in the breast of Carcassonne.

1303

CHAPTER TWELVE

THE SERMON

F OR CARCASSONNE, THE PRECEDING FOUR YEARS had been a whirlwind sown by Bernard Délicieux and the inquisitors, a confusing period of strife, sudden action, and long spells of uneasy calm. Looking back, the townsmen may have had difficulty in making sense of it all, in finding some meaning behind the upheaval and, more important, some spur to clarity and future action.

The signing of the secret accord of 1299 offered Bernard Délicieux the chance to dispel the uncertainty. Of all the events to have taken place during the quadrennium at the turn of the century—ambush at the Franciscan convent, inquisition at Albi, appeal on behalf of Castel Fabre, audience with the king—the occurrence to have the greatest consequences for Carcassonne came first. In skillful hands, the accord was made to seem an injustice, a nefarious agreement pitting rich against poor. Bernard Délicieux found in it the same basis for class resentment that had brought revolt to Bruges.

The agreement had never been made public, which was the root cause of all the mischief to follow. The people of Carcassonne, doubtless encouraged by Bernard and his allies, began to ask what exactly was the nature of the agreement between consuls and inquisitors. Instead of its being recorded in the customary manner, the document had been kept under lock and key for four years in the home of Gui Sicre, a prominent consul of the Bourg. This, in itself, raised hackles and, more dangerously, suggested that the consuls were afraid to disclose its terms. The mere existence of the accord proved that they had collaborated with the loathsome inquisitors, perhaps agreeing to some sinister quid pro quo to be triggered at any time against the less wealthy townsmen of the Bourg. The great consular families had profited from the inquisition, their lesser members serving as notaries, suppliers, and legists for the unjust hounds of the Lord. Perhaps, ran the speculation, the accord was less an olive branch than a heavy club, passed from complaisant consul to corrupt inquisitor.

The normally querulous gossip of the town turned into louder and louder rumors of betrayal, as *la rage carcassonnaise* reared its head once more. Brother Bernard had returned to Carcassonne by early 1303, his residence in the Narbonne convent a forgotten fiction. In addition to fanning suspicions about the accord, he reminded his many admirers in the Bourg that the Wall still stood, that its prisoners still suffered, and that the inquisition was merely dormant, not dead. While the hated Foulques de Saint-Georges had been replaced in Toulouse and Nicolas d'Abbeville's stormy tenure at Carcassonne had concluded, in their place had come Geoffroy d'Ablis, who, the remaining Cathars and Waldenses of Languedoc were soon to learn, would prove to be the most effective inquisitor ever to hold that position in the Cité. As if sensing the building storm, King Philip sent a letter in the spring of 1303 to his subjects in Cordes and Albi, vowing to keep an eye on the newly installed inquistors for signs of overreaching. It was a markedly faint promise. Its moderate tone may have pushed Bernard over the edge, reminding him that talk of revolt was not enough to move the king forward, that he would have to place revolt squarely in the regal lap.

The decision was not as extreme as it might sound to modern ears. Riot and murderous assault were by no means uncommon in the rough-and-tumble medieval city. The pedestrian discipline on the Ponte St. Angelo during the Jubilee was so unusual that the greatest poet of the era, Dante, chose to remark on it through parody in his *Divina Commedia*. The grand civic processions on holy days, with clerics, nobles, consuls, traders, and guildsmen parading in their finery, also displayed a certain discipline, which was hard-won but extremely fragile in the face of seething jealousy and status envy. People pushed to get ahead, but in the medieval iteration of this timeless tendency there was far less inhibition involved—and often a good deal of fisticuffs. The threshold of the intolerable, the moment when the ordinary person feels compelled to take action, may have been more easily reached in the medieval period than in its successors. Certainly, in Brother Bernard's

Languedoc, where a judicial whim might have resulted in one's dear departed mother being dug up and burned in the market square, the intolerable could come calling at any moment.

Yet Bernard and Carcassonne presented a special case. The intolerable for him came not from royal exaction or municipal infighting but from the abuse of power within his own Church, posing the problem of how to lay rough hands on its perpetrators. Nothwithstanding such exceptions as the Avignonet murder of the inquisitors in 1242 and the soon-to-be-enacted Outrage of Anagni in the fall of 1303, the clergy was not considered fair game for the marauding mob. As early as the tenth century, the Church sponsored a Truce of God movement, which, while enjoining boisterous fellows to sheath their swords on certain holy days, carried a further proviso demanding that they refrain from turning their murderous enthusiasms on men of the cloth. Over the years the taboo had held—Henry II's harsh penance over the killing of Thomas Becket points to how strongly the prohibition was felt. Even in the enraged Languedoc of Bernard's day, the men of Albi had had many compelling reasons to string up their reviled bishop or chuck him in the river, yet, when presented with the opportunity, they backed down.

Thus, to reach the untouchable churchmen of the Cité, Bernard had to start with the people of the Bourg. That would open the last stage of the friar's campaign, begun with the ambush at the Franciscan convent. Its culmination, he hoped, would entail dragging in the king, in the person of Jean de Picquigny, Philip's special representative in Languedoc, to quell a revolt by shutting down the inquisition definitively. As a strategy, it was fraught with the danger of matters getting out of hand, but Brother Bernard knew that he had to strike while the inquisitors were weakened.

In 1303 Hélie Patrice, a man of Carcassonne with no previous appearance in the historical record, came to play an important role in the friar's plans. Patrice had become the leader of the Bourg at some point after the turn of the century, having somehow ousted the urban elite from the consulate—the signatories to the accord of 1299—and taken power. Though the circumstances and date of this coup are unknown, what is certain is Patrice's undisputed ascendancy during the long hot summer to come. The inquisitor Bernard Gui contemptuously called Patrice "the little king," in a telling echo of that other meddlesome "king," Pieter de Coninck of Bruges. The Dominican's epithet for the new leader was backed up by testimony at Délicieux's trial, in which witnesses described the high-handed tactics and royal pretensions of Patrice during his tenure as the chief local magistrate. One can reasonably infer that this mysterious leader might well have climbed to prominence from the underrepresented, resentful lower rungs of the class order. If so, his antipathy to the wealthy consuls further aided Bernard Délicieux in his struggle. This reflexive hostility, the friar saw, could be harnessed, put to good use in ending the Dominican monopoly on the inquisition and freeing the unfortunates locked up in the Wall.

Lack of information shrouds the start of Patrice's career as a political figure and the question of whether he rose to prominence independent of the scheming of the powerful Franciscan. The muddiness dissipates in the years 1303–5, however, for unquestionably the two men acted in concert, their aims identical. Henceforth Bernard had a useful partner, able to mobilize his muscular followers. Taken along with Jean de Picquigny, the king's plenipotentiary in Languedoc and Bernard's pliable ally, Hélie Patrice made the friar's position one of great promise.

Picquigny lit the fuse. By midsummer 1303, he saw—or perhaps was told by Bernard—that tempers were running abnormally high in Carcassonne. The rumor mill churned incessantly and the atmosphere in the Bourg bordered on the febrile. The very real prospect of revolt alarmed Picquigny, so much so that he called a meeting to see if he could defuse the situation. The secret accord of 1299, the subject of all conversations, had to reveal its secrets.

The meeting took place some time at the beginning of August 1303. Picquigny summoned his guests to the house of Raimond Costa, the absentee troublemaker turned bishop in the Kingdom of Majorca. No fewer than thirty royal officials were present, as were representatives of the deposed consular elite and Patrice's coterie. Although it was August, the room must have felt chilly. As requested, the former consul Gui Sicre extracted the accord from the strongbox in his home and presented it to Picquigny at the Costa townhouse.

The king's inspector and his lawyers bent over the parchment studiously. So much had been whispered, insinuated, claimed about this agreement that a close reading of it was essential. Jean de Picquigny finally looked up at Gui Sicre. As the latter testified years later at Bernard's trial, Picquigny handed him back the parchment, saying, "My good fellow, here is your agreement. I would have drawn it up the same way had I been there, given the nature of relations between the Bourg and the inquisitor." The ex-consuls breathed a sigh of relief, as this reaction signaled royal satisfaction with them.

Bernard Délicieux then entered the house, approached Sicre, and asked him for the document. Sicre, undoubtedly buoyed by Picquigny's endorsement, handed it over. All eyes watched as Brother Bernard scanned the document. The friar did not hand the parchment back to Sicre. Instead he crossed the room and laid it out again before Picquigny. There were, indeed, objectionable elements in the accord, Bernard explained. What on first reading seemed innocuous turned out to be pernicious, even treacherous. Bernard insisted on having a copy of it and asked Picquigny to withhold judgment until it had been rigorously scrutinized.

Whether Picquigny agreed with Délicieux's analysis is unknown, but the king's man, fatefully, acceded to the friar's request. The meeting, like most meetings, was adjourned without anything having been decided one way or the other. In 1299 the consuls had either acted honorably or betrayed their fellow townsmen. Four years on, it was up to public opinion to judge.

Picquigny must have felt confident that the unanswered question no longer stung so acutely as to spark revolt. Progress had been made toward a resolution of the matter, which no doubt the good people of Carcassonne would appreciate. He left town soon afterward to attend to business in the westernmost reaches of Languedoc.

Similarly, the inquisitor of Carcassonne, Geoffroy d'Ablis, decamped to Toulouse on church business. Whether he was exercising the better part of valor or was truly unconcerned about the situation in the streets did not matter. In practical terms, the senior royal official and inquisitor had quit Carcassonne at the same time, leaving the town to Bernard Délicieux and Hélie Patrice.

Patrice and his men took advantage of the situation to stoke the flames of indignation with tales of covert betrayal and secret plotting, bringing the Bourg to a fever pitch. The head of Bernard's convent and several civic officials appealed to Délicieux to use his great talents to calm the people. His superiors decided that he would preach a sermon the following Sunday, August 4, 1303, in the church of the Franciscan convent. Each household of the town was instructed to have one or two members present to hear what Brother Bernard had to say. An arsonist had been asked to put out a fire.

On that Sunday morning seven centuries ago, the tabula rasa—the long-vanished Franciscan convent in Carcassonne—received its liveliest inscription. When Brother Bernard mounted the pulpit, few in the packed church would have known what to expect. The former consuls no doubt hoped his would be a message of respect and reconciliation. Hélie Patrice and his partisans hoped otherwise. For the majority in the church, belonging to neither faction, there was only fear and foreboding, the alarums of future danger more credible now that the accord had been seen by their leaders.

For Bernard, the congregation was not an audience of one, as at Senlis, but an assembly for which he had been trained in the art of preaching. His listeners were medieval men and women, prone to outbursts of emotion and sudden accesses of depair or joy, fervent believers in the marvelous, profoundly superstitious, spiritual, swayed by eloquent conviction, edified by fable and parable. They were his contemporaries.

The Scripture reading earlier in the service had been taken from the nineteenth chapter of Luke. Disconsolate over the misfortunes that are to befall Jerusalem in the years to come, Jesus tells the city, "For the days will come upon you, when your enemies will build an embankment about you and surround you and hem you in on every side. They will dash you to the ground, you and the children within your walls. They will not leave one stone on another, because you did not recognize the time of God's coming to you."

Bernard took a breath and looked out at the sea of expectant faces. "As He approached Jerusalem and saw the city," the friar read in a whisper, "Jesus wept." A tear welled up, then slowly rolled down his cheek. He remained silent. Then another teardrop, and another. Soon he was crying, his shoulders shuddering beneath his simple brown tunic. His anguished sobs filled the sanctuary, his head bowed down in grief. The congregation watched, amazed, as their guide wept openly for minutes on end.

At last he recovered, wiped the tears away. Eyes glistening, he raised his head and managed to croak, "I am . . . Jesus Christ."

In any era, this would be an astounding thing to say. His listeners must have leaned forward, not believing their ears. He was Jesus, Bernard intoned, his voice rising, because he had been sent to save the people of Carcassonne. Old Jerusalem had not listened to the prophecy of Jesus, and the pagan armies of Rome had destroyed it, stone by stone. Outsiders had come and demolished it.

Carcassonne was Jerusalem, Bernard proclaimed. Men had come intent on its destruction. Outsiders. Evildoers. Dominicans. They would not be satisfied until the city lay in ruins, its people in chains. He begged the people of Carcassonne to heed him and resist the traitors who aided and abetted the inquisitors in their dark designs.

He then proceeded to give the bleakest possible interpretation of the accord of 1299, claiming that the city now lay at the mercy of the Dominicans. In the agreement, the consuls had abjured heresy in the name of the entire town, an admission of guilt that applied to everyone. One slip, one untoward word, he warned the assemblage, and they would be wrongly declared a relapsed heretic, to be bundled off to the bonfire. Their families would be shunned for generations, as all would fear association with them. There was no hope for anyone in Carcassonne in the wake of this betrayal, for no drop of mercy had ever been shown by the inquisition.

Bernard had confirmed the worst of all the rumors. Anyone at any time could be hauled off to the Wall by the inquisitors who, the friar continued, had the gall to call themselves men of the Lord. But, in truth, they were wolves in sheep's clothing. If this sounded familiar to his listeners, there was a reason: Bernard had turned the standard trope of the *sermo generalis*, the sentencing sermon of the inquisitor, on its head, using the Dominicans' rhetorical weapons against them. What they said about heretics now applied to them. They were the ones who preached peace yet sowed discord, endangered souls by encouraging deceit and betrayal. In this, Bernard's argument would not have been much of a stretch for the assembled faithful: for generations in Languedoc, the Dominicans had descended on heretofore peaceable towns and claimed that spirtual outsiders—heretics—disrupted the well-being of the community, though plainly it was the inquisitor, not some long-dead Cathar grandmother, who was causing all the trouble. Even inquisitor manuals acknowledged the difficulty in making the counterinuitive claim that the intrusive nature of inquisition somehow represented the normal, and that the normal tenor of village life constituted the exceptional. For an orator of Bernard's caliber, upending this difficult Dominican argument would have been child's play.

More childlike was the close of the Franciscan's address. As was customary in medieval sermonizing, an exemplum, an illustrative parable or fable, was used to drive home an argument to the unlettered. Bernard chose his story from the time, long ago, when animals had the gift of speech.

A group of rams, he recounted, inhabited a verdant meadow, at peace with each other and enjoying God's good earth. Yet every now and then, one of their number disappeared, abducted by two butchers and led to the slaughter. As time went on, the flock became depleted, morose, endangered. The meadow overlooked the river Aude, Bernard's listeners understood. The rams were the people of the Bourg; the two butchers, the inquisitors at Carcassonne and at Toulouse.

At last the rams could take no more. They huddled together, each one fearful lest he be the next to feel the dread cleaver. One ram then asked, "Have we not horns?" Could they not band together and defend themselves? And this they did: the next time the two butchers came on their hideous errand, the rams attacked, driving them out of the meadow and far, far away. The butchers never came back. The nightmare was over.

The congregation filed out of the church, thoughtful and subdued. A man of God had vilified his fellow friars. Their fellow townsmen, the former consuls, had betrayed them. Like the rams, they would have to defend themselves.

Gui Sicre and two confederates from the town jumped on their horses and galloped to Toulouse, to inform Geoffroy d'Ablis of the extraordinary sermon the people of Carcassonne had just heard. Two Franciscan friars hitched up their mules, their destination the Agenais, in western Languedoc, to catch up with Jean de Picquigny and entreat him to return before a catastrophe unfolded. As in *Romeo and Juliet*, the humble mounts of the friars were outpaced by the swift steeds of the townsmen. The following day, the inquisitor Geoffroy d'Ablis rushed back to Carcassonne.

CHAPTER THIRTEEN
THE INQUISITOR GIVES A READING

<hr>

THE WEEK FOLLOWING BERNARD'S SERMON was unlike any other in the life of Carcassonne. As the inquisitor prepared his rebuttal, a symposium of sedition took place on the streets of the Bourg. Like a speaker at Hyde Park, Bernard harangued his rapt audiences, who stopped their workaday activities to listen to his exhortations. He related more parables, telling of the necessity for the people of Carcassonne to tend to their garden and pull out the bad weeds by the roots. The inquisitors and their accomplices were clearly just such weeds.*

Bernard then began repeating a strange story of an extraordinarily unflappable fellow, a man able to withstand insult and calumny without flinching or losing his self-control. He told the story everywhere, including at the foot of the pulpit. Less an exemplum than a call to action, the tale stuck fast in the memory of the Carcassonnais—so much so that the story was retold several times at his trial. One of the better versions was given by Guillaume Rabaud, a man of the Bourg:

"Once there was a town in which there lived a good man, of whom it was said that nothing could anger him or make him angry. So some wiseacres and knaves said to themselves, 'Let's make this fine fellow lose his temper.' They came up to him and said, 'You are a killer!' He answered, 'May God forgive you.' They tried again. 'You're a thief, you're an adulterer, you're a

<hr>

* Questioned about these weeds at his trial, Bernard gamely responded that he had been referring to heretics, not inquisitors. He was not believed.

murderer!' Whatever the insult, he never lost his temper and
always responded, 'May God forgive you.' At last someone said
that he could make the fellow angry, and he went up to him and
said, 'You're a heretic!' The good man would not put up with
this, and he shouted back in anger that the other was lying
through his teeth, and then he punched him in the face." And
Brother Bernard, having finished his story, said, "Draw your
own conclusions."

Giraud de Meaux, a royal sergeant of Carcassonne, remembered the
story of the unflappable man in more or less the same detail. However,
his version of how Brother Bernard concluded his edifying tale differs
somewhat:

After that, Brother Bernard explained his words, by saying
to the people, "Good people, if anyone calls you a heretic,
defend yourself as best you can, because you have the right to
defend yourself."

The Franciscan worked tirelessly in the week prior to the inquisitor's
riposte. He came in from the streets to give sermons in the parish churches
of the Bourg, grave, accusatory orations in which he singled out individual congregants for opprobrium. He pointed the finger, threateningly,
at those who had helped the inquisition in the past. Some of the accused fled the churches in consternation. They would later say at his
trial that he encouraged the people to murder them, though their survival to give testimony would seem to contradict that assertion. There
can be no question, however, that the friar's campaign intensified as he
steeled his allies for the inevitable confrontation.

It came on or about Saturday, August 10, 1303. Criers ran through
the streets instructing the people to assemble in the courtyard of the
bishop's palace to hear the explanations of Geoffroy d'Ablis, inquisitor
of Carcassonne. At his side, significantly, would be the city's bishop, of
an old Carcassonne family, who had been conspicuously silent in the
dispute between the brash Franciscan and his Dominican foes. In the
distant but fondly remembered days of Carcassonne before the inquisition, his ancestor had been a famously live-and-let-live bishop who

counted several Good Men and Good Women in his immediate circle of kinship. That a cleric of such sensible lineage should support the Dominican might be a sign that the inquisitor had some devastating information to impart.

That information was the accord itself. Scholarly examination of what remains of the secret agreement of 1299 has determined that Picquigny was right when he declared at the meeting with the consuls that there was nothing terribly objectionable in the document. A secret list of a dozen or so townsmen who were to be jailed for heretical leanings could outrage but hardly surprise the people of the Bourg. They had lived in the dread shadow of the Wall all their lives: of course the inquisitors had demanded fresh bodies for its dungeons in exchange for lifting the excommunication.

What did surprise the Bourg was the news that the document purportedly had the consuls, on behalf of everybody, abjuring heretical belief. The consequence of that clause was nothing less than disastrous, for if one renounced a belief, that meant that one once had held it—and in that case, one was guilty in the inquisitor's eyes. Consequently, if one was guilty of once harboring heresy in one's heart, punishment had to follow. Brother Bernard had said as much in his Sunday sermon.

In this reading, the consuls had sold the townsmen down the river by abjuring heresy in the name of everyone. Knowing from experience the implacability of the Dominicans, the people of the Bourg could not possibly have expected them to refrain from using this admission as a weapon some day, vindictively prosecuting anyone who dared oppose them. Four years earlier, with the signing of the accord, they had thought themselves delivered from the inquisition; in fact, they had been delivered to the inquisition.

The only discordant note in this mounting wail of panic might have arisen from the simple fact that the consuls had done no such thing. As a jurist of Carcassonne sniffed at Bernard's trial: "He [Bernard] let it be known through his sermons and other ways that the act concluded between the inquisitors and the consuls . . . was very bad for the city and the people of the Bourg, whereas the agreement, which I have seen and read in my capacity as a jurist and a lawyer, was not in reality bad for the city, but actually good and useful, if given a fair reading." In fact, the word *abjure* appears but once in the document, in a passage of ecclesiastical boilerplate. The men of 1299 had most emphatically not accused their fellows of heresy in any way. One needed only read the document to realize that.

That, however, would have been asking too much. The rumor about the secret agreement reinforced a narrative that had been building for years, a narrative made possible by inquisitorial abuse. Even a level-headed reading of the document had the consuls handing over some citizens to the inquisition, through a list of targets guiltily kept secret— thus they had collaborated and fully deserved public disgrace. But above all else, the inquisition, iniquitous and pitiless, still had license to torment the blameless. Given the strength of the townspeople's revulsion, a public reading of the accord of 1299 would not have changed minds; the citizens of Carcassonne still would have believed that the consuls had called them heretics.

The inquisitor Geoffroy d'Ablis thought otherwise. The learned Dominican was a man of the north, from the town of Ablis, to the southwest of Paris. He had been educated at the venerable school in Chartres, becoming a master of theology. Yet his considerable intellectual achievements did not stand him in good stead at this moment, for he clearly underestimated the degree of hatred he faced. He had arrived in Carcassonne in January 1303, but by that late date too many people had been imprisoned, too many lives snuffed out, too many bodies broken, too many fortunes looted, houses confiscated, children disinherited, conjugal beds emptied, and long lonely nights made sleepless by the ever-present specter of sudden and unmerited punishment. Geoffroy seemed unable to fathom the resentment. He believed that the people had only to be informed of how fundamentally benign the accord of 1299 actually was, and the fever would break.

The bishop and the inquisitor stood before the façade of the episcopal palace in the Cité. In front of them, in the courtyard, the people of the Bourg awaited. The moment for disclosure had arrived. Geoffroy d'Ablis announced that the accord would be read aloud, in full. He motioned for a lawyer on his staff to begin. The man read out a passage in the original Latin, then translated it into the vernacular *langue d'oc*. The crowd listened, brooding, silent.

The lecture went on for a time, but then came the first hisses, the first whistles and catcalls. The inquisitor-theologian had gambled on the sweet voice of reason, but it was too late for that. The people of the Bourg would not listen. The sight of the inquisitor and his men only inflamed them. A hothead in the crowd surged forward and demanded to see the accursed document for himself. The jostling began. There were no unflappable men present. Within minutes the riot was on.

The inquisitor and bishop stepped smartly through a doorway behind them to escape the mayhem. But the crowd had other targets, no doubt suggested by Hélie Patrice and his men, who did not want the people running amok to no good purpose. The rioters ran down from the Cité and spread through the Bourg, calling for death to the traitors and seeking the townhouses of the wealthy consuls of 1299. Their dwellings stood vulnerable, inviting. Windows were smashed, fiery brands thrown in. The mansions of the great burned under the August sun, a black choking thunderhead drifting over the city. Carcassonne had erupted. Within the Franciscan convent, Bernard Délicieux heard the commotion, but was able to finish his prayers with a clear conscience. He hadn't started the riot; the inquisitor had.

C OHAC! COHAC!" Everywhere they went the Dominicans heard the mocking cry, the raucous call of the crow. The people of Carcassonne were jubilant, sardonic, intent on inventing their own *exemplum*. In their view, the Dominicans, enrobed in their black scapulars, were no better than crows, feasting on carrion, poking out eyes with razor-sharp beaks. Ravens swooped and hopped around the gallows set up in every medieval town, coveting their revolting repast, cawing in excitement. So too the Dominicans. For too long had the burghers put up with their rapacious behavior, their digging up and shaming of the dead, their snatching of the living and burying them in the Wall. Those dark times were over, the mocking cry announced.

The rough mistreatment continued as the hot days of August wore on. Small boys ran after the friars in the streets, cawing in derision. Matrons about their business barreled into them, brusquely shoving them aside. Masked men burst into their church, smashing windows and statuary. But the culprits who had spread terror were not now the friars being terrorized: Geoffroy d'Ablis and his staff had prudently fled to Toulouse, leaving their Dominican brethren unconnected to the inquisition to bear the brunt of the people's anger. For the moment, the discomfort of any Dominican had the townsmen crowing in delight.

Bernard Délicieux must have enjoyed the spectacle, but his pleasure was diminished by growing impatience. The king's viceroy was slow in returning to Carcassonne, perhaps out of an understandable reluctance to deal with the mess. When, at last, Jean de Picquigny came to the Bourg, he was accompanied by an impressive retinue of soldiery and magistrates. He had heard that even the seneschal's underlings had been manhandled by the mob; anyone, in fact, who had been party to the 1299 agreement, whether a king's man or not, could expect no forbearance from this latest, most serious manifestation of the *rage carcassonnaise*.

Picquigny learned firsthand of the new arrangements. On reaching the gate of the Bourg, Hélie Patrice's sentries gruffly inspected him and his companions. The cries of joy at his arrival then turned to howls of dismay when the townspeople saw that Picquigny's company included a lawyer who had advised the consuls in 1299. He immediately became the target for brickbats and stones, barely escaping with his life.

Picquigny had hardly settled in when Bernard began hectoring him to do something about the Wall. The town was on fire; only freeing the inquisition's prisoners would put out the conflagration. As always, the king, through the agency of his representative, was expected to protect his loyal subjects from harm, in this instance the relentless persecution visited upon them by the diabolical Dominicans.

Picquigny listened, perturbed. He knew that if he acted according to Bernard's wishes, he, not the Franciscan, would feel the full wrath of the Church, and he would be risking his immortal soul. But if he didn't act, the belligerence of Carcassonne might spread throughout Languedoc. The Bruges Matins and the Golden Spurs had happened only the previous year, and the king's face-saving battle at Mons-en-Pévèle would not occur until the following August. In the summer of 1303 his master certainly did not need another rebellious province on his hands, and the king would not have looked kindly on his viceroy for letting matters get out of hand. Only if he marshaled the mob to act under his orders could Picquigny co-opt the dangerous movement and, afterward, claim that it was on the king's initiative that the inquisition prison had been emptied.

Yet he hesitated. It was a momentous step to take, almost as serious as Guillaume de Nogaret's action in Anagni a fortnight later. For one thing, the Wall was the property of King Philip. His sainted grandfather had built it and the royal treasury underwrote the expenses incurred in maintaining it. If Picquigny attacked the prison, some wise heads in his entourage doubtless pointed out, he would be attacking the king. Yet the Dominicans staffing the prison were unlikely to give

The Porte de l'Aude, the all-important gate in the fortifications of the Cité of Carcassonne that overlooked the Wall, the King's Mill, the river Aude, and the Bourg. Délicieux, Picquigny, inquisitors, the rabble—all trod the path seen here.

The city of Albi viewed from the river Tarn. To the right, the hulking mass at the foot of the bell tower of Sainte Cécile is the notorious bishop's residence, the Palais de la Berbie.

King Philip the Fair of France receiving homage from his vassal for Aquitaine, King Edward I of England, on June 5, 1286. The pointed profusion of fleur-de-lis in Jean Fouquet's illumination can be attributed to the date of its execution (ca. 1455)— immediately after the conclusion of the Hundred Years' War. (Bibliothèque nationale de France)

In a chapel of Avignon, the funerary monument of Bernard Délicieux's judge, the corpulent Jacques Fournier, the bishop-inquisitor of Pamiers who became Pope Benedict XII.

Pope Boniface VIII blessing the flock, in a fresco thought to have been executed by Giotto or his disciples. One of many likenesses of Boniface in Rome, the theater of his anachronistic ambition to dominate Europe as comprehensively as Innocent III had done one hundred years earlier.

Fifteenth-century manuscript depicting Pope John XXII receiving the transcript of an interrogation, in much the same way he would have received the sentence of Bernard Délicieux—and then harshened the punishment.

Detail from the sepulcher of the Dominican Pope Benedict XI in Perugia. Bernard Délicieux and Arnaud de Vilanova were thought to have had a hand in his sudden demise.

Eighteenth-century rendering in Avignon of the beleaguered Pope Clement V, who was forced by Guillaume de Nogaret to look the other way as he crushed the Templars.

A Swiss illustration from an early-sixteenth-century chronicle depicting a prisoner being tortured by strappado to elicit a confession about the murder of his wife. Note the weights that can be attached to his feet.

From Giotto's marvelous sequence depicting the life of St. Francis in the upper basilica at Assisi. Here the pope approves the Franciscan rule, which, as the Spirituals later complained, differed considerably from the saint's last testament.

Detail from Fra Angelico's magisterial high altarpiece in the fifteenth-century Dominican church of Fiesole, near Florence. The friars depicted are all "blessed," hence the haloes and totemic items they carry. The kneeling Dominican nuns are similarly beatified. (National Gallery of Art, London)

The Cité of Carcassonne as seen from the Bourg. In the central complex, the three square towers (with different roof types) housed the inquisition headquarters and torture chambers, as well as part of the bishop's palace. Délicieux was held and tried at this complex in 1319. To the left is the residence of the seneschal, now styled the Château Comtal.

The Church of the Jacobins in Toulouse, viewed from the river Garonne. Once Dominican headquarters in Languedoc, now the magnificently spare Gothic repository of the casket of Thomas Aquinas.

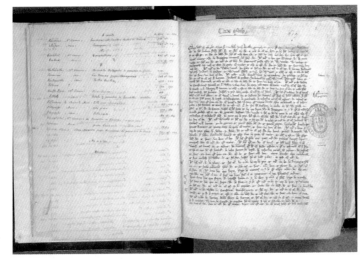

One of the earliest of the dread inquisition registers of medieval Languedoc. Mid-thirteenth century, on display at the Bibliothèque de Toulouse.

The Ponte St. Angelo spanning the Tiber. To the left the Castel St. Angelo, originally built as a mausoleum for the emperor Hadrian.

Pedro Berruguete's late-fifteenth-century rendering of St. Dominic presiding over an auto-da-fé (the victims are lower right). Hanging in Madrid's Prado, it is a celebrated example of the anachronistic "inquisitorializing" of Dominic's biography. The inquisition did not exist in the saint's lifetime.

Giotto's depiction of Pope Innocent III dreaming of Francis of Assisi supporting the weight of St. John Lateran, then the principal church of Christendom and, as such, a symbol of the Church itself.

it up without a fight or some other kind of resistance. Counsels of caution were aired, leading to agonizing indecision. Another consideration to make resolve waver came from the larger opponent the Dominicans represented. To confront the Church head-on, violently, was to flout a long-held taboo and invite the disapprobation of all of Christendom. This would not be a police action of minor moment; this would reverberate across the continent. There is no indication that Jean de Picquigny craved that sort of notoriety.

By the third week of August, the Bourg's ugly equanimity began souring. While it was amusing to rough up the Dominicans of the Bourg, the eyesore on the Aude—the Wall—remained untouched. The voluble Bernard Délicieux seemed to have abandoned his faith in the persuasive power of the word. News reached Picquigny that the Franciscan convent had welcomed several dozen guests from Albi, strapping fellows invited to Carcassonne by Brother Bernard neither as potential novices nor as legal scholars. Their presence made a point without the expenditure of a breath.

Picquigny at last gave the go-ahead. Although the exact date cannot be established, the operation most likely took place during the last week of August 1303. In a country famous for just such an event in 1789, a prison was about to be stormed.

The Wall stood in a no-man's-land between Cité and Bourg, having been built into an outer fortification on the right bank of the Aude. Viewed from the Bourg, it loomed in the middle distance at the foot of the hill crowned by the Cité. Several witnesses at Bernard's trial vividly remembered the morning. Picquigny marched across the old bridge at the head of a company of pikemen and royal sergeants at arms. Behind them came a great gaggle of exuberant townsmen, armed with cudgels, halberds, sticks, clubs, swords, daggers, whatever they could get their hands on. Seeing their number, guards at the outer fortifying wall let the motley soldiery stream through a gate.

The door to the prison was shut tight, locked and bolted. Picquigny called up to a barred window on an upper story that no one would be harmed if the warden opened the door to him. The shouted negotiations stalled, the armed liberators grew restless. The townsmen of

Carcassonne called for the Wall to be razed—not especially difficult, for the prison was built not as a fortress, to repel attack, but as a strongbox, to keep people from escaping. No deadly arrow slits hid archers, no wall walk swarmed with armed defenders.

The standoff could not continue. Picquigny ordered his pikemen to ready themselves for assault. As they were assembling, voluminous parchments wafted into the air from the windows above. They floated downward in the puzzled silence, eventually settling on the cobbles at the attackers' feet.

The documents lodged protests at the outrage about to take place. They contained formal appeals to the pope to reverse the injustice of this day. As with Brother Bernard's magisterial handling of the Castel Fabre matter three years earlier, the Dominicans of the Wall wanted to establish a conspicuous paper trail. These appeals would make Picquigny's action the object of a formal proceeding. The event, far from being a spontaneous calamity, was now duly noted and would one day, the robed jailkeepers hoped, be overturned and avenged in court.

The prison door swung open and Picquigny stepped across the threshold, accompanied by several of his men. The tenor of his conversation with the Dominicans is unknown, but he shortly afterward emerged back out into the yard accompanied by scores of prisoners, blinking in the sunlight. A great cheer went up; hugs were no doubt exchanged between husbands, wives, brothers, sisters, sons, daughters, cousins. The eyewitnesses disagree over whether Bernard Délicieux was present in the crowd, but acquaintance with the workings of the human heart dictates that he must have been there. The day was the culmination of a hard-fought campaign by the agitator of Languedoc, a campaign brilliantly carried out before king, court, magistrate, inquisitor, congregation, and mob. To have missed this moment would have been unthinkable.

Yet the prisoners were not freed. Picquigny showed uncharacteristic indifference to the friar's opinion and instead had them moved to royal custody in the Cité, where they were housed in humane and generous conditions in the towers of the fortifications. The burly ruffians hosted in the Franciscan convent now headed home, to be hastily replaced in Carcassonne by another contingent from Albi—the wives who had complained to the queen of their loneliness.

In keeping the prisoners, the king's man performed an odd act of diplomacy. He had not questioned the verdict of the inquisitors; if he had, he would have set everyone free. Rather, he was addressing the problems of the conditions of detention and possible abuses of legal procedure. That nicety may have amounted to shutting the barn door after the horse had bolted, but the administrative fiction was necessary. His action had effectively placed his king in opposition to the inquisition and the Dominican Order. Already another of the king's ministers, Guillaume de Nogaret, had accused the pope of heresy and was preparing to lead a squad of mercenaries to the papal residence in Anagni. Picquigny would not throw oil on the fire by declaring the whole enterprise of inquisition to be a sham and thereby set up the king for charges of abetting heresy.

From the larger perspective, what Délicieux made happen on that day, no matter what the status of the prisoners, stands as a landmark in the course of medieval history. He had bucked the tide. To a culture of increasing persecution, of a developing Christianity of fear, of a renewed intolerance of Jews, of a nascent fear of witchcraft and sorcery—ultimately, to a culture intent on demonizing dissent and difference—the man who pried open the Wall had said no. Brother Bernard saw violent persecution as incompatible with his religion. It was a stark and simple position. He refused to allow the arguments of expediency and institutional loyalty to construct a worldview fundamentally at odds with his point of departure, as some Dominicans had done in their elaboration of a system of sincere persecution, righteous torture, and judicial killing. A century after Bernard's time a German bishop, horrified by the schism afflicting the Church in the wake of the Avignon exile of the papacy, would write: "When the existence of the Church is threatened, she is released from the commandments of morality. With unity as the end, the use of every means is sanctified, even cunning, treachery, violence, simony, prison, death. For all order is for the sake of the community, and the individual must be sacrificed to the common good."

Bernard Délicieux could never condone such sentiment. He and a few kindred spirits stood up and decried the direction their church was heading. It had joined hands with the torturer and the executioner, effectively seconding the argument that Cathars had put forth for nearly a century: Roma was the opposite of Amor. The Franciscan could not have known that inquisition, once in the control of men far less scrupulous than the medieval Dominicans, would plague Catholic Europe and Latin America for centuries, but he could already see with his own eyes the spiritual corruption it brought in its wake. Bernard was exceptional in that he actually took effective action against this sickness of spirit. Somewhat as the amoral German bishop had advised for the defense of his Church, Bernard had used guile, politicking, demagoguery, oratory, persuasion, perhaps bribery, and even the threat of force to achieve his objective, but he had nonetheless done the unthinkable: overturn the inquisition. And, in contradistinction to the bishop, he had accomplished this without the effusion of blood or the flash of swordplay. He was a man of peace, true to Francis of Assisi. As one simple woman of Carcassonne is said to have exclaimed on hearing him speak: "Behold, the Lord has sent down an angel to help us!"

CHAPTER FIFTEEN

TORURE EXPOSED

ERNARD NOW LABORED to make his victory permanent. The Wall had disgorged a valuable group of informants. These people had been tortured, made to accuse their neighbors, their enemies, their friends. Bernard, combining the instincts of an investigative reporter and an activist lawyer, set out to construct his own version of an inquisition register. He went to the towers of the Cité and interviewed the prisoners, beseeching them to scour their memories and recall the treatment they had received and the words they had spoken. In one part of this "register," Bernard recounted the tortures awaiting those who fell afoul of the inquisition, specifying what had been done to whom, and when. The full panoply of cruel Christianity was laid bare.

This torture section, given Bernard's persuasive proclivities, must have been riveting. Although the document itself has not survived, the nearly indignant references to it contained in the formal charges against him at his trial suggest that, at the very least, it was distressingly colorful. Doubtless the friar evoked the torture in common use in his day, the strappado, the "queen of torments," which was used to elicit confession, the "queen of proofs." In this operation, the victim's hands were tied behind his back and then, the loose end of the rope coil having been played across a ceiling beam, he was raised into the air, his outstretched, distended arms bearing his full weight. Heavy weights could be tied to his feet, to make the contortion even more unbearable. Depending on the whim of the torturer, the rope could be loosed for a split second, causing the victim to drop, then be reimmobilized in midair, the resultant jolt dislocating his arms or pulling them out of their sockets. The strappado might initially last only a few minutes—the time it took for the holy inquisitor to intone a prayer, it was suggested piously—before being renewed if the results proved unsatisfactory.

The inquisitor had many other refinements, which Bernard would have taken care to relate in detail. For women and children, binding of the wrists tightly by coarse wet cord, then unbinding them and starting up the process once again, with even more force, was considered humane. Other extremities could be useful as well. Savagely beating the soles of the feet was fairly common. This sent pain rioting up through the body. For obdurate people, an inflammable liquid could be splashed on the feet and then set alight. This attention to the body's extremities arose from the duty of the thoughtful jurist, then as now, to avoid causing major organ failure. Another common technique entailed sleep deprivation. Forty hours of enforced sleeplessness came to be considered the happy mean. Further treatments common in Carcassonne included the rack, other means of stretching and dislocating (which sometimes came accompanied by the judicious application of hot brands), and the shock of freezing cold water.

In his complementary section, Bernard pieced together the confessions and accusations. He compiled a long list of names, organized by town, of people who were still blithely going about their business, unaware that the inquisitor had plans for them. They had been denounced as supporters of heresy. Were it not for Bernard's and his allies' ability to stymie the inquisitors in both Albi and Carcassonne, the persons bearing these names would have been manacled in the filth of the Wall, awaiting their next beating and strappado. His collating done, he had copies of his work made and disseminated far and wide.

The Franciscan barnstormed the towns and villages between Carcassonne and Albi. He convened meetings at which he told the inhabitants of the brutality and deceit of the inquisitors; for the illiterate, he pointed to their names on his lists. He elicited the expected reaction: horror and anger. Donations flowed into his treasury—only Bernard Délicieux could permanently lift this plague from the land.

Jean de Picquigny had more immediate concerns. Unable to countenance the injury done to the inquisition, Geoffroy d'Ablis had excommunicated Picquigny in September. The king's man would burn in Hell for what he had done. In the same month, the beleaguered Pope

Boniface VIII was shouting *"E le cole, e le cape!"* to the intruders in his residence at Anagni. The outrageous slap took place on September 7; the pope was dead on October 11. Guillaume de Nogaret then quickly joined Jean de Picquigny in the ranks of the excommunicated, an occupational hazard of working for King Philip the Fair.

Whereas, incredibly, Nogaret then labored for seven years to have the dead pontiff disgraced and posthumously excommunicated, Picquigny took another tack. He appealed the sentence of d'Ablis. In October, he and Brother Bernard made the long journey once more to Paris. The Franciscan had been badgering Picquigny to make the voyage to see the king ever since the emptying of the Wall; he had suggested bringing along the prisoners who had been freed from it so that the monarch could see the marks of torture and mistreatment on the bodies of his loyal and blameless subjects. The king's man, perhaps regretting how well he had been played by Délicieux, showed himself once again not to be entirely the friar's creature. He refused to take the men of Albi with him, wisely wishing not to enmesh his master further in Bernard's schemes. Picquigny had paid the price: now he was an excommunicate, with little chance of a speedy reprieve from Rome. He knew that the events at Carcassonne and at Anagni would hardly dispose the new pontiff to think fondly of the French. In any event, given the turmoil usually attendant on the conclave charged with electing a pope, several months, even years, could pass before the throne of St. Peter was once again occupied. The cardinals would not lift his excommunication in the interim.

The Dominicans, not surprisingly, decided to exacerbate Picquigny's difficulties. At a general chapter held in Paris in the fall of 1303, the leaders of the Friars Preachers in France proclaimed his appeal invalid and confirmed the sentence of excommunication. Brother Geoffroy d'Ablis, they declared, had done the right thing in throwing this godless hypocrite out of the sacred communion of the Church.

Picquigny viewed this intervention in his appeal process as gratuitous, malicious, and infuriating. In a letter he asked for support from the consuls and townspeople of Toulouse, Carcassonne, Albi, Cordes, Pamiers, Montauban, Béziers, Gaillac, and Rabastens. It is an extraordinary document, so vehement in its language that it was included in the transcripts of Bernard's trial. One can divine the reason for this odd inclusion, for the excerpt below, even given the shroud of translation, leaves no doubt as to the identity of Picquigny's ghostwriter:

> There are no words, no expressions that We could use to convey just how spitefully, irreligiously, monstrously and deceitfully some lying, perfidious, iniquitous men, who are ravening wolves disguised as lambs, have falsely denounced Us before our lord the king, our lady the queen and all the great of their court. Namely, Fr. Geoffroy d'Ablis, inquisitor, along with other friars, who in reality do not preach, but rather breach divine law and infallible truth. Repaying us evil for good, hate for love, in their distress at seeing our lord the king, his advisors and other men of good faith refusing to believe, as they had hoped, their poisonous words, they struck out higher and higher, reaching at last the weapon of excommunication. Abusing power, forsaking truth and embracing error, like madmen and dullards, they declared in a public sermon at the Dominican house in Paris that We were de facto excommunicate, thus offending our lord the king, madame the queen and their privy council, and that We were a supporter of heretics and a notorious troubler of the office of the Inqusition—this, after and in spite of a canonical appeal that We have submitted to the Apostolic See . . . [Their action] constitutes a manifest attack on the truth and an offense to justice.

The blistering missive had its desired effect. The good burghers of Languedoc opened their purses to fund Picquigny's defense. But by October 29, the date of this letter, news may already have reached Paris of what had transpired in Rome four days earlier. Contrary to custom, a new pope had been elected with remarkable dispatch, prompted by the unprecedented insult administered to the papacy at Anagni. The process had taken but eleven days.

The new pontiff called himself Benedict XI, in tribute to Benedetto Caetani, the late, great Pope Boniface VIII. Prior to his elevation to Christendom's highest perch, Niccolò Boccasini had lectured in theology and written commentaries on the Psalms, Job, Matthew and Revelation. He had then gone on to other, more prestigious positions. For the previous seven years, he had been the Master-General of the Order of Friars Preachers. The new pope was a leader of the Dominicans.

Other startling news quickly followed. Although the nature of Brother Bernard's conversations with the king in October of that year has not survived the passage of time, we do know that at one point Philip informed Délicieux and Picquigny that their oft-extended invitation had finally been accepted.

The king wanted to see for himself what was going in Languedoc. King Philip and Queen Joan would come to Toulouse on Christmas Day, 1303.

1304

CHAPTER SIXTEEN

THE KING AND QUEEN IN LANGUEDOC

OULOUSE SPREADS ITS PINK EMBRACE over both banks of the river Garonne. The capital of Languedoc in the time of Bernard Délicieux, the modern city still has an immense old quarter filled with a hodgepodge of half-timbered houses, medieval towers, and Renaissance mansions. Its basilica, St. Sernin, is the largest and loveliest Romanesque church in southern France. Across town and nearer the river, its splendid Gothic grace notes given their finishing touches in Brother Bernard's day, rises the Church of the Jacobins. Now a public monument, the sanctuary possesses a quiet cloister that was home to meditative Dominicans and an impossibly lofty nave that soars high above the golden casket of Thomas Aquinas.

This is not to suggest that Toulouse's history has been as harmonious as the city appears at first glance. Like its lesser sisters in the region, *la ville rose* has had its moments of tensions and unrest. Early in the thirteenth century, Toulouse had been a protagonist in the Albigensian Crusade, stoutly resisting occupation by the invading northerners and, on one memorable afternoon in 1218, catapulting a rocky payload directly through the skull of the French leader of the Crusaders then besieging the city. That murderous event, and others of its kind, is remembered in a profusion of giant tableaux executed by history painter Jean-Paul Laurens and hung in the city's grand Capitole, the town hall from which the *capitouls*—consuls—once governed their prosperous fellow citizens.

In a great city with such a long and checkered history, there cannot help but be layers of memory on any given street. One such place is the southern entrance to the old town, where the Narbonne Gate once stood. So called for the road leading to the Roman provincial capital of Narbonne, by medieval times the gate stood in the shadow of the similarly named Château Narbonnais, a hulking, impregnable fortress astride the city's fortifications that lodged the family of the most powerful lord of the moment. That château is long gone, its inhabitants replaced by the Parlement, a dispenser of the king's justice—Martin Guerre, the famed identity thief, was tried here—and nowadays of French republican law.

Across a small triangular plaza from the modern Parlement building stands a modest medieval house, of an unremarkable reddish brown color punctuated by curious half-moon windows on its upper floor. This is the Maison Seilhan, so named for the man who gave this dwelling in 1215 to St. Dominic. The building then became the headquarters of the inquisition in Toulouse. The ordinary Dominicans lived near the Church of the Jacobins; their persecuting brethren practiced their nonroyal, nonrepublican form of jurisprudence here.

The layering of memory increases in complexity as the triangular plaza, called place du Parlement, gives way to a slightly larger and more regular square, place du Salin. The *salin* refers to the salt tax, which was collected here by agents of the king housed in the Maison du Roi, on the square's north side, well in sight of the inquisitor's offices. The Gothic royal house, however, has been a Protestant church since 1911, a metamorphosis that no doubt would have the defenders of the faith across the way tearing at their tonsures in confusion.

Yet distant posterity has not been altogether unkind to inquisitor Bernard Gui and his fellows. In 1988, the Maison Seilhan—which had undergone many uses over the centuries, including housing a spice shop—was purchased and lovingly restored by a group associated with the modern-day Dominican order. The rehabilitation of the house of the inquisition did not go unnoticed. Several years later, on a traffic island close to the Maison Seilhan, a signpost was installed bearing an inscription that reads, in part (in French):

> *Homage*
> *To the precursors of the Enlightment*
> *Victims of obscurantism*
> *Who studied or taught at Toulouse:*

Giulio Cesare Vanini   (1585–1619)
Italian philosopher, burned alive on this spot for atheism on
*   February 9, 1619*
Etienne Dolet   burned in Paris   (1509–1546)
Michel Servet   burned in Geneva   (1511–1553)
Giordano Bruno   burned in Rome   (1548–1600)
They prefigured free thought and reason
The matter in the sky is no different from that of a man or a beetle
*   (G. C. Vanini,* Amphitheatrum)

This showdown in the present is discreet, a faint but distinct echo of
the resentments associated with the area ever since the Maison Seilhan
became home to the inquisitors. Indeed, the traffic thunders through
the two squares, heedless of past commotions. Such a carefree passage
was impossible on Christmas Day, 1303. On that occasion, King Philip
IV of France rode through the Narbonne Gate, past the Château Narbonnais on his right and the Maison Seilhan on his left, amidst a scene
of indescribable chaos.

The progress of the king and queen to their southern possessions was
stately in the late autumn of 1303. The king made this journey only
once in his thirty-year reign. The towns on the monarchs' itinerary had
received them with the deference due their exalted rank. None of the
swank that had greeted them two years earlier in Flanders was on display, just a dignified solicitude toward this feared lord and his much
beloved lady. They undertook the extended tour to dispel fears of further weakness in the wake of the Flemish debacle. The king would attend to Flanders; his people need only support and trust him. There
may also have been the matter of a much-needed ordering of the royal
establishment. Perhaps as a result of Philip's preoccupation with the
late pope, or, more likely, through the usual human frailties, corruption seems to have run deep in the king's administration. In the months
and years to follow this tour, several senior officials were dismissed and
replaced, and the chancery in Paris regularly issued royal ordinances
promising to root out abusive practices. The Dominicans were not the
only irritants in the provinces—other grievances could spark revolt.

The orchestrated stateliness of the tour evaporated instantly once the royal party reached the great city on the Garonne. Philip installed Queen Joan in the Château Narbonnais before heading into town on Christmas Day. At once, he was met by a near hysterical mob, the handiwork of Délicieux. The people of Albi, Cordes, Carcassonne, and other towns had been recruited to join with the Toulousains in calling for action. They cheered vociferously, yelled out their desire for justice, begged the king to put an end to their woes.

Bernard had used near-riot to good effect before, by making Jean de Picquigny's return to Carcassonne the previous August frighteningly raucous. Now it was Philip's turn to receive the same treatment. The commoners pressed in on their king, waving clubs and jostling his escort. The clamor deafened, the horses reared. Whether the crowd welcomed or threatened was at best ambiguous, perhaps deliberately so.

The king was not amused. A biographer of the great Capetian monarch states that Philip had two religions, Christianity and sacred kingship—and that the latter was more important to him than the former. Thus Philip could indeed really believe that the pope was a heretic, the Templars traitors, the inquisitors dishonest, the Lombards treacherous, the Jews extortionate, if the action of any of these parties somehow impeded the exercise of his divine office. Such a view accorded a great place to the dignity of the king's person, which had been seriously ill-used by the Christmas scrum in the streets of Toulouse. Bernard's rabble-rousing tactic had clearly been a mistake. The king was shaken and furious, not intimidated.

Philip's ministers called a meeting in early January 1304 to hear all sides in the ongoing struggle for the soul of Languedoc. This was not to be an audience of one. Dominicans, Franciscans, bishops, royal officials, and a delegation from Carcassonne and Albi led by Délicieux were invited to a large hall in the Château Narbonnais. However grandiose the setting, the atmosphere cannot have been relaxed. The king was surrounded by his counselors, including Guillaume de Nogaret, who had directly joined the royal tour after making historic mischief in Italy. Thus, the churchmen in attendance had to put up with the presence of two notorious excommunicates, Nogaret and Jean de Picquigny.

Picquigny was invited to speak first. He reiterated what he had told the king the previous October when he and Bernard had traveled to

Paris: the inquisitions at Albi and at Carcassonne were corrupt and unjust, and he had been unreasonably excommunicated. He had just done his duty as a loyal officer of the crown and moved to correct what was a serious and dangerous situation. There were some in the Dominican order who had proved unworthy of the responsibilities given them by their superiors. The king's subjects were restive, unhappy.

At this point he was interrupted. Brother Guilhem Peire de Godin, the head of the Dominicans in Languedoc, stood to speak. The king nodded. The friar read from a document obtained from the desk of none other than Jean de Picquigny. It was a letter addressed but not yet sent to the king, a letter of unusually violent language, warning—even threatening—the monarch that unless he acted decisively against the inquisitors, the people would rise up as they had in Flanders. As one witness recalled at Bernard's trial: "[Picquigny] had found the whole country to be in a very bad state because of the bishop and the inquisitors, and that unless his lordship [Philip] came down to the country to remedy the situation, the people of the country would make themselves a king the way the Flemings had."

The allusion to De Coninck and his rebellious allies sent a scandalized murmur through the hall. Some things were best left unsaid. The king could not have been pleased. Only a week or two previously, just a few steps from where this disputation was being held, he had been accorded a nearly rebellious reception in the streets of Toulouse—and now his officer had the temerity to invoke the disgraceful treason of Bruges and the Golden Spurs! Philip's famously impassive demeanor turned icy. Faced with his master's dark countenance, Picquigny set about making excuses, claiming the letter was merely a draft and that the inflammatory clause about Flanders was the result of a clerical error by an inexperienced scribe.

Picquigny continued his presentation, but it was effectively over. He had lost the king's attention and, no doubt, his own eloquence. The purloined letter had dealt a body blow from which he never recovered. As if he had displeased an even greater power, within eight months Picquigny was dead, succumbing to some sudden malady, an excommunicate to the end. At the time he was in Italy, desperately trying to make his case to the papal curia. He died disconsolate, not knowing that he would be posthumously pardoned four years later.

After Picquigny meekly sat down, the provincial of the Dominicans in Languedoc rose once again to take the floor. Brother Guilhem cannot have been happy with Philip, given the actions taken by his agent in Carcassonne and at Anagni by the man who now sat, serene in his sinfulness, at the king's right hand. Still, there was a silver lining to Nogaret's action: Guilhem's esteemed colleague Brother Niccolò had ascended to the papacy.

As could only have been expected, Brother Guilhem launched into a rousing defense of his Dominican brethren and an equally rousing denunciation of their enemies. Unexpectedly, the Dominican superior then veered back to the case of Foulques de Saint-Georges, arguing that he had been badly treated. King Philip had publicly excoriated inquisitor Foulques and had spent months pressuring the Dominicans in Paris to relieve him of his post—which they eventually did. Now the head of the Dominicans in Languedoc had dredged up the affair all over again, as if to remind the king of how much the friars had enraged and defied him two years earlier. Possibly Brother Guilhem could not let any slight to his organization pass without comment. Or perhaps somewhere in a single-minded fanaticism lay a belief that he could change the monarch's mind, make him view things the correct—Dominican—way. Whatever his reasoning, Brother Guilhem had shown himself devoid of diplomatic instinct, and his presentation turned out to be as ineffective as Picquigny's, which he had so adroitly sabotaged.

Bernard Délicieux then rose to speak. No doubt all in attendance expected, with either dread or delight, a performance worthy of his reputation. Once again the friar of Carcassonne did not disappoint.

He began by picking away at something Brother Guilhem had apparently said either in his oration or at an earlier meeting. The head of the Dominicans in Languedoc had admitted there could be no more than forty or fifty heretics in all of the country around Carcassonne and Albi. Why then, Bernard asked, was an inquisition necessary? Why the horrendous architecture of repression, making multitudes unhappy, if there was only a handful of heretics still out there? Why were those innocent men of Albi still incarcerated? The king, Délicieux argued, was wasting resources, creating ill will, giving the impression of approving a brotherhood bent on prolonging pain, even as their provincial in Languedoc admitted that heresy was a fast-vanishing problem.

At this point, Bernard switched from extemporaneous commentary to the rhetorical assault he would have prepared in advance. Up until this moment, Bernard had delivered his tirades solely for the edification of the laity, the townspeople and villagers of Languedoc and the king and his court in France. At this meeting he was face-to-face with the people he wished to destroy and who wished to destroy him. He condemned the inquisition in front of the inquisitors. While Bernard's speech in Toulouse went well beyond the particularities of his story to teach a universal lesson in courage, within the constraints of his own times it was a remarkable moment. One can only imagine the expression of amazement—perhaps even admiration—on the face of Guillaume de Nogaret, that master of backroom treachery, as the Franciscan launched his very public attack.

At his trial Bernard recounted the scene. On October 10, 1319, some fifteen years after this speech, after being tortured and knowing full well that he might face death, he continued to stand by what he argued to the king, his court and the inquisitors:

> I said that if Saint Peter and Saint Paul were alive today and that if that they were accused of adoring the Perfect, and if they were proceeded against as certain inquisitors have proceeded against so many people, they would have no way of defending themselves. Because if they were asked about their faith, they would respond as Doctors and Masters of the faith. But when they were told they had adored the Perfect, they would ask who had said this—and they would be given only last and Christian names so common that Saints Peter and Paul would say, "We do not know them. Tell us where they're from, when they came here, where they went, what their language is, their appearance, their occupation?" And they would be told nothing that would allow them to know who were the Perfect that they had been accused of adoring. If they then asked when this adoration took place, they would not be told the day, the month or the year; if they asked the names of the witnesses, they would not be given them, and no one could say that these most holy apostles could defend themselves of such a charge before such men, all the more so since anyone coming to their defense would be suspect of supporting heresy: . . . So that's what I said then.

The manner of delivery of Bernard's speech in Toulouse, given his flair for the theatrical, must have been incandescent. In the sober setting of the trial fifteen years later, he spoke dispassionately, clearly describing the workings of an infernal machine. The imposture of the Carcassonne inquisition, worthy of Kafka, was fully laid bare. And in portraying the two greatest figures of early Christianity as powerless before the inquisitor, the Franciscan's argument strangely anticipates Dostoevsky, before whose Grand Inquisitor in *The Brothers Karamazov* even Jesus Christ himself is helpless. Paul, Peter, and Jesus could have done nothing before the implacable injustice of inquisition.

The meeting in Toulouse was not going the way the king and his ministers had planned. The archbishop of Narbonne held up a hand to silence Délicieux. Gilles Aycelin, who at Senlis had acted for the king in investigating the competing claims of Jean de Picquigny and Foulques de Saint-Georges, rose to his feet and looked directly at the fiery Franciscan. The king, he reminded the friar, had addressed the problems brought to his attention. He had taken the temporal offices away from Bishop Bernard de Castanet and made sure the unsatisfactory inquisitors were removed from office.

Speaking as the king's proxy, Archbishop Aycelin was, in effect, telling Bernard Délicieux what Philip and his counselors had already decided to do. The inquisitors, Aycelin continued, would still be under the control of their local bishops. No arrests would be made without the assent of parties outside the Dominican order. An inquisitor could no longer act with impunity. The senior royal officials of the district had to be consulted and give their approval for any proceeding to move forward.

Bernard realized that the proposed policy constituted a return to the concessions won in the 1290s by the lawyers of Carcassonne. It notably did not wrest control of the inquisition from the Dominicans. The Wall would stand. And the men and women transferred from the Dominican dungeon the previous summer would remain incarcerated.

Surely these conditions were satisfactory to the people of Albi and Carcassonne, the archbishop concluded. The inquisition, which had been charged by the Holy Father to stamp out the leprosy of heresy, would be surrounded by safeguards to ensure that no further abuse was possible.

The bishop sat down. The king, Nogaret, and the entire court looked at the lone figure in front of them. The message delivered by this collective gaze was simple: Délicieux should step back. Too much was at stake here. The king had narrowly escaped excommunication in his struggle with the late pope. The new pontiff had to be given a peace offering. The French monarchy could not attack the Dominicans when a Dominican wore the papal tiara. The politics of the day were complex. There were rebels in Flanders, restive burghers in different reaches of the kingdom, problems of finance and diplomacy, swirling intrigues, rumors of war. The king could not afford another major crisis.

Bernard Délicieux considered his options. Picquigny had crumpled when challenged, and his message went unheard. The Franciscan had labored so long and so hard to have the Dominicans ousted—and now that prospect was slipping beyond his grasp. He knew only too well that Pope Benedict XI, as a Dominican, would one day come after him, and that this moment was his last chance. A streak of fanaticism may have played in his mind as well, leading him to think that with one more effort he could bring the king around to see things from the correct—Franciscan—point of view.

He resumed his speech. After the first few words, the assembly knew that Délicieux had chosen to ignore Aycelin's conciliatory message and the unspoken supplication of those now looking at him. His trust in the wisdom of the king and his court, Bernard stated bluntly, was shaken. In deciding this policy, they were acting neither competently nor rationally. If the inquisition was so blameless, he asked his king rhetorically, then why should there have been a need to take any action at all? He turned witheringly sardonic: if the inquisitors were just and good men, then they should be rewarded. Even at his trial, in recollecting this speech, he could not resist sarcasm, saying that these supposedly good inquisitors "should be congratulated in many ways, honored like golden candelabras of the church, to the sound of trumpets." Why shame them in the people's eyes by installing bishops to look over their shoulders?

But if they had done wrong, then what precisely was the point of these half measures? Evil men will evil do. When a doctor was faced with a sick man, Bernard argued, he had to determine the type of disease afflicting his patient. Common sense called for the physician to find out exactly what was wrong and then take drastic action to combat the illness. And Languedoc was gravely ill, Bernard declared; the sickness of Dominican inquisitors afflicted the land, a sickness that demanded a drastic cure. His voice rose, his temper flared.

It was a wonder, he exclaimed, that the people of Languedoc did not rise up against the French who ruled them and shout as one: "Get out!" The last he spat out in the *langue d'oc.*

The king started in anger. Nogaret crossed the room and stood before the friar, who was to speak no more. Délicieux had said the unforgivable. He had committed the trespass of Bernard Saisset, treating the sacred rule of Philip over Languedoc as a foreign occupation. Jean de Picquigny, who had been the Franciscan's midwife in court manners at Senlis, must have looked at his protégé in astonishment. He had worked so diligently on behalf of the people of Albi and Carcassonne—he must have wondered if Bernard's talk of the king's loyal subjects in the south had all been a tale told to a fool.

The Franciscan regained his seat. He added his voice to the chorus of whispers that followed the abrupt termination of his speech. He sought the ear of a man of Albi who was to speak next, Arnaud Garsie, his longtime confederate and fellow advocate in Senlis. Arnaud, whose mocking likeness still adorned the Dominican convent in Albi, must have winced as Bernard whispered to him an outlandish accusation and instructed him to repeat it in front of the king. The Franciscan believed it to be his trump card, to be played as part of a last-ditch effort to shake the king from his complacency about the Dominicans. Since Bernard had shattered a taboo about southern resentment toward the northerners, he no doubt thought he could bring up again the forbidden topic of Flanders. The extraordinary meeting held one more extraordinary surprise

Arnaud bowed to his monarch, who knew him from Senlis, then announced that the king's inner circle harbored a traitor. He pointed to a Dominican, Brother Nicolas de Fréauville, the king's personal confessor and one of the most powerful men at court. Arnaud had it on good authority that Brother Nicolas was in the pay of the Flemish rebels. Every word uttered in court about the king's plans to put down the rebellion reached their ears, thanks to their spy in high places.

Stupefaction greeted this revelation. The king ordered one of his ministers to question Arnaud, which was done in a tone of peremptory skepticism. The brave man of Albi did not reveal the source of this tale—Bernard Délicieux, who had in turn heard it from a high-placed cardinal in Paris the year before. Arnaud did admit, however, that the story of Fréauville's alleged treachery was hearsay, which earned him a swingeing rebuke from the king. He too would not be allowed to speak again.

A last speaker from Castres, Peire Pros, finished the proceedings, but the serial uproars of the day worked to drown out whatever he said. King Philip had heard quite enough for one afternoon: first Picquigny threatening him with a Flemish-like revolt; then the Dominican returning to the matter of Foulques de Saint-George; then the insolent Franciscan daring to lecture his king on the nature of his rule and even suggesting he ruled illegitimately; and this last outrage, sordid gossip about his confessor from a desperate, unscrupulous man. The impassive *roi de marbre* must have shown his displeasure for all to see. The king's patience had been tried to its limits—from the moment he entered Toulouse, tribulations had beset him. His decision was made and it would be enforced.

A sad, almost comical, cavalcade crossed the wintry countryside in the opening months of 1304. The trees were barren, the vineyards a parade ground of shriveled stumps, their last spindly growths already snapped off and stored to dry for the fire in the hearth. A few dark stands of cypress bent under the February wind. The king and queen, accompanied by their retinue of lords, ladies, and ministers, took to the old Roman thoroughfares and rode through the villages of Languedoc to hold court in each of its major towns. Following them, at a safe distance, came a swarm of petitioners and hangers-on, hoping to get the ear of the powerful for a few precious minutes. Among these were the men of Albi, Castres, and Carcassonne and the disappointed Franciscan, mulling over what to do next.

The first stop was Carcassonne, which had been decked out in finery to celebrate the arrival of the royal couple. The little king, Hélie Patrice, seems to have learned nothing from the real king's displeasure at the antics of his subjects in Toulouse on Christmas Day. Annoyingly overfamiliar, Patrice dogged the king's heels as the monarch approached his troubled city, offering advice and veiled threats. One witness claimed Patrice said to the king, "My lord, you must do us justice quickly, else we will turn toward another lord." Even if he had not been so foolish to say this, which was a variant of the Franciscan's ill-advised cry of "Get out," Patrice could not have been a welcome presence to the king. Philip's seneschal had told him that Patrice's militia controlled the Bourg and showed no aversion to disarming the king's officers and roughing them up. And if, as is speculated, the little king rose from the lower ranks and usurped the power of local nobles and respectable burghers, Philip would have been even less well disposed to have the ruffian as constant companion.

The inevitable at last occurred at the governor's palace of the Cité. As Philip mounted the monumental stairway, an exasperated Patrice yelled out from the bottom, "Lord! Lord! Have pity on your wretched city which suffers so!"

The king turned and addressed his sergeants, gesturing toward Patrice and his men: "Throw them out of here!"

Disgusted, Patrice got on his horse and rode down to the Bourg. The townspeople awaited the good news of his royal interview. Instead, Patrice ordered them to rip down the garlands and banners and tear them apart, to give this king no sign that his subjects bore him any love whatsoever. Carcassonne was soon as bare as its surrounding orchards and vineyards. The queen subsequently made the conciliatory gesture of visiting the men of Albi held in custody in the Cité, but no move was made to release them. Still, that the queen of France had visited these prisoners, convicted sympathizers of heresy, was remarkable in and of itself, proof that the monarch still believed what Bernard Délicieux had argued. The problem lay in the fact that the king was not going to do anything about it at this time.

Further indignities followed as the cavalcade set off again toward Narbonne, then Béziers. Witnesses at Bernard's trial tell a strange tale of two large silver vases, paid for by civic subscription, that were to be offered to the king and queen as a token of the city's gratitude. They had not been ready in time for the monarchs' stay at Carcassonne, but the silversmiths delivered them to the townsmen during the journey eastward. At Béziers, Queen Joan accepted hers. Philip did not—and then ordered his lady to give back her vase. The men of Carcassonne now looked, as one historian notes, "ridiculous."

The humiliating cavalcade continued, toward Montpellier and Nîmes. Hélie Patrice, Arnaud Garsie, Peire Pros, Bernard Délicieux, and their frustrated allies tagged along, vases clanging in their luggage, hoping against hope. Bernard was not permitted to address a single word to the king.

Guillaume de Nogaret finally took the Franciscan aside. Clearly the king's minister must have had a good deal of respect and compassion for his fellow southerner, and perhaps he was tickled that the friar had so successfully indulged in Nogaret's specialty—giving the Church grief. His customary behavior would certainly not have included divulging the thinking of the king's inner circle, yet with the Franciscan he opened up. Guillaume may actually have liked Bernard.

It's over, he told the friar. The king would not be moved, and he could not be persuaded to defy the Dominican pope. The struggle with Boniface had brought the king to the brink of disaster—as Nogaret, of all people, knew—and now was not the time to pick another fight. The moment called for reconciliation. Wait, he advised Bernard, until circumstances became more favorable.

What had been understood implicitly was conveyed explicitly to Bernard by the most powerful man in France, aside from the king himself. The men of Carcassonne and Albi made their farewells and rode home through the barren landscape, disheartened, dejected, but pensive.

CHAPTER SEVENTEEN

INTRIGUE IN THE ROUSSILLON

O NE DAY SHORTLY AFTER EASTER IN 1304, two robed figures on horseback picked their way southward alongside the Mediterranean Sea. Once past the border town of Salses, they had left the kingdom of France and come within sight of their destination, Perpignan, home to their Catalan cousins and capital of the Kingdom of Majorca. The red city slumbered in the warm spring sunshine. Beyond its church spires and russet warren of brick dwellings, in the distance, the sculpted line of the Pyrenees stretched into the clouds. The tallest peak, the Canigou, still had the snows of winter on its majestic summit. At its foot lay the well-watered plain of the Roussillon, its fertile bounty a source of amazement for visitors from arid Languedoc.

Within the travelers' pack was a letter bearing the seal of the consuls of Carcassonne. It was addressed to a prince of Majorca. The consuls were asking him to place their city under his protection. If the prince showed himself willing to be their lord, they would gladly slip the traces of Capetian France. Secession was its goal.

Bernard Délicieux was the letter's bearer and author. He and a fellow friar sought the third of four sons sired by King Jaume II of Majorca, Prince Ferran, a man renowned for his warrior prowess and possessed of an ambition thwarted by his status as a younger brother. Brother Bernard was offering him the kingdom he craved. In so doing, he was also committing high treason.

The events of the winter had pushed Bernard and his allies to this extremity. Following the disastrous disputation in Toulouse, the humiliation of the calvacade, the insult of the silver vases, and, in the end, the explicit advice delivered by Guillaume de Nogaret, the men of

Languedoc desirous of lifting the yoke of the Dominican inquisition knew that they could no longer look to their king for help. Philip the Fair was determined to preserve a situation and an institution they could not abide. The corruption, the corvine pecking at the body of an agonized Languedoc, had to be halted another way.

The scheme seems to have been first mooted a month earlier, during King Philip's visit to Montpellier. The great university city was, at the time, a part of the kingdom of Majorca, surrounded by Capetian holdings, so its suzerain, King Jaume II, journeyed north from the Roussillon to extend his hospitality to the French monarch. Philip was the Majorcan king's ally in keeping the armies of Jaume's cousin, the mighty king of Aragon, safely south of the Pyrenees, away from the kingdom of Majorca—thus France's friendship mattered greatly to the Catalan monarch. From Perpignan, Jaume had traveled to Montpellier amid the requisite pomp to welcome his distinguished visitors, accompanied by his court and his family, including Prince Ferran.

Testimony at Bernard's trial—the source of the scarce information concerning the nebulous plot—states that the Franciscan was seen twice conferring with the thirty-year-old prince during Philip's visit to Languedoc. On the second occasion, at Nîmes, in the company of Hélie Patrice this time, the parties appeared deep in conversation, saying "sinister words." By then, presumably, the spurned silver vases were being rerouted south, to Perpignan, and not north to Paris.

In Carcassonne, a few of the consuls reacted with horror when informed of their allies' intentions to secede from France. They refused to go along with the scheme. The same reaction, only stronger, occurred in Albi, to which Arnaud Garsie had returned to rally support, albeit unsuccessfully. The Albigeois knew their detested bishop was still in trouble with his hierarchy and that his expulsion from their midst would be only a matter of time (it occurred in 1307). With Bishop de Castanet defanged and the Dominicans of Albi demoralized, no inquisition troubled the city on the Tarn. Other towns they approached, such as Limoux and Cordes, had turned them down, too. Thus the Carcassonnais were on their own in this new adventure.

When Bernard rode into Perpignan on that spring day, he found the Palace of the Kings of Majorca—a stunningly beautiful Mediterranean fortress-residence that still stands—to be empty of its royal occupants.

They had decamped to their country quarters, at Saint-Jean-Pla-de-Corts (in Catalan, Sant Joan de Pladecorts), in the shadow of the Pyrenees. Bernard would have to travel there, a half day's ride, to meet with the prince. He and his companion, whose identity is uncertain, set out again, riding south, in all likelihood past the town of Elne. There is no record of Bernard stopping to see Bishop Raimond Costa, to thank him for the use of his Carcassonne townhouse as the breeding ground for so many anti-inquisitorial initiatives. Equally absent is a record of Bernard's confiding the strategy underpinning this audacious plot to any like-minded cleric. That can only be conjectured.

The idea must have been not to raise an army—there were so few in on the plot—but to spark an insurrection. Like medieval Bolsheviks, Ferran and his handful of conspirators were to somehow seize an important choke point, and from that action a chain reaction of rebellion would begin, its end result the ejection of the French from the lands of Languedoc. That happy outcome would not be easy to accomplish, but an attempt had to be made to reverse the return to the wretched status quo: the inquisitor working hand in hand with the royal seneschal. Historians have judged the plan "silly" and "hopeless," but the mere fact of entertaining such a scheme—and then acting on it—speaks volumes about the desperation of the men of Languedoc at the mercy of the inquisitors.

Bernard knew just how deep resentments ran toward the French and the inquisitors; he had toured Languedoc more thoroughly than any foreign royal functionary. From that knowledge he must have concluded that the seditious enterprise could work. The French had struggled mightily to subdue Languedoc during the Albigensian Crusade eighty years earlier, having done this with reinforcements from all over Europe. Subsequent armed repressions in the region during the thirteenth century had been effected through the use of local Languedoc muscle, paid in the king's coin. Turn these men, he no doubt thought, and the French presence in Languedoc would be exposed as a paper tiger.

In the spring of 1304, the Flemish rebels still stood defiant on the battlements of their cities. Even if the revolt in Languedoc did not succeed as decisively as its forerunner in Flanders, a king made desperate by two rebellions might be more inclined to negotiate—or rather accede to the anti-inquisitorial demands of the south. For Bernard, there was also the distinct probability that the long arm of a Dominican pope might soon reach out to snatch him, with Philip's consent. He surely thought that to act boldly was more sensible than to submit meekly. However much he took risks, Bernard would not have courted death—as he did by riding to meet Prince Ferran—had he thought himself engaged in an enterprise automatically doomed to failure.

Saint-Jean-Pla-de-Corts sits on a small rise overlooking the rushing river Tech, now the southernmost watercourse in mainland France. Just beyond the stream rises the green wall of the Albères, the last range of the Pyrenees on their march to sudden, almost operatic conclusion as rocky cliffs plunging into the bright blue sea. When Bernard glanced up at the Albères, he would have known that less than ten years earlier the negotiations to end the latest war between Majorca and Aragon had opened in a chapel at the mountain range's Perthus Pass. They were concluded in Italy with the signing of the Treaty of Anagni.

Of King Jaume's summer palace, little remains in the present day: a few roofless enclosures, their ancient wooden beams once supporting elegant upper stories; a solid royal chapel turned art gallery; and tawny medieval fortifications into which villagers have burrowed all manner of dwellings over the centuries. The hamlet is quiet, the motes of dust drifting lazily through the air illumined by the stark sunlight. Visitors are remarked, as they would have been seven centuries ago, especially if they were Franciscans speaking the *langue d'oc* and venturing into the royal precinct of the Catalans.* These friars would have been recognized as men of learning, only heightening curiosity as to the purpose of their visit.

Bernard and his companion called in at a local church and found lodging. The prince and his father the king were out hunting wild boar, still one of the principal inducements behind leaving the cramped streets of Perpignan for the verdant woods of Saint-Jean. On their return, Ferran slipped down to the Franciscan's hostelry for a meeting.

---

* The French Catalans of the Roussillon refer to the "foreigners" north of the Corbières—i.e., Languedoc—as *gavatx* (pronounced "ga-batch"), meaning "rustic oafs."

Bernard, fifteen years later at his trial, claimed that he then tried to dissuade the hotheaded prince from going through with the scheme. He also claimed to have destroyed the consuls' letter before reaching Saint-Jean-Pla-de-Corts by tearing up the document, digging a hole, stuffing the parchment fragments into it, covering up the hole with dirt, and then peeing on the spot. Why he would go to such absurd lengths to destroy the letter, if indeed he had had a change of heart, must remain a mystery. Or he is simply not to be believed. His recollection of this visit to Saint-Jean-Pla-de-Corts changed over the course of his trial, subject as he was to the attentions of aggressive interrogators.

Two Catalans who testified at Bernard's trial stated that King Jaume had got wind of the plot by the time the friars arrived. How this happened is unknown: perhaps, on receiving reports that the famed Bernard Délicieux had been sighted in Perpignan and had met secretly with his impetuous son, Jaume astutely put two and two together. More likely he had been tipped off. One of the many consuls of Carcassonne or Albi horrified by the proposed revolt—and by what would be the fearful, bloodthirsty roar of the vengeful French monarch—probably got word to the Catalan king of the dangerous game his son was playing.

Whatever the source, the king knew. The next afternoon, after having ridden out on the hunt with the prince once again, Jaume forsook his habitual siesta and instead called for Ferran to attend him in his royal apartments. The prince arrived as summoned. His father then proceeded to beat the living daylights out of him. Whether Ferran admitted or denied the Carcassonne scheme is unknown; regardless, the king went berserk. Sounds of his rage echoed down the stone corridors. A footman rushed in and restrained the king from clubbing his son senseless. The royal chamberlain, late to the scene, saw a flushed and battered Ferran stagger down a hallway, clumps of hair his father had just torn out falling from his shoulders. The king had administered a brutal lesson on just how vital to the kingdom of Majorca was its alliance with France.

Bernard, waiting at his inn for a feast of wildfowl promised to him by his princely host, was accosted by a man sent by the king. The newcomer informed him that His Majesty was mightily displeased with the Franciscan for speaking to his son without first presenting himself to the king and making a formal request for such a meeting. Bernard hotly replied that he had met with sons of far more important kings and hadn't needed anyone's permission.

The king's emissary told Bernard that he and his companion had to leave Saint-Jean-Pla-de-Corts immediately. The king did not care about the late hour. And the next day, he insisted, they were to leave the kingdom altogether. Despite the order to quit the kingdom as quickly as possible, the Franciscans should have been thankful that King Jaume did not have them both thrown in a dungeon. Their status as clergymen may have stayed his hand, but so too would the reputation of his family have weighed on the king's mind.

His last hope crushed, Bernard obediently left Saint-Jean as commanded and found shelter in the neighboring town of Le Boulou. The years of revolt had come to an end. The following day he rode north, and within the week had returned to Carcassonne with the bad news for the conspirators. If word of this debacle spread north to Paris, Bernard and his confederates knew, they were dead men.

At about the same time, on April 16, 1304, His Holiness Benedict XI had, from his residence in Viterbo, sent a bull entitled *Ea nobis* to the head of the Franciscans in Languedoc. It read, in part:

> We have heard reports about Fr. Bernard Délicieux of your Order, saying such things as we must not and shall not allow to go unpunished . . . [wherefore] we order you, under pain of excommunication, deprivation of your office and of the right to hold any future office should you fail to execute this mandate, to arrest, to place under close guard, and to bring personally into our presence Fr. Bernard Délicieux.

Part III

The Time of Repression

CHAPTER EIGHTEEN

SURVIVAL

I N THE SUMMER OF 1305, Geoffroy d'Ablis received an unexpected visitor. His secretary announced that Guilhem Peyre-Cavaillé, from the town of Limoux just a few leagues south of Carcassonne, was at the door of the inquisitor's headquarters in the Cité. The name was familiar: Peyre-Cavaillé had been picked up on suspicion of heretical leanings in late 1304 and held in the Wall until the following spring, then released. Proof of guilt needed to be ironclad for a new proceeding to take place, given the probity embraced by the inquisition in the wake of the disastrous *rage carcassonnaise* of recent years.

Peyre-Cavaillé surprised the inquisitor by claiming that there were indeed heretics abroad in Languedoc, but not of the kind the Dominicans had been picking off in Carcassonne and Albi, wealthy townsmen with sentimental ties to the faith of their fathers. The heretics of whom he spoke formed an established Church, run by a dozen or so well-trained and much beloved Good Men, who in the past five years had rekindled the flame of old. They had followers by the hundreds, in the meadows, villages, and mountains, men and women, noble and peasant, who had conscientiously supported and concealed them as they went about their missionary task. Peyre-Cavaillé knew this for a fact because he had managed their affairs and organized their travels—a refusal to pay him back all of his expenses motivated him to talk to the inquisitor.* The people broke bread with these Good Men, housed them in their attics and hayricks, gathered for their sermons, and, when the end

---

* Specifically, expenses incurred for food during his most recent imprisonment in the Wall.

came, entrusted them their souls. The creed of the Cathars, alive and well, had spread its message of hope and love far and wide.

The inquisitor, like other Dominicans on learning the news, recalled the bitter fight with Bernard Délicieux. The Franciscan had been the focus of their fear and fury, to the exclusion of all else. In their view, while they had been occupied beating Brother Bernard back, the servants of Lucifer had gone about their diabolical business, unmolested by the justice of the Lord. This was what the actions of the foolish Franciscan had sown: a harvest of heresy, hardy and perennial in the ever-fertile fields of error that blanketed this corner of Christendom.

The Cathars' leader was Peire Autier, formerly a prosperous notary in the mountain town of Ax, in the county of Foix, south of Toulouse. Some time in the 1290s Autier grew dissatisfied with his comfortable life, in much the same way as Francis of Assisi had tired of his. Autier then traveled to Italy with his similarly disillusioned brother to find salvation. In corners of Lombardy and the Piedmont, where the fervid stew of politics surrounding partisans of emperor, pope, guild, and merchant militated against a sustained effort at religious repression, the Cathar Church had survived and still clung to a semblance of structure, its hidden hierarchs instructing and confirming Good Men and Good Women as in the days long gone. The Autier brothers from Languedoc, men in their fifties, yearned to stage a rebirth of the faith in their homeland before the embers of belief had gone cold. They stayed and studied in their Italian retreats for two to three years before being conferred the *consolamentum*, the sacrament making them Good Men and the spiritual equivalent of Jesus' apostles.

These highly literate and educated holy men, disguised as unlettered knife merchants, then headed homeward. They chose their time carefully, the winter of 1299–1300, when roads were overrun with pilgrims buoyed at the prospect of the Jubilee. Boniface VIII surveyed with satisfaction his flock surging across the Tiber, but his direst enemies, lost in the flow of the crowds, had soon forded the Rhône, the Aude, and the Garonne to meet with their followers. What transpired in the years to follow, Peyre-Cavaillé told the aghast Geoffroy d'Ablis, was a sturdy flowering of the faith, first in the mountains near Ax and Foix, where ties of kinship linked the Good Men to their followers, then in the downlands to the south and west of Carcassonne, respectively the

Razès and the Lauragais, and then in important towns such as Limoux and Pamiers, and finally in the workingmen's neighborhoods at the gates of Toulouse itself. Peire Autier presided over a church, a growing number of people who had achieved the *entendensa del Be*, the understanding of the Good. And there was no secret to the flip side of this understanding. As Autier preached: "There are two Churches, one which flees and forgives, the other which fetters and flays. The Church which flees and forgives takes the right path of the Apostles. It neither lies nor deceives. And the Church which fetters and flays is the Roman Church."

The meeting with Peyre-Cavaillé forged in Geoffroy d'Ablis a steely new determination. Circumspection in the conduct of inquisition was no longer an option: to act timorously was now a dereliction in the exercise of his sacred function. There had to be a return to the days of burning. From that moment on, and for the rest of his career, the inquisitor at Carcassonne mounted a ferocious offensive against spiritual dissent. He would soon be joined by inquisitors of even grimmer determination and greater talent than his own: the Dominican Bernard Gui in Toulouse and the Cistercian bishop of Pamiers, Jacques Fournier. Together, d'Ablis, Gui, and Fournier became avengers of scandalized orthodoxy through a sustained and coordinated campaign of arrest, imprisonment, interrogation, torture, punishment, and execution. The indignities visited upon the inquisition by the *rage carcassonnaise* were but pinpricks in comparison to the injuries now in store for Languedoc.

Campaigns, like wars, have starting points. The inquisitor's began in September 1305. Summoned to Limoux by the treacherous Peyre-Cavaillé, two Good Men of the Cathar revival—one of whom was Peire Autier's charismatic son—fell into the trap set by Geoffroy d'Ablis. In the same period, squads of soldiery accompanied by Dominicans made raids on dozens of dwellings and manors in the countryside. One of the most remarkable moments in this opening salvo of repression concerned Verdun-en-Lauragais, a village of several hundred souls, where the entire populace was arrested and thrown into the Wall of Carcassonne. Restraint was no longer required. Contrary to what the king's churchman, Archbishop Gilles Aycelin, had smoothly assured Bernard Délicieux at the great disputation in Toulouse the preceding year, the king no longer placed a brake on the inquisition. There was no authority to oversee the Dominicans; there was only complicity.

D'Ablis knew also that the Bourg would offer no resistance whatso-ever to his vigorous persecution. His enemies had been silenced by the royal seneschal. From a gibbet high above the waters of the Aude swung the lifeless bodies of Hélie Patrice and fourteen other consuls of Carcassonne. Found guilty of treason, they had been hanged on Sep-tember 20, 1305, after being flogged mercilessly and then tied to horses, to be dragged facedown through the streets to the gallows. They would be left there for weeks, to edify the Bourg. Not everyone would turn his head in revulsion. In the words of an eminent historian: "As Ber-nard Gui observes with savage exultation, those who had croaked like ravens against the Dominicans were exposed to the ravens."

Gui's happiness, however, was not complete. For among the eyeless corpses submitting to the pecking of the crows, there was no man of the cloth dangling in the wind, no Franciscan.

Remarkably, the return in force of the inquisition did not spell the end for Bernard Délicieux. Nor did the exposure of the plot to secede from France. Nor did the enmity of Pope Benedict XI. Given this array of menace, Bernard's itinerary from 1304 to 1310 can be seen as a feat of survival as unlikely as his brave but ultimately failed campaign to chase the inquisitors from Languedoc.

The most immediate threat was dealt with first. The Franciscans had proved dilatory in executing the pope's order to haul Délicieux to Rome, perhaps because the pontiff was a Dominican, but more likely because Brother Bernard was a valued and respected member of the Order, protected by senior friars and cardinals and revered by common man and wealthy burgher alike. When, at last, on July 6, 1304, the vicar of the Franciscan provincial of Aquitaine arrived in Carcassonne to arrest him, Bernard, guarded by Patrice's rough-and-ready militia of the Bourg, simply refused to go with him. Given his quarry's muscular entourage, the vicar thought better of insisting.

The next day, the heretofore hale Dominican pope dropped dead, at age sixty-three, of acute dysentery, in Perugia. Luck had intervened, spectacularly—too much luck, his enemies would say at his trial fifteen years later. Bernard had been heard predicting Benedict XI's untimely demise in the spring of 1304. Charged with the pope's murder, Bernard had to convince his judges he had no hand in the felicitous disappearance of his greatest enemy.

Whatever the truth behind the rumor, the sudden demise of the Dominican pope—and the subsequent vacancy of the Holy See—took the pressure off Bernard at precisely the moment when he needed to concentrate on an even graver threat: the wrath of King Philip the Fair. In the fall of 1304, ominous news came from Brother Durand de Champagne, Queen Joan's Franciscan confessor: the king had caught wind of the aborted plot to make Prince Ferrand of Majorca sovereign of Languedoc. Who informed Philip is not known, but the sheer number of people aware of the plot, not least King Jaume II, suggests he heard it from multiple sources.

On receiving this distressing intelligence, Bernard Délicieux went on the offensive. True to form, he urged a subscription from the burghers of Carcassonne, Albi, and other towns to fund a delegation. It would be headed by him and travel north to confront the king and beat down the accusations. The townspeople, many of them innocent of involvement in the plot yet terrified of indiscriminate royal vengeance, raised the funds for Brother Bernard's last mission to the north.

Once at court in October 1304, the men of the south immediately entreated Brother Durand to intervene with the queen on their behalf. According to testimony given at Bernard's trial, they somewhat impudently requested that she elicit some pillow talk from her husband that night as to whom, exactly, he had in his sights. Queen Joan obliged, reporting the next morning that only the men of Carcassonne had been accused. Delighted to be off the hook, the men of Albi packed up and went home. They were free—though they, innocent or guilty, would later have to pay a huge bribe to Jean d'Aunay, the corrupt seneschal of Carcassonne, to squelch any further investigation of them.

Uncertainty shrouds the question of whether Bernard ever saw the king, or when the men of Carcassonne returned to the south. However, during the winter of 1304–5 the king did not lift a finger to punish the plotters. Hélie Patrice and his doomed fellows went about their business in the south, unaware of the ugly fate awaiting them the following summer. Bernard seems to have stayed in Paris, untouched and, in all likelihood, engaged in rallying surreptitious support at court for his survival.

There are several possible explanations for the curious royal inaction. The king simply may have been too busy with the various crises besetting the kingdom to deal with a quixotic plot that had failed before even getting off the ground. Royal distraction—which had been Bernard's bane at the Estates General of 1302—may have worked in his favor. Another reason behind the king's delicacy could have had something to do with the memory of Anagni. Three years previously, the last time the king had arrested a prominent member of the clergy, Bernard Saisset, all hell had broken loose. Bernard Délicieux was nothing if not a prominent clergyman, a hero in some quarters, a respected colleague in others. The great Arnaud de Vilanova, whose advice Philip is known to have solicited in other matters, counted the Franciscan among his peers. Brother Bernard, an important member of the Franciscan order, had friends in high places.

Thus it is not unreasonable to assume that someone entreated the king for mercy behind closed doors. Perhaps it was Guillaume de Nogaret, then nearing the height of his power, who may have formed a bond with his fellow southerner and who, it is important to note, was one of the few at court with enough clout to stay the king's hand. But a more plausible conjecture is the queen.

Throughout the agitation led by Délicieux, he and Jean de Picquigny repeatedly appealed to Queen Joan. Her Franciscan confessor, Durand de Champagne, admired Délicieux; she herself met with him several times, once in the company of the women of Albi. During the visit to Carcassonne in the winter of 1304, she visited their menfolk freed from the Wall but still incarcerated in the Cité. She then graciously accepted the gift of the silver vase, returning it only when ordered to by Philip.

A compassionate and vivacious woman, admired by her subjects in a way that her husband was not, Joan may very well have been Bernard's advocate in the royal apartments. If the king made a promise not to harm him, he upheld it during his years of mourning for the wife he seems to have loved sincerely—for in April 1305 Joan died, age thirty-two, in childbirth, it is thought. The trial and hanging of Hélie Patrice and his allies later that year, significantly, did not take place at the behest of the king. Testimony at Bernard's trial demonstrates that the seneschal Jean d'Aunay came across the plot independently of any royal instructions and prosecuted its perpetrators. All of which suggests that Bernard's survival, alone among the prominent plotters of Carcassonne, can be laid at the feet of Queen Joan. Certainly there is something attractive, even romantic, in a whispered vow of clemency from a stern king to his doomed young queen, but however elegant that may be as explanation, the truth of the matter will forever remain elusive.

Less murkiness clouds the fate of Brother Bernard following his mysterious reprieve. As his name echoed loudly in the torture chambers of the royal seneschal during the trial of Patrice and the others in the summer of 1305, the king had little choice but to take some action with regard to the Franciscan. Tellingly, Philip chose the mildest course possible—he requested that the Franciscans in Paris keep Bernard under house arrest. The gentleness of the punishment suggests, once again, an unspoken commitment on the part of the king. When a new pope, Clement V, was finally chosen in the autumn of that year, Délicieux was moved to the custody of the papal court and the charges against him were eventually dropped.

As events transpired, Bernard's new captivity did not mean exile to Rome. His change of fortune came during an epochal moment in the history of the Church. The riotous influence of urban mobs and rival sister cities in the affairs of Rome finally took its toll, and the rising power north of the Alps could no longer be resisted. For the next seventy years, starting in 1309, the papacy was to be French, centered near the mouth of the Rhône in the Comtat Venaissin, a patchwork of feudal principalities held by the pope and his vassals. In choosing Avignon as his capital, its population (five thousand or so) paltry even in comparison to other towns of the Comtat, the pope signaled the need for a fresh start and for the complete independence of his institution. In reality, his new lodgings sat squarely in the long shadow cast by Paris, and seven successive vicars of Christ, all of them French, became entwined in the very material affairs of the kingdom. The medieval imperial pontificate was over; a new grasping boomtown rose on the banks of the Rhône.

The first of the Avignon popes, Bertrand de Got, came from near Bordeaux, from the Gascon nobility whose feudal overlord was, technically, the king of England. As Clement V, he distinguished himself for over-the-top nepotism in an age of nepotism: five of his kinsmen were made cardinals and, on his death, the papal treasury was bequeathed to his family, sparking an unseemly lawsuit from his successor. However magnificently flawed, and unceasingly pressured by Philip and Nogaret in the affair of the Templars and the posthumous persecution of Boniface VIII, Clement seems to have been a judicious man who attempted to steer a middle course through the choppy waters of his fractious Church. He dispatched envoys to investigate the newly invigorated inquisition in Languedoc, to make sure that conditions of incarceration were humane and that there was no overzealousness on the part of Dominican inquisitors electrified by the discovery of the Autier revival of Catharism. As a result of this embassy, dozens of prisoners were released from the Wall, and steps were taken to correct the grotesque conditions of the bishop's jail in Albi. Clement lifted the excommunication of the deceased Jean de Picquigny. Behind these actions may have been the hand of Brother Bernard, who was present in the curia in the early years of Clement's papacy.

Clement did not decide definitively to move to Avignon until 1309, and even then the move was considered provisional. His court traveled around France for four long years. As the curia moved from town to town, Délicieux nipped at the pope's heels, reminding him of past injustice, calling for the disbanding of the Dominicans. In principle a captive but in reality a free and noisy advocate, Bernard attended the pope's coronation in Lyon and followed him to Mâcon, Nevers, Bourges, Limoges, Périgueux, and Bordeaux. In Poitiers in 1307, the Franciscan stationed himself outside the pope's residence in the hope of buttonholing the visiting King Philip. On successive days as the king entered the building Bernard badgered him about injustice done at the trial of Carcassonne and about inquisitorial abuse—and was stonily ignored. Three powerful cardinals, friends and protectors of his, eventually felt compelled to take Bernard aside and tell him in no uncertain terms to let sleeping dogs lie. Do not provoke the king or the pope. Theirs was a clear echo of the moment during the great meeting at Toulouse three years earlier when scores of glances had implored Bernard to step back. It was also a variation of Nogaret's warning in Béziers in the same year, 1304, to wait until circumstances were ripe. At Poitiers, the combative Franciscan at last stepped back.

In the years following this retreat, Bernard fought to wriggle out of the tight embrace of the curia, to which he was repeatedly summoned after sojourns in Languedoc. He could not have been a welcome sight to all of the cardinals, especially to those affiliated with the Dominicans. His presence was an affront, a source of painful memories. Bernard could not have been happy as a hanger-on in the acquisitive snakepit of Avignon; his subsequent activity suggests that the spectacle of power helped him come to a decision on how to further his view of the way in which the Church should conduct itself. The king would not help him, the pope took half measures, and his allies in the cities were either dead or cowering in terror. He resolved to take the route he himself had shunned during the days of rage at the turn of the century: to work from within the Church, at ground level, to effect the change he saw necessary. He would adhere to his long-held view of spirituality to work a revolution.

By the beginning of the second decade of the fourteenth century, Bernard had finally slipped the soft shackles of his confinement. Pope Clement had forgiven him all, as had King Philip. The pope declared any lingering excommunications delivered in the years of strife by angry Dominicans to be invalid. Délicieux was given permission to go to whichever Franciscan convent he pleased.

The friar returned home to Languedoc. He chose the convent at Béziers. The city was the base of his most powerful cardinal protector in the curia, Bérenger Frédol, and, more important, the rebellious star of the Spiritual Franciscans shone truest there. No quiet retirement, Bernard's personal itinerary now merged into the larger currents of thought that played themselves out in the effervescent Languedoc of the early fourteenth century.

CHAPTER NINETEEN

CATHARS AND SPIRITUALS, INQUISITORS AND CONVENTUALS

OVERTY AND SALVATION, or wealth and damnation—for the people of Languedoc, the question burned bright in the soul. The opening of the fourteenth century may have differed considerably from the opening of the thirteenth, as attested by the nature of the crowds on the Ponte St. Angelo, but a constant of the medieval period concerned the welfare of the individual before God. Like their predecessors, Bernard's contemporaries asked plaintively where their Church had gone in this time of spiritual need. The pope was no longer in Rome, surrounded instead by moneychangers at his temple on the Rhône. The Holy Land was delivered to the infidel, and its protectors, the Templars, had been declared heretics. To some, the promise of the mendicant movement seemed teetering on the verge of collapse. Too many friars were worldly now, their convents and churches as large and lavish as those they had once decried. Brothers were bishops, cardinals, popes, their vow of poverty long forgotten. For the clear-eyed in Languedoc the friars were agents of hatred and cruelty who hunted, maimed, and killed. They said they were saving souls, yet they promised fire and brimstone from their pulpits. The Church and its robed brotherhoods seemed concerned first and foremost with spreading fear, all in the service of inculcating a cowed obedience. However much the fruits of labor satisfied, the ties of family comforted, the pleasures of love transported, the streets of the city stimulated, people were told again and again to be afraid: of God, of Jesus, of Hell, of Purgatory, of the Church, of inquisitors. Of strangers. Of neighbors. Of their own humanity.

For some the reappearance of the Cathars came as a ray of light. The

Good Men were, indisputably, holy and poor. They fasted often, comforted the sick and the dying, asked for nothing in return. Their message, unlike the threats and warnings thundering under the great naves of Languedoc, was hopeful: There was no Purgatory, no Hell. One was fated to take on a material tunic in successive lives until ready to find the moral fortitude necessary to join the ascetic ranks of the Good Men and Good Women in one's final incarnation on this earth. Then one would join the Good God in eternal bliss. So in the meantime believers should be kind to one another, live well, find contentment, and ignore the lies. The ferocity of the inquisitor was proof of the rightness of the cause. As Peire Autier preached:

> I'll tell you why they call us heretics. It's because they hate us.
> And it's no wonder that they hate us, since they hated Our Lord,
> whom they persecuted along with his apostles. We are hated and
> persecuted because we firmly uphold His law. Those who are
> good and wish to remain true to their faith must let themselves
> be crucified and stoned to death when they fall into their enemies'
> power, just as the apostles did.

The magnificence of the Church was a siren song of delusion; praying before its statues was an occupation for fools. "Those who adore such images are idiots," Autier said bluntly. "Because they are the same people who made them, those statues, with their axes and metal tools." As for the cross, the object of veneration, the instrument of Christ's martyrdom, the ever-present icon of a living faith, the Cathars saw it as a Roman instrument of torture and nothing more. The cross did not symbolize Christianity, it symbolized death—which was Rome's message, not that of Jesus. When asked by a shepherd whether it was wrong to make the sign of the cross, if only to deflect suspicion, Autier advised: "Oh no, it's a fine thing. In summer, it's a very good way of shooing the flies away from your face. As for the words, here's what you can say: 'This is my brow, this is my beard, this is one ear and this is the other.'"

Others in Languedoc, though not sharing Autier's corrosive heterodoxy, would have understood many things the Good Man had to say. When he railed against "the Church that fetters"—that is, fetters itself with material goods—heads nodded, tonsured or not. Among the Franciscans, especially in Languedoc and Italy, the seeds of discord that were Francis' exemplary life and, especially, his last testament would finally bear fruit. Shortly before his death in 1226, Francis had dictated a radical testament in which he commanded his brothers to respect the dictates of destitution. At the request of the Franciscan leadership, this testament was declared nonbinding on the Order of Friars Minor in 1230 by Pope Gregory IX, but the document still hovered over their spiritual landscape as a reminder and a reproach. The life of apostolic poverty had been embraced by the Cathars and the first mendicants; later generations of friars were never really interested in going about in rags, as many men were attracted to the order by its success and prestige. To these were added brothers of an institutional and organizational bent, who saw mass mendicancy on a continent-wide scale as woefully impractical and, more to the point, downright uncomfortable. They came to be called the Conventuals.

Opposing them in Brother Bernard's time were the Spirituals, a movement of many factions that had grown in strength and numbers in the second half of the thirteenth century. A large theoretical framework had been built around the notion of Franciscan poverty, notably by a friar of Narbonne, Pierre Jean Olivi. After his death in 1298, Olivi's grave in that city had become a shrine and the man an unofficial saint. On a more political level, the struggle between Conventuals and Spirituals afflicted convents throughout Europe, with successive popes growing concerned about the threat to orthodoxy such internecine fighting posed. In the early 1290s, Pope Nicholas IV, himself a Franciscan, severely punished the Spirituals, thereby radicalizing them even more. His successor was the hermit pope, Celestine, whose holiness and poverty inspired the foundation of a new branch of Spiritual friars, the Celestines, who were then declared heterodox by his successor Boniface VIII. Pope Clement, hounded by Guillaume de Nogaret in his campaign of posthumous vilification of Boniface, reluctantly made Celestine a saint—though as a confessor and not, as Nogaret had wanted, as a martyr. This canonization was seen as a boon to the Spirituals, and the compromise-seeking Clement allowed them control over several convents in select provinces, of which Bernard's Languedoc was foremost.

The divide in the Franciscan Order over poverty was carried to extremes, many of which brought the fight down from the understandable level of control and disposal of resources to a place that, to the eyes of outsiders seven hundred years later, can seem bewilderingly petty. Disputes arose over how many tunics an individual friar could have, and how the habit was to be worn. Many Spirituals opted for a sole habit made of the coarsest cloth, unwashed and in tatters, worn short to ensure mortification of the flesh—all of which drove Conventual abbots to angry reprisals of expulsion or imprisonment. The Spirituals excoriated the feasting at convents; the Conventuals responded by saying that they were simply obeying Francis' injunction to eat what was put before them and not question the workings of divine providence. It was not their fault that, as often happened, some grateful benefactor prepared for them meals of suckling pig and roast capon, to be washed down with a demijohn of the finest from the vineyards of the Lord.

Debating whether a Franciscan could own anything, the rigorists claimed that Jesus had owned nothing, and neither had his disciples. Polemic flew back and forth over whether the apostles had handled money, possessed a purse. This led to an ingenious solution: the operative working fiction held that the Order possessed nothing at all and that the friars just borrowed from the pope, who was the owner of all things Franciscan. The Spirituals countered that by using these things, one made a de facto proprietary claim to them. The wisdom contained in the book-lined study of the scholastic friar raised the issue of whether all those volumes, bought and used exclusively by the scholar, were in fact the property of the pope. Some of the more radical Spirituals asked whether such abstruse learning furthered the goal of poverty and preaching or fostered the sin of intellectual pride. "So it goes, there is no more religion," lamented a Spiritual in the 1290s. "We see a bad Paris that has destroyed Assisi with its learning."

The bickering over detail might have remained just lively material for a footnote in Franciscan annals, full of colorful charges about gluttonous Conventuals and holier-than-thou Spirituals, were it not for the growing involvement of the laity in the matter. The Franciscans had originally been an order of laymen; under the Spirituals the tradition was strengthened. Two of their greatest defenders, Arnaud de Vilanova and Ramon Llull, were laymen. On a far humbler but more important level, thousands of ordinary people joined auxiliary Franciscan groups, called the Third Order, its members known in Languedoc as Beguins. These latter, whose numbers included a large share of women, embraced some of the strictures of poverty and much of the fervent piety of their tonsured guides. Alarm bells went off in the papal curia, which was always leery of unauthorized associations in which the unordained might approach the Scripture and its interpretation. Sacerdotal professionalism was as important to the medieval Church as the immunity of the clergy to secular prosecution.

In practice, the Spirituals and the Beguins seem surprisingly close to the Good Men and their believers. Simple, austere meals were shared, the blessing and breaking of bread performed, the cup of wine passed around, followed by injunctions to lead a simple, pious life in imitation of the apostles. The Cathar believers of the mountains sat at the feet of Peire Autier; the Beguins of the coast gathered round the table of Bernard Délicieux—for Brother Bernard, according to a horrified Dominican contemporary in Béziers, had by 1314 become the undisputed leader of the Spirituals there. The Dominican wrote that Bernard and other prominent Spirituals were viewed by the common people and the local clergy as "saints of God and the foundation of His church." What Délicieux offered, as did Autier, was access to a humane spirituality denied by an authoritarian, sometimes terrifying Church hierarchy.

In fact, the result of Brother Bernard's actions may be seen as justification of what he had been saying all along, even during the heady days of the *rage carcassonnaise*. Catharism was nonexistent in the lands where the Beguins were thick on the ground. The most effective antidote to doctrinal heresy may have been not, as the inquisitor believed, campaigns of prosecution and punishment, but, as Bernard had long insisted, the offering of an alternative gentler Christianity for those impatient with the imperfections of the Church. Heresy—the root of the word comes from the Greek for "choice"—could be defeated by choosing another pastoral mode.

Fatally for Bernard, some in the Spiritual movements strayed dangerously out on a limb. Smarting from severe disciplinary measures, radical Spirituals echoed the Cathar Autier almost to the letter by holding up their victimhood as a proof of the justice of their cause. That position, of course, was diametrically opposed to the radical Dominican one, which viewed persecution in the service of the Church as a divine command, and thus it was the persecutor, not the persecuted, whose cause was automatically just. Where the inquisitors, especially Conventual Franciscan inquisitors, became truly interested in the Spirituals as targets of persecution occurred when some of the more ecstatic of the brethren left the bounds of orthodoxy. The struggle no longer took place in the convent, between two factions within the Order; rather, it moved to the larger ontological stage where the suppression of the Cathars also unfolded.

The heterodoxy of the later Spirituals arose from a lush forest of apocalyptic and mystical thought. Baldly stated, some Spirituals, by the second decade of the fourteenth century, believed themselves freed of their vow of obedience to the pope. They arrived at this remarkable view through an intellectual journey that reflected the persistent uncertainties and terrors of their time.

Although a definitive beginning to any movement of thought is difficult to pinpoint, the foundation for the more heterodox of Spiritual assertions was laid prior even to the emergence of St. Francis. At the close of the twelfth century a Calabrian abbot, Joachim of Fiore, produced texts concerning the three ages of mankind, the nature of the Trinity, and various prophetic declarations drawn from the Book of Daniel and the Book of Revelations, among others. His complex, riddle-filled schema of speculative eschatology influenced thinkers throughout the thirteenth century, leading some to identify the Antichrist as Emperor Frederick II and prophesy an end time beginning, or concluding, in the year 1260. Even after that year came and went with neither bang nor whimper, Joachite thinking, as it is called, remained a constant underground source of speculation and prophecy.

In the Franciscan context, the Joachite notion of the ages of mankind, along with theories about different epochs of Church history, took the order down several winding roads. If Jesus had introduced the First Age of the Church, then Francis inaugurated the Second. A third and final stage, after the age of Father and Son, would involve the Holy Spirit.* Alternatively, Francis might have been an angel, breaking

---

* There were other, competing traditions that divided history into a different number of ages.

the sixth seal of apocalyptic tradition and ushering in the arrival of a seventh and concluding seal breaker. Perhaps this would be the Antichrist, once thought to be the *Stupor Mundi*—who was christened in the same baptismal font in Assisi that had served to christen Francis—or perhaps the personage to usher in the end times was an angelic pope, such as Celestine, or a bad pope, Boniface, whose pontificate saw the persecution of the Spirituals, a persecution not only welcomed but foreseen by prophecy.

Whichever the variant—and there were many—on these rich speculative themes, the figure of Francis of Assisi invariably stood at the center of them all. Over time the charismatic visionary of the early thirteenth century, the figure who had seized and shaped his moment of history, came himself to be shaped by later generations who poured their fears and hopes into him. Like his contemporary Dominic, hapless before a posterity that had transformed him into an inquisitor, Francis was changed into something he would not have recognized. The self-proclaimed holy fool was championed as a prophet who had transcended the institutional Church, a figure of revolutionary piety standing outside the flow of normal time. In the most radical iteration put forth by the Spirituals, the testament of Francis carried as much authority as the Gospels, and the man of Assisi became the equal of the man of Nazareth. If the pope ordered the Franciscans to make compromises with the world that were at odds with Francis' sacred testament, then in the eyes of these Spirituals the pope was wrong.

Heresy was the logical climax of the process. The papacy was swept away, the first thousand years of sanctioned Christianity, so recently celebrated in Jubilee, definitively closed, as the Joachite prophecies had foretold. Jesus and Peter had founded a church to supersede Judaism; Francis had come to supersede that church and usher in a new era. Whereas the Cathars saw themselves as continuators of the Church of the apostles, the more radical Spirituals knew themselves to be trailblazers into a mystical future. And while the Judeo-Christian thread in this speculative enterprise has often been underlined, to observers of other traditions another comparison springs to mind—these Spirituals were to Christianity what the Shia are to Islam. Just as the murdered

Ali (and his murdered son Huseyn) came to assume as much sanctity as the founder of Islam in the eyes of some Shia, with their cause destined to be vindicated by the arrival of a hidden imam, or providential figure, to bring on a new dispensation, so too had Francis, in the eyes of the radicalized Spirituals, achieved parity with Jesus, Christianity's avatar, with the friar's followers scouring their prophecies to predict the as yet undisclosed arrival of a world-shaking figure to further the Franciscan revolution.

Bernard may have been one of their number, awaiting the Franciscan imam. Certainly, the soothsaying straws at which he grasped in predicting the early demise of two popes most certainly came from the prophetic literature produced in Spiritual circles at the time.* And, more speculatively, the astonishing trope used in his great sermon of 1303, during which a weeping Bernard claimed to be Jesus Christ, may have been less an eccentric stroke of rhetoric than an indication of familiarity with the more radical Spiritual claims about the status of St. Francis.

Whatever Bernard's implication in this conjecture, a swirl of conflicting influences washed over his rich and inventive homeland.† A deadly tug-of-war took place between two sets of opposing parties in Languedoc, with the majority of the populace, pious or impious, looking on in consternation. Inland, the inquisitors fought the Cathars, their sympathizers, and anyone who impeded the inquisition. On the coast, in such places as Béziers and Narbonne, the Spirituals faced off against the Franciscan hierarchy, its Conventual leadership whispering in the pope's ear at Avignon. In both arenas, a muffled hatred was animated on all sides by a shared love of Jesus Christ. It was a singular moment, not destined to last. And alone among the dissident parties in the second decade of the fourteenth century, one man had made

---

* In the spring of 1304, Bernard predicted the death of Pope Benedict XI, which occurred in the summer of that year. In 1319, while being brought to Carcassonne for his trial, he predicted the early demise of Pope John XXII, who lived another dozen years. For the latter prediction he described to his captors a book of prophecy circulating among Spirituals.

† At about the same time as these upheavals in Christianity, the Jews of Languedoc, especially on the littoral north and south of Béziers, were engaged in developing the Kabbalah.

enemies of both the inquisitors and the Conventuals. That man was Bernard Délicieux.

Geoffroy d'Ablis had reason to be pleased with himself since receiving Guilhem Peyre-Cavaillé five years earlier. In Toulouse in 1310 for a *sermo generalis* that lasted for days, on April 10 of that year he stood alongside his esteemed colleague, Bernard Gui, as the body of Peire Autier was consumed by flames before the Cathedral of St. Stephen. Autier had been finally tracked down and captured near Toulouse in August 1309. Over the next nine months, he was tortured, tried, and convicted. His Cathar revival was dead, or at least its leadership destroyed. One Good Man had committed suicide to elude capture; another had tried to undertake the *endura*, or hunger strike, earlier in the year, but Brother Bernard Gui burned the impudent fellow before peaceful death snatched him from his deserved fate. All the others had been caught and burned, save one, who had disappeared over the mountains into Aragon.

The inquisition in the two decades to follow was unstoppable. Succeeding and surpassing the work of Gui and d'Ablis, Bishop Jacques Fournier brought a methodical, almost sociological approach to interrogation out of what was obviously a passion for prosecution. The bishop, a corpulent man of the south with boundless energy, seems to have been more interested in getting convictions than in handing down sentences, given his occasional leniency toward those found guilty. Nonetheless, his see, Pamiers, once notorious for sedition under Bernard Saisset, became even more notorious as the center of a rapacious dragnet that no one could escape. The inhabitants of the mountain village of Montaillou had successfully pulled the wool over D'Ablis' eyes about the extent of their heretical leanings; not so with Fournier, who revived the investigation to reveal that the entire town was Cathar, even the curé. That proceeding has come down to us because the transcripts of Fournier's activities survived in the archives of the Vatican—the brilliant, ruthless bishop eventually became an Avignon pope, Benedict XII.

Thanks to Fournier's remarkable industry, the remaining network of Cathar sympathizers was painstakingly dismantled, as informants and spies thrived under the bishop's generous stewardship. Even those who were orthodox yet refused to turn in their heretical neighbors fell afoul of his tribunal. "I did nothing to denounce them," one Catholic protested to Fournier, "because they did no harm to me." The man was jailed. And the last Good Man of Languedoc was lured across the Pyrenees from his safe house far to the south, beyond Tarragona, by a sleeper Fournier operative who had lived among the émigré Cathar faithful there for more than a year. The Good Man was burned in 1321.* After Fournier shut down his machine five years later, there were no further convictions for heresy in the diocese of Pamiers. This can be ascribed either to the complete extermination of Cathar belief or to his successors' willingness to leave well enough alone. If the experience of Albi is any indication, where Bishop de Castanet's last frenetic inquisition of 1300 was succeeded by a judicial flatline toward heresy, we can assume that the blessings of peace to descend on Pamiers had less to do with the disappearance of residual spiritual disagreement than with the departure of a driven prosecutor.

On the coast, events moved inexorably to a conclusion through the departures of the great, rather than by the burning conviction of a few gifted inquisitors. The pivotal moment came on April 20, 1314, when Pope Clement V passed away. As if to explain how the disease-ridden old man had managed to hang on for so long, a debunked but still tantalizing historical legend attributes his death to a curse that Jacques de Molay, the last Templar Grand Master, had shouted out six weeks earlier as the fire roared beneath his feet on an island in the Seine—within the year, the expiring Knight howled, those responsible for this murder most foul would themselves be dead. Clement promptly obliged, as did Philip the Fair, on November 29, 1314, following a stroke while out hunting in Picardy. The last great Capetian monarch left a country soon to be visited by war, disease, and famine as the disastrous fourteenth century progressed. Jacques de Molay's greatest nemesis, Guillaume de Nogaret, had died in the year preceding the apocryphal curse, carried off by some revolting illness that resulted in

---

* The story exemplifies the poison spread by inquisition. The operative, Arnaud Sicre, agreed to undertake the treachery if Fournier would restore to him the property confiscated from his heretical mother, Sébélia Peyre, who was burned at the stake.

a death rictus unusual for the way the tongue of the deceased was found sticking far out of his mouth. Whether supernatural in character or not, the disappearance of these three figures ushered in a time of great peril for the Spirituals, and in particular for Bernard Délicieux, who had lost support in court and curia.

The jockeying to choose Clement's successor lasted twenty-seven months, an indecorous pageant of riotous assembly and sordid deal making. The man who at last emerged from the fray was Jacques Duèse, who secured election as John XXII by promising skittish Italian cardinals to move the papacy back to Rome and assuring the conclave as a whole that, as pope, he would defer to their decisions. Of course he had no intention of keeping these promises. A man of Cahors, a town that in medieval times was synonymous with wealth and banking, John immediately took a hard look at Church accounts to ensure sufficient revenues for his person and entourage. Although able, learned, and active as leader, the second Avignon pope embodied the entire episode of the curia's exile to the Rhône by embracing splendor throughout his pontificate, even to the very end. Inaugurating a new style for papal sarcophagi, John's costly mausoleum stands as a mini-cathedral of Gothic daring—its stone forest of spires and towers later to be likened by Renaissance critics to "quills upon a fretful porcupine."

The new pope, above all else, wanted to put his house in order. Unlike Clement, whose adopted papal name befitted a man capable of compromise and forgiveness, John was impatient with division and disagreement—a trait of character that ensured him a rocky tenure riven with dissension. At the outset of his pontificate, no doubt exasperated by the clamor in the convents, he sought to bring the Spirituals to heel. A quiet phrase in a letter of 1317 summed up his view of the Franciscan imbroglio with deadly simplicity: "For poverty is good, and chastity is greater, but obedience is greatest of all."

At the end of April 1317, the dread summons came. The friars of Béziers and Narbonne were to come to Avignon to explain themselves. The pope had heard distressing reports of disobedience from the head of the Franciscan order, a Conventual with no love for his

Spiritual brethren. During the vacancy of the Holy See, attempts to install Conventual abbots in the convents of Béziers and Narbonne had been met with assault and injury. The pope demanded to know what had happened.

The friars assembled for their journey, no doubt worried about the pope's intentions. Wisely, given his gifts, they chose Brother Bernard to be their spokesman. For his part, Bernard entrusted his few belongings to a notary of Béziers, in the event his sojourn in Avignon turned out to be protracted. He knew he was taking an enormous risk.

Fifty-four brothers traveled through Montpellier, Nîmes, and Arles en route to Avignon. At last they arrived at the famous bridge spanning one arm of the Rhône, late on Pentecost Sunday, 1317. The magnificent Palais des Papes that can be seen today was then still a twinkle in the eye of a venal curia, so the Languedoc Franciscans headed toward the door of the episcopal residence, where the pope had his headquarters. They were not admitted.

It was a warm night and the friars were in a state of nervous excitement. They decided to sleep out in the square before the bishop's palace. The following day, May 23, the men of Béziers and Narbonne were ushered into the pope's presence. The audience chamber was packed with great prelates and cardinals as Brother Bernard stepped forward to speak.

Two eyewitnesses left accounts of what happened next. The hostile witness, a Conventual, claimed that the famous Franciscan launched into an unreasonable and offensive tirade. The friendly witness, Angelo Clareno, a Spiritual, characterized Bernard's opening remarks as the sweet sound of reason and humility.

Which version of the event is correct matters not. Where the two men agree wholeheartedly is far more important. Both state that Bernard, early on, was interrupted. Many of his listeners stood up to hurl accusations and abuse at him. There was a storm of indignation, a collective shriek of protest. His past deeds were shouted out in anger; the pope was begged not to listen to the man. The audience turned tumultuous, out of control.

John XXII signaled his guards. He had a choice: calm the exercised or remove the source of their displeasure. The pope ordered his men to seize Brother Bernard Délicieux. He was to be escorted down to the dungeon, where chains and manacles awaited.

It had been a setup, a trap. As Bernard left the room, he may have turned back, in his very last instant as a free man, to see the triumphant smiles on the faces of his many enemies. The crows had come home to roost.

CHAPTER TWENTY
THE TRIAL

A LONE IN A DANK, dark cell in the dungeons of Avignon, Brother Bernard was beyond the reach of the network of friendships and alliances deployed to protect him in the past. So many were dead and gone. Queen Joan and Jean de Picquigny had vanished long before. More recently, Pope Clement V, King Philip the Fair, and Guillaume de Nogaret had passed. Bernard's ally and Picquigny's colleague in reforming Languedoc, Richard Leneveu, was *Leneveu* gone as well, his last miserable days spent as a leper in a lazaretto of Béziers—a fate that the reliably unpleasant Bernard Gui celebrated in his memoir. The allies remaining to the Franciscan, the prelates of the Frédol family of Béziers, no longer had a voice in the affairs of the Church, as Pope John XXII viewed their complaisance toward Bernard's Spiritual brethren as a badge of infamy. The leader of the Spirituals, Angelo Clareno, had fled to the relative safety of Italy. As for Bernard's two brilliant friends, Arnaud de Vilanova had drowned in a shipwreck off Genoa in 1311 and the ever mysterious Ramon Llull died two or three years later, in either Palma de Majorca or Tunis.

Though Bernard's enemies now had him under lock and key, the challenge lay in what to do with him, and who should do it. The friar had angered so many in the course of his career that any number of people were eager to rough him up. The Franciscans got to the head of the queue. One of the leaders of the Conventuals, Bonagratia de Bergamo, questioned and tortured Bernard throughout late 1317 on his relation to the Spirituals, over whom the cloud of heresy had now permanently settled. In 1318, while still an agonized captive in Avignon, Bernard heard that four of his companions who made the trip with him from Languedoc had been burned at the stake in Marseille. The inquisitor was Franciscan, his victims Franciscans.

Among the common people and, especially, the Beguins, news of the gruesome deed caused dismay. Burning a Cathar was one thing; killing a holy friar was quite another. Talk of martyrdom arose, of men who had embraced death rather than renounce their faith, like the saints of old who had sacrificed themselves before the brutish power of pagan Rome. No fool, the pope realized that he had to proceed more carefully from then on, and particularly in the case of Bernard Délicieux. Initial gloating over having landed such a big fish gave way to disquiet, for holding a prisoner of his stature came fraught with danger. Bernard's web of protection may have been shredded, but his reputation remained intact—and his name was known throughout the entire Midi and beyond, among people of all stations in life. All knew that were he to be burned on pettifogging charges of Franciscan misbehavior unlikely to be understood outside the overheated confines of the convent, Bernard Délicieux would remain as much a threat to authority in death as he ever had been in life.

Plans were made to snuff him out quietly—and in such a manner that no one could describe the process as a judicial murder or see its outcome as a martyrdom. Bernard's Conventual tormentor, Brother Bonagratia, was permitted to continue his cruel games with his captive, but the serious business of engineering the elimination of the prisoner was carried out elsewhere. The first step was taken by Bernard de Castanet, no longer the bishop of Albi but by then a respected member of the curia. During the last months of Cardinal de Castanet's life in 1317, he drew up the initial list of forty charges against his Franciscan foe. Subsequently, over a period that stretched for months, depositions and evidence were sought from different parties throughout Languedoc by roving papal investigators. A second, more comprehensive list of sixty-four charges was then compiled—by, it is believed, Bernard Gui. An expert in prosecution and a champion of vindictiveness, Gui crafted his charges carefully. By the spring of 1318, the dossiers were ready and the judges, called commissioners in the transcripts, had been chosen. A haggard Bernard was haled before a court in Avignon to answer to the charges on Gui's masterful list.

The Avignon investigation, unlike the subsequent and more thorough 1319 trial in Carcassonne, is not rich in documentation. We know some of its activities—particularly the reading into the record of Castanet's and Gui's lists of charges—because portions of the proceedings were folded into the larger transcripts of the later and final trial. What can be determined with certainty from the fragments is that the three commissioners—all middle-level clerics with careers to further—had mixed success with the defendant. His enemies seem to have forgotten that, among other things, he was a master tactician. Taking the measure of the monstrous machination that had been building against him during his year of harsh confinement, Bernard refused on numerous occasions to answer to the charges.

On June 28, 1318, Bernard stood up and sternly proclaimed that the three men before him were not qualified to judge him: "I will not respond to the question . . . because the commissioners are simple men of a lowly station . . . I hereby demand that my judges be strong and powerful officials, cardinals who knew of the inquisition affair during the time of My Lord Pope Clement." Bernard also said to their faces that they were stooges in the service of his enemies in the cardinalate, particularly the late king's Dominican confessor, Nicolas de Fréauville, whom he had accused in the Toulouse disputation almost two decades earlier of treasonous activities with the Flemish. These so-called commissioners, Bernard insisted, were unworthy of judging a man of his eminence and sorely lacking in knowledge of what had transpired in Languedoc at the turn of the century. Shrouded by ignorance and inexperience, they could not be trusted to render a fair verdict.

The friar's foes, in their scrupulous preparations to bring down such a towering figure with as little commotion as possible, had forgotten one other thing: Bernard knew he was a big fish, and had astutely identified the weaknesses in the pope's position. Anything less than the appearance of impeccable fairness worked in Bernard's favor. He had supporters everywhere. A hasty trial conducted by his enemies' flunkies would not look good at all, no matter how well prepared the paperwork. He demanded to be tried by his peers, churchmen of distinction, in the place where his actions were known, in Languedoc.

The commissioners, showing their own resolve, did not buckle before the great man's scorn. They excommunicated him on the spot. To return to the body of Church, Bernard had to agree to cooperate, which, apparently, he did. The historical record then goes dark, with very little in the way of documentation until the hearing of witnesses in Avignon the following spring.

Despite his grudging cooperation in the face of excommunication, Bernard had nonetheless fired a loud warning shot. Pope John XXII heard it. One can imagine an annoyed but admiring shake of the papal head on learning of Bernard's insults. Even after months of torture and a year of solitude in the darkness, fed on the meagerest of fare, the friar of Carcassonne was yet a shrewd, dangerous adversary. The seventy-five-year-old pope from Cahors, a no-nonsense town of cash and credit, realized that exceptional men would have to be found to take him down.

The trial was moved to Languedoc. Lest anyone at that destination dare forget what the pope expected, his letter preceding the transfer stated at the very top:

> Whereas inaction before those who cause harm to others must rightly be odious to all men of good sense, the sanction of justice here must be most severely pursued against those who, although having submitted to the vows of an Order, acted as wolves in sheep's clothing and wore the raiment of holiness and good works all while seeking the destruction of others through hateful machinations.

Thus condemned in advance, Bernard was taken from Avignon under guard in late August. His traveling companions, prepped on the nature of the charges against him, tried to elicit damning admissions from him in the course of casual conversation, which they would later repeat at his trial. Bernard, freed from the cold stone of his cell and able to breathe in the warm air of his beloved homeland, became expansive, voluble even, as the journey progressed. He freely admitted to being a Spiritual, versed in Joachite prophecy. He explained to his escort, by means of describing a figure in a book, how John XXII was fated to die soon. He did not take the bait and declare the inquisition corrupt, but he did not hide his feeling that many inquisitors had behaved corruptly. When an interlocutor questioned him about rumors of corruption on his side, about how Jean de Picquigny had accepted bribes to work with the Bourg, Bernard snarled at the man: "You lie through your teeth! Picquigny was a honest man!"

In early September, an initial audience of the full court was held in Castelnaudary, a town between Toulouse and Carcassonne. The setting proved unsatisfactory, perhaps because a great number of witnesses still to be called resided in Carcassonne. It was, after all, the scene of the crime. The entire retinue—one lone accused man surrounded by a host of hostile guards, notaries, lawyers, and judges—then decamped to the city on the Aude. Bernard was probably not thrown in the Wall there, where he would have had a poignant reunion with the surviving men of Albi, who had never been released. In 1305, when the seditious plot of the Carcassonnais had been uncovered, these poor pawns had been transferred from royal custody in the Cité back to the Wall, where all would eventually die.

For his captors, however ardently they wished that fate for Bernard Délicieux, the Wall was in all likelihood not the place to confine their celebrated prisoner. For one thing, escapes from that prison were not unknown, especially for high-profile captives with rich and powerful friends. In the days of the Autier revival, four Good Men had managed to escape the Wall through the judicious greasing of palms. Although all were eventually recaptured and burned, and the prison's corrupt wardens replaced at the behest of Pope Clement's investigators in 1308, the lesson had been learned—no chances were going to be taken with Brother Bernard.

Further, the trial was to take place in the Cité, in the bishop's palace. Between that residence and the fortress of the seneschal stood the headquarters of the inquisition. The baleful registers were hung high on the inner wall of a great round tower of the fortifications there. Its neighboring tower, square in shape, also belonged to the inquisitor; it contained several chambers and, at its base, a handful of cells replete with manacles and other restraints. In the center of this area the torturer plied his trade. As the friar was expected to be available at almost all times during his trial, holding him here was only a matter of convenience, as well as security. This was Bernard's home in Carcassonne for the last public act of his life.*

The trial at Carcassonne began on September 12, 1319, and concluded on December 8. For the very first session in the Cité, Bernard was seated in front of his judges. Originally Pope John had named three to preside, but one, the archbishop of Toulouse, had begged off, claiming an administrative burden too great to permit him to do a thorough job. He was politely allowed to shirk the difficult task of tackling Brother Bernard. That left two.

Of those two, neither was a Dominican. One was an intimate of the pope's, Raimond de Mostuéjouls, the bishop of St. Papoul, a diocese to the northwest of Carcassonne. He was a reliable, efficient servant of the pope. The other judge came from farther south, from the shadow of the Pyrenees. His diocesan see was Pamiers.

Bernard Délicieux sat down on that first day under the steady gaze of Jacques Fournier.

The people of Carcassonne began their autumn of unease. Brother Bernard was back among them at last, but now, for the first time, he was unseen and unheard. Visitors arrived from far and near, summoned to testify at the solemn trial being held in the Cité. The inns of the Bourg reverberated with rumor, as strangers from Perpignan, Albi, Castres, Limoux, and Alet told of what they had seen and what they had said. More common in these months of September and October was the sight of men of Carcassonne crossing the bridge over the Aude and then mounting the path of the Trivalle to the gate of the fortress-city that led to the bishop's palace. Dozens from the Bourg were called to remember days nearly twenty years distant. As they took their oath to tell the truth, they had to meet the eyes of the defendant, Bernard Délicieux, present in the hall. Almost daily, then, a small drama of reunion took place, between enemies, acquaintances, friends. For some, revenge hung in the air, for slights suffered at the hands of Bernard's allies so long ago, but so too did compassion, for a great man brought

---

* Unlike the tabula rasa of Bernard's convent in the Bourg, the place has survived from his day and can be visited. Even on the warmest days, it gives off a chill.

low, ensnared in the awful gears of ecclesiastical justice. Yet this was no inquisition trial. Bernard saw who accused him, heard or read some of their testimony. He knew what the charges against him were. And he was allowed to defend himself, repeatedly, and in writing. Whether the trial was legitimate in the first place is another question entirely.

The charges against him can today be grouped under four headings: adherence to the Spirituals, treason against Philip the Fair, the murder of Pope Benedict XI, and obstruction of the inquisition.

The first became inconsequential. Although the effective cause of his arrest—Bernard had traveled to Avignon in 1317 to defend the Spirituals of Languedoc—support for them was not what the judges were attempting to pin on him. The Spirituals were being fiercely denounced by then as heretics, and Bernard freely admitted to being sympathetic to their cause, but he had to confess to crimes that were uniquely his, separate from the intra-Franciscan fracas that was rocking the Church. Punishing him solely for that would have set him up for martyrhood among a dissident faction of the Order. Besides, one can suspect that Fournier and Mostuéjouls, respectively a Cistercian and a Benedictine, had little time for the self-inflicted woes of the self-important mendicants. As such, his belonging to the Spiritual movement occupied almost no time during the three-month proceeding.

The treason charge formed the subject of Bernard's first of many appearances in the dock at Carcassonne, on October 2. Why the Church was trying him in this matter remains open to question. If King Philip had not given assurances that Bernard had been absolved, then Pope Clement never would have let the Franciscan leave the curia at Avignon to go to Béziers. One sees here the same reasoning behind the conflict surrounding Bernard Saisset: Délicieux was a churchman, ergo he had to be tried by a Church court jealous of its prerogatives. If, in the future, Philip's successors wished to resurrect the charges, the reasoning went, he could not be tried by royal justice. So he would be tried in Carcassonne about that matter now, by the Church. Added to that institutional scruple was the far weightier reality that Pope John wanted to throw everything he could at Bernard.

We know, from the narrative constructed of the events at Saint-Jean-Pla-de-Corts earlier, that Bernard confessed to his treasonous activity (his confession was supplemented by two witnesses to the stormy scene between King Jaume and his son). What retains attention in the story of his trial is the way in which the confession was extracted. In his first appearance, Bernard gave a patently unbelievable story about how he had broken up the plot, in what was a grave underestimation of the acumen of his judges. Many of the witnesses called from Carcassonne and Albi, including Bernard's former allies, had testified that this was not the case. Fournier must have been insulted. He ordered Bernard tortured—not severely, to avoid incapacitating him or causing organ failure, but tortured nonetheless. The notaries of the transcript duly noted his cries of pain and distress but did not specify the technique used. We can infer that on this or a subsequent occasion a few weeks later it may have been the strappado, being suspended from a beam with one's distended arms tied behind one's back, given a reference late in the transcript to Bernard's badly damaged hands.

In the event, Bernard confessed nothing to the torturer. But he did sleep on the matter and offer a partial confession on October 4. This, too, was dubious, but here the skill of Fournier and his colleague emerged—the treason discussion was shelved for the moment, and subsequent interrogations covered other matters entirely. In what would come to be a pattern in October and November, Bernard did not know what he was going to be asked about when he was unshackled and taken into the bishop's palace. The seemingly scattershot approach may have been unfair, designed to confuse and confound the accused, but when the prosecutor was judge no holds were barred. Bernard must at last have realized that he had gotten what he wished for: judges who were equal to his gifts.

In the thicket of interrogation sessions the matter of the killing of the pope arose on October 27 and November 17. The passing of a prominent personage in the Middle Ages almost always occasioned such suspicions, in the same way that secular courts usually got around to charging whoever was the enemy of the moment with sodomy, heresy, blasphemy, and the like. In this part of the charge sheet against him there were nonetheless several important pieces of circumstantial evidence. Three men of Albi—those who were deposed in Avignon in June 1319—claimed to have been in Bernard's presence in the spring of 1304 when he prepared a mysterious package to be sent to his friend Arnaud de Vilanova, then in Perugia locked in conflict with the Dominican pope, Benedict XI, resident there. Further, Bernard had said not long before the pope's sudden death that no bird could fly to Rome fast enough from Languedoc to see the pontiff alive. And, last, found in the possessions Bernard had entrusted to a notary of Béziers before leaving for Avignon in 1317 was a book of necromancy and spells, its margins covered in annotations by a reader. The Franciscan rule forbade such books, so he had transgressed.

As with the story of treason, Bernard made implausible denials. The book was not his, or perhaps it was. He may have read a few pages, but he had forgotten everything. And those notes in the margin could not possibly be his. Exasperated once again, on November 20 his judges ordered him tortured, and his screams were once again duly noted. Again he admitted nothing. On reflection, several days later he admitted to owning and marking up the magic book, but he vehemently denied having any hand in the death of the pope. He did not add the obvious—that the immensely learned Arnaud de Vilanova would hardly have needed a tutorial on magic from France to pharmaceutically terminate anyone he pleased.

The bulk of the interrogations concerned his actions against the inquisitors. These testimonies in the transcripts—the accounts given by the dozens of witness—breathe life into the ambush at the convent, the appeal of Castel Fabre, the audience at Senlis, the colorful sermons, the taking of the Wall, the disputation at Toulouse, the silver vases. What compels in considering the conduct of the trial is the way in which an ever-weakening Délicieux and an ever-vigilant Fournier—two great minds and consciences—dueled for almost two months.

The judges uncovered events in Délicieux's life in the same seemingly unmethodical but entirely destabilizing manner of unexpected return to subjects already raised. Fournier also raised the question of the disputed inquisition registers. Welcoming the opportunity, Bernard demolished them. He told a lengthy and entirely credible story of a Dominican friar, no less, warning a prelate of Narbonne of their outright falsehoods. Bernard named the inquisition clerks he believed behind what was essentially a scheme to keep the inquisition active in Carcassonne so that the two clerks, both men of the south, could retain their feared positions and collect the fortunes confiscated. He enumerated once again his complaints about imaginary Good Men, then recited a devastating taxonomy of the type of people whom the inquisitors of the 1280s and 1290s convicted and despoiled: they were always dead, thus defenseless; they had always been hereticated on their deathbed; they were never accused of heresy while alive; many of those who supposedly attended such heretications never knew the deceased until that moment, and were only in turn accused after their own decease; and, most damningly, the living witnesses to the heretications, the informants, were never pursued. Bernard's arguments, given in a steady voice in the stone chamber, were not challenged by the court. Fournier must have known the friar was right, for he was aware of the workings of inquisition and the opportunities for abuse.

The bishop of Pamiers, however, had been sent to do a job, which he did on his own terms. Fournier was, above all, a man of principle—however much his prosecutorial ethic is unappealing to most modern eyes. Unlike many of his fellow churchmen, he was not venal or nepotistic. Alone among Avignon popes, Fournier, as Benedict XII, tried to rein in the circus of luxury by the Rhône. Yet in 1319, he had been clearly charged by Pope John to take down Bernard one way or the other. The challenge for Jacques Fournier lay in how to do this in a way that he thought just. It is bold but not unreasonable to conjecture that this brilliant, principled prosecutor did not really care about the other charges: he could have seen the murder charge as the usual farrago of fantastic rumor, the long-dead treason conspiracy as an exercise in the Church's guarding its jurisdictional turf, the Spiritual affiliation as a matter of mendicant madness. Efficient and workmanlike, he and his colleague had wrung out confessions on the last two charges and a ringing denial on the first. But only the matter of inquisition—for which, significantly, torture was not applied—could give Fournier satisfaction.

In late October, he threw the book at Bernard. In a written warning, the judges told Bernard that he had been an excommunicate for years. They spelled out the law of the inquisitors: anyone who caused to be released from the custody of the inquisition any duly convicted prisoner, without the permission of the competent church authority (inquisitor or bishop), was automatically, as a result of that action, excommunicated.

And if the situation was not rectified within a year and the excommunication not lifted, that person was a heretic.

Faced with this sobering statute, Bernard confessed his role in undoing the work of the inquisitors and asked for absolution. Despite this admission, the judges knew it was insufficient. Public sentiment held that the conduct of inquisition in Languedoc in the two decades prior to the year 1300 had been scandalous. Bernard had merely confessed to opposing unjust inquisitors—which was what he had been arguing all along. The judges needed more than a confirmation of what everyone already knew and not a few still applauded.

If Fournier silently agreed with Bernard about the iniquitous registers and incompetent or corrupt inquisitors, he had to establish that the Franciscan's antipathy went far beyond that. Bernard maintained that he had gone only after particular inquisitors, not the inquisition. Both men knew the significance of the distinction. Arguing for the destruction of the inquisition, the sanctified tool for combating heresy, aided and abetted heresy. That was a capital crime. It was not, like freeing the prisoners, an action that triggered an automatic excommunication measure. It was not tantamount to heresy—it was heresy, not stumbled into through the expiration of a one-year grace period but held sincerely and criminally over time.

The dance between the two men on this fundamental matter continued throughout the month of November. Fournier stated that witnesses had spoken of a system of anti-inquisitorial opposition that Bernard had wanted to make permanent. A witness deposed in Avignon on June 7, 1319, had stated in a matter-of-fact manner that Bernard's goal in going to Senlis for his momentous audience was "to ensure the inquisition was completely paralyzed and persuade the king of France to abolish it altogether." There were damning letters to consuls of Languedoc towns, demanding money for organizing. Bernard allowed that he might have overstepped his bounds as a simple Franciscan friar, but it was all in the service of fighting the unjust among the inquisitors. Around 1300, Bernard had claimed that there were no heretics left in Languedoc, yet that had been demonstrably proven untrue in subsequent years. In an exchange of November 8, Fournier asked a seemingly innocent question: who, at time of the disputation of Toulouse in 1304, were the inquisitors at Carcassonne and Toulouse? Bernard gave the names: Geoffroy d'Ablis and Guillaume de Morières. Yet they were not the ones Bernard had earlier identified to the court as objectionable, namely, Jean Galand, Guillaume de Saint-Seine, Foulques de Saint-Georges, and Nicolas d'Abbeville. They no longer held office at the time of the disputation, when Délicieux had lectured the king on diagnosing and extirpating an illness. The implication of this point of fact was clear: the friar would never approve of an inquisitor, any inquisitor.

November drew to a close. Bernard was failing, the constant interrogations and traps having taken their toll. So too had torture and captivity. Fournier, sensing the kill, opted then to take out his heaviest cudgel. Bernard was informed he had a choice. He could stop all his cavils and evasions on the charges, confess to obstructing not just inquisitors but the inquisition as a whole, thereby aiding heresy, and then ask for forgiveness, or he could persist in his denials and excuses. If he chose the latter, he should be under no illusion: he would then be convicted on the charge of heresy, which would incur excommunication, execution, and an eternity in Hell.

The Franciscan was given a few days to think it over. Now that his body was broken, he had to think of his soul.

On December 3, he was brought before Fournier and Mostuéjouls. He had decided to end the exhausting game of cat-and-mouse. The germane passage of the transcript reads: "[The judges], seeking and attempting to effect the conversion of Brother Bernard and the salvation of his soul, warned him once, twice, thrice and demanded he confess without any further diversions and frivolous excuses to having favored the heretics and obstructed the inquisition." Bernard, in the first part of his surrender, at last uttered the words Fournier had long sought: "Despite the justifications and excuses put forth by me in my statements and responses on favoring and obstructing, I now admit my guilt."

The "queen of proofs" had been delivered. If Bernard had indeed wanted to topple the inquisition, no matter who staffed it, then by the logic of the day this was a moment of justice long delayed. If, on the other hand, he had done only what he had originally claimed—attack corrupt inquisitors—then on this day in Carcassonne there must have been darkness at noon. He had condemned himself to spare the Church embarrassment.

On Saturday, December 8, 1319, crowds jammed the market square of the Bourg of Carcassonne. The great and the mean had gathered together. Of the former, there were prelates and noblemen and notables in their splendid finery, among them the bishops of Carcassonne, Mirepoix, and Elne, the abbots of Lagrasse and Montolieu, the count of Forez, the seneschal of Carcassonne, the knights François de Lévis, Guillaume de Voisins, Dalmas de Marciac, and Raimond Accurat-Comte, the judges of Verdun and Rivière, the eminent law professor Frisco Ricomanni, the lawyers Peire Vital and Peire Guille, and the consuls of Carcassonne. The humbler of the multitude—merchant and maiden, tradesman and alewife, friar and widow—had come from the streets leading to the marketplace, a variegated stream of medieval humanity. All had come to see Bernard, their enemy, their friend, their former nemesis, their erstwhile champion, the man they had heard vilified or praised, the holy or unholy priest their parents had told them so much about.

There was no *sermo generalis*. This was not an inquisitorial proceeding. There was no stake, no chanting Dominicans, no talk of dogs returning to their vomit.

Bernard stood in full view of the assembly, failing, sickly, undone. The judgments against him were to be read aloud. No mention of the friar's adherence to the Spirituals was made. The original pretext for prosecution had been abandoned. Judgment was rendered.

On the charge of killing the pope: not guilty.

On the charge of treason: guilty.

On the charge of obstructing the Holy Office: guilty.

The reading began, a long, detailed, and sententious monument of stately prose and stern outrage. As his offenses were recounted Bernard stood silent, as thousands looked at him for the last time.

His sentence arrived at the end of the reading. He was to be defrocked—he would no longer be member of the clergy, no longer be Brother Bernard. Although he had confessed and been given absolution, a just punishment, a penance, had to be inflicted. He was sentenced to life imprisonment in the Wall of Carcassonne—to the *murus strictus*, shackled solitary confinement and a diet of bread and water.

Whether the sentence was too harsh or too lenient came to be answered conclusively later in the day at the episcopal palace, where Bernard was taken one last time for a formal ceremony to exclude him from the clergy. Following that moment of further degradation, a letter was addressed by Jacques Fournier and Raimond de Mostuéjouls to his new jailer, Jean de Beaune, the inquisitor of Carcassonne. Once beyond the customary flowery formalities, a surprising passage leaps out:

> Having finally assigned him to strict confinement in the Wall, situated between the Cité of Carcassonne and the Aude, subjecting him to perpetual imprisonment in irons and a diet of bread and water, We, out of consideration for his age and weakness, and particularly at this moment for the weakness that can be discerned in his hands, believe that he should be dispensed from performing this penance . . . and [thus] give you by this document the permission to exempt him from irons and fasting.

This was a final twist, and, for his enemies, the last straw. The legal representatives of the French king, Philip V, demanded that Bernard be turned over to them for execution. He no longer could claim the immunity of the cloth—he was no longer a clergyman. Their appeal was lodged the next day. Although a formal gesture, a type of jurisidictional chest-puffing between state and Church, the document stands out for the vehemence of its language. The last-minute clemency clearly had grated—and produced last-minute prose:

> He [Bernard] committed or encouraged others to commit many great and shameful crimes, shameful acts that were both criminal and harmful and that cannot be detailed without a long speech, that should stir up a tempest of the elements, and for which he should suffer death not once, but many times, if human nature would only allow it.

Fournier and his colleague were having none of it. They flatly rejected the appeal. They had punished Bernard enough by putting him in the Wall he so detested and which he would never leave. For his contemporaries, the softened sentence seemed lenient. If, indeed, he was guilty of heresy through systematically trying to bring down the inquisition, then by the cruel standards of the day he deserved not imprisonment but death.

Yet behind Fournier's final act of compassion, there might be another consideration. Fournier, for all his rectitude, was not a softhearted man: to be an inquisitor of his stature, one had to have no compunction about ruining lives for matters that could very well have been ignored—and were, by other churchmen of his own day. The mercy Fournier accorded Délicieux may have proceeded from scruple. He had been dispatched by the pope to do a job, and he had done it. Yet if the final confession made by Bernard had been false, extracted under threat and given to save ecclesiastical face, Fournier would have known that only too well. It would have nagged at his conscience. If, as the Franciscan had maintained until the very last moment, he had acted only against inquisitorial abuse and not the inquisition itself, then he had done no wrong. In showing mercy to Bernard, Jacques Fournier may have been asking God for mercy for himself.

The pope had no such scruples. Inserted in an inquisition register of Bernard Gui conserved in the British Museum, a papal letter of February 27, 1320, informs Jacques Fournier and Raimond de Mostuéjouls that they had been mistaken to reduce the severity of the punishment. A marginal notation appears, written by an unknown but deferential clerk:

My Lord the Most Holy Pope John XXII, after the sentence delivered against Brother Bernard Délicieux had been read before him and the lord cardinals in a private consistory, and after learning the retention of the right to mitigate the punishment, revoked this stipulation entirely and ordered that Bernard Délicieux be subject to the full rigor of the sentence and that the conditions of his punishment be completely observed.

By the time this icy blast of malice was received, Bernard Délicieux was, in all probability, already dead. If not, its implementation finished him off. We do not know the date of his demise or where he was buried, only that it occurred in early 1320. The pope, in his final letter on the subject, clearly wanted Bernard to suffer and die quickly.

The trial at Carcassonne had been staged to make that happen. Had he been burned, he might have entered legend. Pope John, through the grinding machinery of a trial, wanted Bernard to confess and disappear into the Wall, where he would be forgotten. And he was.

But the fourteenth-century pope could not have foreseen one last thing: it is precisely because of that same trial that the friar of Carcassonne can be remembered by us.

AFTERWORD

BROTHER BERNARD DÉLICIEUX WAS A CREATURE—AND a victim—of his times. As is true of all historical figures, the temptation to imagine his pertinence to the present day must be resisted, but not entirely rejected. Even in the nineteenth-century heyday of exuberant anachronism, when freethinkers and liberators were found hidden under every rock in a historical landscape stretching back to Cro-Magnon times, the story of Brother Bernard was treated with unusual care. Biographer Jean-Barthélemy Hauréau, although unable to resist viewing the Franciscan as a patriot of Languedoc independence, warned in the first major work on the Carcassonne revolt that the medieval critics of inquisition were not proceeding from a premise held by nineteenth-century democrats like himself:

> It should be noted that in all the arguments put forth by the reformers there is not one word about freedom of conscience. The right to believe or not to believe, the right to reason or rant freely on any metaphysical subject, the right surrendered by some of the faithful in the early days of the Church then abolished subsequently by the decrees of Constantine—this sentiment was lost, and many centuries would have to pass before it awoke again in the soul of man. All the complaints concerned iniquitous condemnation and scandalous expropriation. Very few people even dared question whether the inquisition was necessary; only the conduct of the inquisitor was open to accusation.

No civil libertarian, Bernard Délicieux nonetheless saw grievous wrong and summoned up the courage to try to redress it. In this he was a man for all seasons—but still just a man. As a hero, certainly, he fell short. The friar's feet of clay were prominently on display at his trial: the testimony clearly showed that he embraced duplicity and counseled treason in the service of his cause and that he was not above the most pusillanimous of tale-telling in his failed attempt to escape punishment at that same trial. Hardly the paragon of judicial virtue, he was no saint, either, his misrepresentations of the accord of 1299 an unedifying instance of demagoguery. Bernard was a follower of Francis, not an imitator.

This humanity—this imperfection—may be what makes Brother Bernard compelling. Far more appealing than the spotless victor, the flawed vanquished presents a figure with which most people can identify, especially when the cause—standing up to oppression—seems universal in its nobility. Yet a note of caution has to be sounded loudly here, for however resonant the story may be in the present day, the irrevocable chasm carved by the passage of time should always be kept in mind. The writer of history attempts to bridge that chasm, but his or her construction must necessarily be flimsy, subject to collapse in the winds stirred up by new scholarship or, more likely, the new circumstances born with every generation.

Added to the fragile is the foreign: the strange people moving at a distance of several centuries, their outlook unfamiliar, alien even, like figures crossing a faraway field on a moonless night, to be distinguished only in the dimmest of half-lights. The reasoning of Bernard's judges, for example, seems reassuringly rational until a passage in their act of formal sentencing heads straight into a fog of magical thinking, its wording fit for the card catalogue at the library of Hogwarts. The passage concerns a book found in Délicieux's possession:

> This little book contains many characters, the names of demons, the manner in which to conjure them, to offer sacrifices to them, to demolish through their aid houses and fortresses, to sink ships at sea, to gain the affection, the confidence and the ear of the great and others, to have women in marriage or for the act of love, to induce in people present, or even absent,

blindness, broken limbs and other infirmities, even death, thanks to images and other magical acts, and in general to cause many other evils.

Not that attempting to peer into a past darkened by the march of centuries should ever be abandoned, for even from Bernard's distant day distinctly recognizable silhouettes appear. Guillaume de Nogaret is the man who will say or do anything in the service of the regime to which he owes allegiance; Jacques Fournier, the brilliant prosecutor on a mission; Pope Boniface, the leader masking, or perhaps revealing, weakness through a show of pomp; the inquisitors, men who discern an existential threat to their world order and invent, or rewrite, the rules by which they are to conduct themselves.

Of all the facets of Bernard's story, the inquisition is the one that must be approached with the greatest care, given its enduring notoriety. It is, in a sense, a celebrity of intolerance. The targets of inquisition in the years immediately after Bernard's time switched from heretics to witches, as the two categories of enemies became conflated. The inquisition also eventually became the Inquisition, a formalized institution with a permanent bureaucracy established at different times, in different countries. As with the switch from heresy to sorcery, it changed its targets according to perceived need, which is yet another figure recognizable in almost any age: an institution that alters its original mission to ensure its perennity.

In the Holy Office's most dread iteration of the early modern period—the Spanish Inquisition—first the covert practice of Judaism and then any trace of "Jewish blood" became grounds for prosecution, as the Church undertook to erase the memory of Iberia's multiconfessional past. As with other inquisitions in the Mediterranean world, the Spanish institution also sought to punish renegades—Christian converts to Islam captured in the piratical corsairs they sailed for the Ottomans and their allies off the Barbary Coast. Much of Catholic Europe and the Catholic New World were saddled with these tribunals until the dawn of the nineteenth century, so the well of legend runs deep and dark. So tenacious is the hold of inquisition on memory that the pope of the year 2000, John Paul II, felt compelled, in a speech decried as anachronism by some and hailed as olive branch by others, to apologize on behalf of the Church for the excesses of its inquisitors.

If the pope knew the particulars of the cause of the friar of Carcassone, his apology must also have been destined for the people of medieval Languedoc. Although modern scholarship, at a distance of so many years, has difficulty in determining from the disputed inquisition registers whether Bernard's misgivings about them were correct, the Franciscan's clerical contemporaries did not labor under the disadvantage of remoteness. The Church came to doubt the contents of Registers X and XI. They were minutely examined on several occasions by suspicious authority, which performed the historian's task, in a sense, at a time when the evidence was fresh.

Pope Boniface VIII forbade their use as grounds for prosecution; Clement V examined them personally, affixing the papal seal onto each of their pages. The most thorough of these reviews, commissioned by a pontiff, John XXII, wholly unsympathetic to the cause of Carcassonne, was conducted some eleven years after Délicieux's death by the men who had sat in judgment of him in 1319. His denunciations of the registers at the trial had planted hardy seeds of doubt in their minds. While not accepting Bernard's maximalist reading of the documents as top-to-bottom deceitful, Jacques Fournier and Raimond de Mostué-jouls concluded that they contained enough error and evidence of shoddy methods to be no longer considered accurate and trustworthy. As for the question of Guilhem Pagès and Bernard Costa—the Good Men with the bland John Smith names—no conclusion could be drawn as to their having existed or not. Significantly, however, no one took up the gauntlet thrown down by Bernard during the Castel Fabre matter. No one ever came forward with information about these men. Délicieux was thus vindicated—and from the camp of his enemies emerges another familiar silhouette, the practice of lying in the pursuit of power.

Without Bernard Délicieux and his mixture of talents and flaws there would probably never have been such successful agitation against a judicial practice so perfectly in step with the persecuting ethos of its day. That in itself was his greatest accomplishment—taking a stand against the corruption and the cruel certainty of his times. What he did was never repeated. He was aided by his profound attachment to the Franciscan ideal, as well as his political acumen and tremendous gifts of persuasion and oratory. Yet these qualities are of limited reach, almost anecdotal, unlikely to coalesce as a distinct or universal shape. Perhaps where Bernard ultimately resides is not in the outward realm of archetype; rather, he uncomfortably touches the nerve within, where principles are housed and decisions must be made. In the end, the Agitateur du Languedoc may be pointing his finger at us all, demanding that no matter what confronts us, we be true to our convictions.

ACKNOWLEDGMENTS

ANY PEOPLE HAVE CONTRIBUTED to the making of this book, through their help, consideration, and kindness. In the southwest of France, home to the story of Brother Bernard, the invaluable assistance of the indefatigable journalist Pascal Alquier, aka Monsieur Toulouse, opened doors for me, led me to scholars and scholarship, and provided welcome shelter for me in his flat near the Basilica of St. Sernin. In the countryside Jean-Pierre Pétermann and his wife, Joelle, welcomed me into their home in Auterive several times, and when Jean-Pierre (a medical professional in real life but in truth a modern-day Cathar) and I returned from our photographic safaris of Languedoc, a hearty meal always awaited, as did a fine bottle from the local bounty. In the mornings after the nights before, Jean-Pierre and Joelle's young, voluble triplets, Aymeri, Aurenca, and Aélis, made sure that we did not shirk our duty to hit the road again brightish and earlyish.

Other denizens of Languedoc edified, informed, and welcomed, including scholar Father Georges Passerat, troubadour Christian Salès, cultural impresario Robert Cavalié, radio journalist Laura Haydon, and writer Suzanne Lowry. In Carcassonne, my thanks also to Jean-Louis Gasc, who conducted me on a tour of the ramparts that was exclusively devoted to the trial of Bernard Délicieux. In the Bourg, at the Centre d'Études Cathares, the staff assembled hard-to-get monographs and articles on the history of *la rage carcassonnaise*. They simplified my research immensely and—Francophobes take note and repent—went out of their way to do their job, even to the point of making up for a missed rendezvous (because of a hospitalized child!) by going to the center and photocopying documents for me during its August closing, no less.

In the Roussillon, on the tracks of Bernard's failed plot, I was welcomed in Camélas once again by Vladimir and Yovanka Djurovic and Martine and Francis Péron. Farther north, in King Philip the Fair's scheming metropolis, my research sojourns in Paris were made even more enjoyable by the hospitality of Heidi Ellison and Sandy and Elisabeth Whitelaw. In London, home to so many good bookstores, my stays there were always enlivened by the warm welcome of Kate Griffin and her daughters Flo and Georgie. In Toronto, I would like to thank Helen Mercer and Eleanor Wachtel for their hospitality and support. In Ottawa, a similar thank-you to artist Patrick Cocklin and, of course, to my dad, Daniel O'Shea.

Most of this book was written and researched in Providence, Rhode Island. As in the past, the eagle eye and writerly advice of novelist pal Eli Gottlieb, out in Boulder, Colorado, have been much appreciated. I'd like also to thank two hyperliterate lawyers, Fred Stolle of Providence and Edward Hernstadt of New York City, for training their gaze on the manuscript—particularly the third chapter—for signs betraying the legal neophyte. Ed and his wife, Maia Wechsler, old friends from our Paris days together, have made their Dumbo loft in Brooklyn a second home for me in my frequent stays in the city.

Here in my first home, as ever, a heartfelt thank-you to my family, Jill, Rachel, and Eve, for their support—even though daughters Rachel and Eve insist on taking obscure revenge for my monomania by always referring to my heretics as "Cathires." To those friends here who did not take the subject of my research as an instance of rôtisserie-league Catholicism, I say thank you: Claude Goldstein, Allen Kurzweil, Rosemary Mahoney, Bill Viall. To those who did, I say nothing. A debt of gratitude is also owed to two medievalists resident in Rhode Island, both specialists of the fourteenth century (providential, no?), who led me from the path of error: Joëlle Rollo-Koster and Alizah Holstein.

Professionally, I owe much to agent Chuck Verrill, who guided this project expertly from the outset. I am also indebted to talented designer Cara T. Collins for escorting me onto the Web in style (stephenoshea online.com—please feel free to check it out and leave comments, suggestions, brickbats, etc., for me on this present work at the contact point provided; I am much better at responding to e-mail than to snail mail). And thanks again to publishers Scott McIntyre (Canada), George Gibson (United States), and Peter Carson (United Kingdom) for their un-

AGMENTS | 211

tiring support and confidence. I, alas, am wholly responsible for whatever infelicities and inaccuracies the book contains.

Last, but most important, a word about research. Whatever else one may say about America, here in New England the sheer profusion of great libraries, digital archives, easy access to interlibrary loans and the like is nothing less than world-class, a true example of democracy in action. Many thanks to my research assistant, Jennifer Schneider, for attacking the stacks when I couldn't. A recent graduate of Brown, Jenny was able to find just about anything at the libraries of her alma mater.

Elsewhere, the staff at the Fox Point branch of the Providence public library system pulled some rabbits out of their hats, as did the friendly librarians of the Providence Athenæum. And for those mendicant obscurities unavailable anywhere else, I am indebted to Providence College and its research library, its stacks admirably open to the general public. I enjoyed slipping in there, with Brother Bernard hidden in my backpack, for Providence College is the only university in North America run by the Dominicans. It has a good men's basketball team, the Friars.

NOTES

A narrative with a claim to immediacy on events long past necessitates a good deal of notes. As many, but not all, of the details about Brother Bernard's activities come from his trial, I will point the skeptical reader frequently to Jean Duvernoy's French translation of the trial transcript. Decisions and inferences made by me and others will also be discussed. Mundane matters of fact found in all his previous biographies will not be cited, as that would put everyone to sleep. Where the biographers differ, however, will be flagged.

Also cited are sources not directly germane to Bernard, such as, for example, those dealing with the affair of the Templars. And I will also provide additional material in the notes that I could not somehow shoehorn into the main narrative. These digressions, I hope, may lead in a roundabout way to a better understanding of Délicieux and his place in history. Some are amusing, some appalling.

Bibliographical detail in the notes is provided the first time a work is cited. After that, abbreviated entries are the rule. If you don't want to lose your temper flipping back through the notes to see where such-and-such a book is first mentioned, save yourself the trouble and go to the bibliography. Last, the publishing date covers the edition I used.

BROTHER BERNARD

2 **Those who commissioned him sought to bolster local pride and regional identity, and to instruct and edify:** Tastes changed and the history painting went out of fashion. The most memorable epitaph for the genre came from the savagely witty pen of Saki (Hector Hugh Munro) in his story "The Reticence of Lady Anne": "They leaned towards the honest and explicit in art, a picture, for instance, that told its own story, with generous assistance from its title. A riderless warhorse with harness in obvious disarray, staggering into a courtyard full of pale swooning women, and marginally noted 'Bad News,' suggested to their minds a

distinct interpretation of some military catastrophe. They could see what it was meant to convey, and explain it to friends of duller intelligence." *The Complete Saki*, London, 1998, pp. 46–48. For immediate gratification, the story can be found online: http://haytom.us/showarticle .php?id=119.

4 **his three major biographers:** Jean-Barthélemy Hauréau, *Bernard Délicieux et l'inquisition albigeoise (1300–1320)*, Paris, 1877; Michel de Dmitrewski, "Fr. Bernard Délicieux, O.F.M. Sa lutte contre L'Inquisition de Carcassonne et d'Albi, son procès, 1297–1319," *Archivum Franciscanum Historicam*, 17, 1924, pp. 183–218, 313–337, 457–488; 18, 1925, pp. 3–32; Alan Friedlander, *The Hammer of the Inquisitors: Brother Bernard Délicieux and the Struggle Against the Inquisition in Fourteenth-Century France*, Leiden, 2000. To these larger works must be added two invaluable monographs: Jean-Louis Biget, "Autour de Bernard Délicieux. Franciscanisme et société en Languedoc entre 1295 et 1330," *Revue d'histoire de l'Eglise de France*, 70, 1984, pp. 75–93; Yves Dossat, "Les origines de la querelle entre Prêcheurs et Mineurs provençaux," *Cahiers de Fanjeaux*, 10, 1975, pp. 315–354. These scholars produced other works germane to Bernard's story, but the five works cited here form the core material, aside from the transcripts of the trial. Their other works, and those of other scholars to treat the story, appear in the bibliography.

7 **an American historian undertook the task of collating, transcribing and publishing:** Alan Friedlander, *Processus Bernardi Delitiosi: The Trial of Fr. Bernard Délicieux, 3 September–8 September 1319*, Philadelphia, 1996.

7 **rendered the Latin of the original into a modern vernacular:** Jean Duvernoy, *Le Procès de Bernard Délicieux 1319*, Toulouse, 2001.

7 **the memory of Brother Bernard Délicieux:** The Franciscan is not universally revered. While inspecting the lower town of Carcassonne (called the Bourg in the main narrative) in the summer of 2009, I entered an old cathedral, St. Michel, which stands more or less unchanged since Bernard's time. I was alone. I took notes, which I didn't end up using, on the interior of this fine example of Languedocian Gothic. A figure approached from a side aisle, smiling, thirtysomething, in priestly attire. I asked him about his church, its past and present. He was very affable, knowledgeable, a learned clergyman affiliated with the Dominicans. His edifying explanations drawing to a close, he asked me why I was so interested in the church. I told him I was researching a

book on Bernard Délicieux. It was if I had slapped his face with a large, wet fish. He recovered his smile, then snapped in premature parting, "On dit tout et n'importe quoi à son sujet!"—don't believe what you hear about him.

1. The Bridge at Rome

11 **the drudges of his *Wasteland*:** The passage is found in T.S. Eliot, *The Wasteland: i The Burial of the Dead*, 60–64. From T. S. Eliot, *Collected Poems, 1909–1962*, New York, 1963.

11 **the Ponte St. Angelo:** The beautiful bridge still stands and is reserved exclusively for pedestrians, a measure enacted by Mussolini in the early 1930s.

11 **Dante commanded his underworld denizens:** Dante, *Inferno*, xviii 27–32:

> come i Roman per l'essercito molto,
> l'anno del giubileo, su per lo ponte
> hanno a passar la gente modo colto,

> che da l'un lato tutti hanno la fronte
> verso 'l castello e vanno a Santo Pietro,
> de l'altra sponda vanno verso 'l monte.

I used in the narrative the verse translation of Pinsky, *Inferno*. It is clear. A more stately, but not altogether transparent, translation of the passage was made by Henry Wadsworth Longfellow, published to great fanfare in 1867:

> Even as the Romans, for the mighty host,
> The year of Jubilee, upon the bridge,
> Have chosen a mode to pass the people over;

> For all upon one side towards the Castle
> Their faces have, and go unto St. Peter's;
> On the other side they go towards the Mountain

The Castle is undoubtedly Hadrian's mausoleuem, aka the Castel St. Angelo. The Mountain or mount is the Gianicolo (Janiculum), the tall, distant ridge beyond the Borgo of central Rome and another bend of the Tiber. It is not one of the Seven Hills.

12 **"Day and night two priests stood at the altar of St. Paul's":** The chronicler is William Ventura, cited in Paul Hetherington, *Medieval Rome: A Portrait of the the City and Its Life*, New York, 1994, p. 79.

12 **he was moved to undertake his *Nuova Cronica*:** Rome impressed him
so much that he thought of Florence: "It was the most marvellous
thing that was ever seen . . . Finding myself on that blessed pilgrimage
in the holy city of Rome, beholding the great and ancient things
therein, and reading the stories and the great doings of the Romans,
written by Virgil and Sallust and Lucas and Titus Livius and Valerius
and Paulus Orosius, and other masters of history . . . I resolved myself
to preserve memorials . . . for those who should come after . . . But
considering that our city of Florence, the daughter and creature of
Rome, was rising, and had great things before her, whilst Rome was de-
clining, it seemed to me fitting to collect in this volume and new
chronicle all the deeds and beginnings of the city of Florence . . . and
to follow the doings of the Florentines in detail." Giovanni Villani,
Nuova Cronica, viii 36. From translator Rose E. Selfe, *Villani's Chronicle, Being Selections from the First Nine Books of the Croniche Fiorentine
of Giovanni Villani*, London, 1906, p. 321. In this section Villani estimates a crowd of 200,000 pilgrims is present every day of that year in
Rome.

13 **his massive marble tomb . . . apostolic deputy:** Both details in Herbert
L. Kessler and Johanna Zacharias, *Rome 1300: On the Path of the Pilgrim*, New Haven, 2000, pp. 215–16.

13 **The expansive pope had called the Jubilee to celebrate the commonwealth of Christendom:** Like Christianity itself, the notion of Jubilee is
derived from Judaism. The traditional Jewish jubilee, like the timing of
the Sabbath, was connected to the number seven. Thus, every forty-
nine years—that is, seven times seven years—was a jubilee year. Kessler
and Zacharias, *Rome 1300*, p. 2.

13 **a despairing Pope Celestine:** Details of the papal politicking are found
in many of the books consulted. I found most useful to have at hand:
J. N. D. Kelly, *The Oxford Dictionary of Popes*, Oxford, 1986; Walter Ullmann, *A Short History of the Papacy in the Middle Ages*, London, 2003.

13 **the old man dutifully died:** Celestine's imprisonment and demise had
two important consequences: it would be used by Guillaume de Nogaret to accuse Boniface of murder, and in the eyes of radical Spirituals
and Joachites, Celestine became the "angel pope" foreseen in apocalyptic prophecy.

14 **a newly completed fresco:** Kessler and Zacharias, *Rome 1300*, p. 30.

16 **Holy beggars stripped to the waist, fakirs at fairgrounds:** The literature on the rise of heresy and the notion of apostolic poverty is very
large and very entertaining. The bibliography should be consulted. I
especially recommend two excellent one-volume works: R. I. Moore,
The Origins of European Dissent, Toronto, 1994; Malcolm Lambert, *Medieval Heresy: Popular Movements from the Gregorian Reform to the Reformation*, Oxford, 2002.

16 **It had excommunicated orthodox proponents of poverty:** The
Waldenses were the subject of a bull of excommunication issued at Verona in 1184 by Pope Lucius III. The followers of a certain Valdes, or
Waldo, a rich merchant of Lyon who gave away all his wordly wealth,
the Waldenses were, in fact, no more radical than the Franciscans were
at the time of their foundation. Innocent III was shrewd enough to
embrace the mendicant movement; Lucius lacked his acumen and
needlessly expelled the Waldenses. According to historian Jonathan
Wright: "Sometimes people like Valdes were denounced as heretics;
sometimes very similar people were lauded as pious harbingers of a new
and better age. This only goes to show how hard it was to draw the line
between heresy and challenging, acceptable Christianity. There is no
better proof of this than the story of Valdes's close contemporary, Francis of Assisi, who did many of the same things but, instead of being
persecuted, ended up being revered as a saint." Jonathan Wright, *Heretics: The Creation of Christianity from the Gnostics to the Modern Church*,
New York, 2011, p. 137.

18 **Giovanni Francesco di Bernadone:** His second name is thought to
have been given him as a token of his father's respect for France. Francis
spoke French and most certainly attended the fairs of Champagne in
his father's company.

18 **other sons of affluent traders:** C. H. Lawrence, *Medieval Monasticism:
Forms of Religious Life in Western Europe in the Middle Ages*, London,
1990, p. 248.

18 **the Ayyubid sultan, Malik al-Kamil:** The remarkable meeting occurred near Damietta in 1219. The sultan was a supremely intelligent
man, as proven by his negotiations with Emperor Frederick II (*Stupor
Mundi*), which allowed the latter to take the title of King of Jerusalem
and hold the holy city on a fixed-term lease. The arrangement scandalized both Christendom and the lands of Islam, but through it the

bloodshed of yet another Crusade was avoided. The two rulers showed exceptional judgment and statesmanship in the matter. For more on this agreement: Stephen O'Shea, *Sea of Faith: Islam and Christianity in the Medieval Mediterranean World*, London, 2009, pp. 238–239.

19 **hotbeds of recruitment and brotherly achievement:** The mendicants were by no means welcomed to the universities with open arms, as the competition for students and their fees, faculty positions, and comfortable quarters was fierce. Guillaume de St. Amour led the charge of the secular faculty in Paris and managed to have the friars expelled for a time. The first half of the 1250s were particularly trying for the friars, as Pope Innocent IV sided with their critics. Their rights and privileges were reinstated by his successor, Alexander IV, in 1256.

18 **The saint's first biographer:** Thomas of Celano. For an edifying treatment of the life of this remarkable man: Julien Green, *God's Fool: The Life and Times of Francis of Assisi*, trans. Peter Heinegg, San Francisco, 1985.

19 **They were discharged from their duties . . . because of their venality:** David Burr, *The Spiritual Franciscans: From Protest to Persecution in the Century After Saint Francis*, University Park, PA, 2001, p. 5.

20 **the evangelization of Bosnia . . . was held up for several years as Franciscans and Dominicans fought:** Dossat, "Les origines de la querelle," p. 318.

20 **metanoia:** Lawrence, *Medieval Monasticism*, p. 239.

20 **"the greater jihad":** Islamophobes may be surprised, but the "lesser jihad" is the struggle with others. The struggle with one's self, in striving in the way of Allah, is considered the greater and more important task.

21 **Commercial Revolution:** This passage on the vigor of the medieval economy covers ground explored by many historians. For the general reader, I recommend the widely available Joseph and Frances Gies, *Life in a Medieval City*, New York, 1981, a wonderful evocation of life circa 1250 in Troyes, Champagne. Another, more general treatment is found in Francis Oakley, *The Medieval Experience*, Toronto, 2005. The chapter "Making and Doing: The Nature of Medieval Economic Life" (pp. 73–107) is a particularly deft introduction to the complex subject.

22 **Latin westerners ruled Greek Constantinople:** The so-called Latin Empire of Constantinople lasted from 1204 to 1261. The Paleologus

family, an old and powerful Byzantine clan, reasserted Greek control after a lengthy siege.

22 **The precious number zero:** Its promotion in the Latin West is commonly attributed to Fibonacci (1170–1250), the son of a Pisan merchant. He learned of the Hindu-Arabic numeral system during extended stays in Algeria, where his father ran a trading post for the Republic of Pisa. He subsequently became a honored guest at the Sicilian court of the ever-curious *Stupor Mundi*, Emperor Frederick II.

2. THE KING'S MEN AT THE DOOR

23 **the day of reckoning for the Knights Templar:** The Templars have spawned entire libraries of speculative and historical literature. The best of the recent works for the general reader is from the reliably clear-headed Piers Paul Read, *The Templars: The Dramatic History of the Knights Templar, the Most Powerful Military Order of the Crusades*, London, 1999. The opening of King Philip's order for their arrest reads: "A bitter thing, a lamentable thing, a thing which is horrible to contemplate, terrible to hear of, a detestable crime, an execrable evil, an abominable work, a detestable disgrace, a thing almost inhuman, indeed set apart from all humanity." Cited in Michael Haag, *The Templars: History and Myth*, London, 2008, p. 216.

23 **the obscene kiss:** This involved the rear end of a cat. It was a common charge leveled against heretics, who were thought to perform this particular osculation as part of their nocturnal orgies. Indeed, the word *Cathar* may not originate from the Greek for pure, *katharos*, but from the Low German for a cat lover, *Ketzer*. As for other specifics of the heresy charge: "It was claimed that new initiates were required to deny Christ three times and spit on a crucifix. Then, having stripped naked, they would be kissed on the mouth, the navel, and the spine by their superiors: a foretaste, it was suggested, of the life of sodomy and bestiality that awaited them. A life, so the accusations continued, that was punctuated by the despoiling of sacraments and the worshipping of idols— including jewel-encrusted human skulls." Wright, *Heretics*, p. 124.

23 **"drink like a Templar":** Alistair Horne, *La Belle France*, New York, 2006, p. 59: "For centuries after their demise 'Boire comme un templier' was common currency in France, while the old German word Tempelhaus became synonymous with a house of ill repute."

23 **Only very recently has a scholar found in the archives of the Vatican:** Barbara Frale, "The Chinon Chart, Papal Absolution to the Last Templar, Master Jacques de Molay," *Journal of Medieval History* 30, 2, 2004, pp. 109–134.

24 **long-lived monarchs in the Capetian line:** Philip II (Philip Augustus) reigned 1180–1223; Louis IX (St. Louis) reigned 1226–1270; Philip IV (Philip the Fair) reigned 1285–1314.

25 **Stupor Mundi:** Frederick II is a singular figure in European history and has received considerable well-deserved scholarly attention. The modern foundation text of Frederick studies is Ernst H. Kantorowicz, *Frederick the Second, 1194–1250*, trans. E. O. Lorimer, New York, 1957. Norman F. Cantor devotes a chapter to the odd Hitlerian backdrop behind Kantorowicz's scholarship in his entertaining, if controversial, *Inventing the Middle Ages: The Lives, Works, and Ideas of the Great Medievalists of the Twentieth Century*, New York, 1991.

25 **the 1268 beheading:** With the execution of Conradin, the once-mighty Hohenstaufen line became extinct. The event was romanticized in later centuries in a sort of homoerotic haze. Genre paintings show the beautiful Conradin in the company of his dearest friend, the nineteen-year-old and equally beautiful Frederick of Baden, calmly playing chess in their prison cell in Naples as they are informed that death is imminent.

25 **a pivotal event:** The extinction of the Hohenstaufen is not just marked as a key event in German history. There is a remarkable passage on its significance in Friedrich Heer, *The Medieval World*, trans. Janet Sondheimer, New York, 1961, an enduringly useful one-volume overview of the Middle Ages. Heer writes (p. 331):

> The public execution of the last of the Hohenstaufen in the marketplace of Naples was a revolutionary event, without precedent in the history of Europe; until it had happened anyone would have said it was unthinkable. In terms of "the logic of history" it may seem the "right" conclusion to the papal revolt against the Emperor. It was only papal approval and the tenor of papal propaganda over the past two centuries that made the deed possible. The Popes, by diminishing the status of imperial descent, had prepared the scaffold for future princes of noble birth (or of "divine descent," according to popular belief): for the execution Charles I and Louis XVI. It was fruitless for Popes of more modern times, from the sixteenth to the nineteenth centuries, to set themselves up as the sworn allies of

"Christian princes" in the task of crushing "infamous rebellions" instigated by heretics and "the scum of society"; it was fruitless for papal ideologists to try to breathe fresh life and meaning into post-revolutionary attempts at restoration. The Papacy had encompassed the destruction of the Empire only by a revolutionary breach of the continuity of European history; the transformation of the popular image of the Christian monarch from a sacred and sacrosanct figure into a diabolical object of execration had called for the most blatant techniques of propaganda and political manoeuvering. Scarcely a generation elapsed after the execution of Conradin before the Pope was forced to pay the first instalment of the penalty for having degraded and dishallowed the highest office in Christendom apart from his own. In 1303 Boniface VIII was taken prisoner at Anagni by William of Nogaret, Councillor to Philip IV of France. Subjected to all manner of ignominy, the Pope's pride and self-confidence were mortally wounded and he died in Rome only a few weeks after his release.

25 **"the Church's eldest daughter"**: The expression, in the original, is *la fille aînée de l'Eglise*. It got a lot of play from the seventeenth through the nineteenth centuries as factions in the French church disputed its place vis-à-vis Rome. The party who saw their church as a national one were known as the Gallican wing, while those who looked south to the Pope for guidance formed the ultramontane wing, that is, "beyond the mountains"—the mountains in question being the Alps. In the square in front of the Church of St. Sulpice in Paris, recently made famous by Dan Brown, there is a fountain bearing statues of four prominent Gallican churchmen. They face the four cardinal points of the compass. Thus, with the usual Parisian love of wordplay, the fountain is known as *Les Point(s) Cardinaux*, which means "the cardinal points" with the silent *s*, but means "the not-at-all cardinals" (*point cardinaux*) without the *s*. As the four great Gallican churchmen favored the national church, their respective popes, all of whom had reason to be annoyed with them, never made them cardinals.

25 **His biographers**: I have used, primarily, Jean Favier, *Un Roi de Marbre, Philippe le Bel, Enguerran de Marigny*, Paris, 2005, and Joseph R. Strayer, *The Reign of Philip the Fair*, Princeton, 1980.

26 **"a captious, sternly moralistic"**: E. A. R. Brown, "The Prince Is Father of the King: The Character and Childhood of Philip the Fair of France," *Medieval Studies*, 49, 1987, pp. 282–334.

26 **the French king's holdings . . . were dwarfed:** Lucien Romer, *A History of France*, trans. A. L. Rowse, New York, 1953, p. 107.

27 **penned by Giles of Rome for Philip the Fair in 1286:** Joseph Canning, *A History of Medieval Political Thought 300–1450*, London, 1996, p. 133.

27 **another political thinker, Marsilius of Padua:** Canning, *Political Thought*, pp. 154–61.

27 **"O God, who has sown discord":** A good single volume on the fascinating rise of the secular class is Alexander Murray, *Reason and Society in the Middle Ages*, Oxford, 1978.

28 **a well-attended conclave of Cathars:** Stephen O'Shea, *The Perfect Heresy*, London, 2000, pp. 17–31.

28 **his grandfather had been a Cathar sympathizer:** Yves Dossat, "Guillaume de Nogaret, petit-fils d'hérétique," *Annales du Midi*, 53, 1941, pp. 391–402.

29 **Philip's expensive new palace:** Nogaret did not live to see the building finished. Parts of it are incorporated into the magnificent Conciergerie complex on the Ile de la Cité, including the great hall.

29 **Together they hatched extraordinary schemes:** Information on the machinations of Philip and Guillaume is drawn from Favier, *Roi de Marbre*, and Strayer, *Philip the Fair*.

30 **which Philip's men tossed into the fireplace:** The bull-tosser was Robert of Artois. Martin Gosman, *Les Sujets du Père: Les Rois de France face aux Représantants du Peuple dans les Assemblées de Notables et les États Généraux 1302–1615*, Leuven, 2007, p. 155.

30 **the document he held had been edited by royal lawyers:** Gosman, *Les Sujets*, p. 161.

31 **The pope . . . might even be a heretic:** Lambert underscores the novelty of a king charging a pope with heresy (*Medieval Heresy*, p. 198). He then goes on to detail Nogaret's cynical use of the inquisition in declaring the Templars heretics.

31 **Many were brave enough to go:** Boniface's and Philip's actions at this time are well discussed in a small, annotated anthology of articles: Charles T. Wood, ed., *Philip the Fair and Boniface VIII*, New York, 1967. Of Boniface's summons to the French clergy, Wood writes in a

footnote (p. 52): "Boniface had summoned seventy-eight French bishops; thirty-six actually attended. That so many obeyed the papal summons is largely explained by the extent to which men viewed Courtrai [the Golden Spurs] as a judgment of God on Philip's policies. This was particularly the case because the three men Boniface had specifically accused of being the cause of royal hostility—Pierre Flote, Robert of Artois, and the Count of St. Pol—were all slain on the field of battle."

32 **a military catastrophe dealt to Philip:** The Battle of the Golden Spurs, July 11, 1302.

33 *"E le cole, e le cape!":* The chronicler is William of Hundlehy, "William of Hundlehy's Account of the Anagni Outrage," trans. H. G. J. Beck, *Catholic Historical Review,* 32, 1947, pp. 200–201.

33 **"new Pilate" . . . "two thieves":** Dante, *Purgatorio,* xx, 87–90.

33 **the same Dante who despised Boniface:** On Dante's going into exile, banished from Florence by Charles of Valois, the pope's ally:
> As he rode on, shocked and anguished, he reviewed in his mind what had occurred. He knew that Charles of Valois had been charged to respect the constitution of Florence and to function justly as peacemaker. It was now obvious that he had had no intention of doing so. This was deliberate treachery and Dante would later refer to him contemptuously as being "armed with the lance of Judas." But he saw clearly now that the real villain was Pope Boniface, who had all along schemed and intrigued to gain control of Florence, even to the point of preventing Dante, the most able of the deputies, from putting his fellow Whites on their guard. A fierce hatred, never to be extinguished, flared up in Dante's heart and would ultimately fuel the great work he was to write.

Barbara Reynolds, *Dante: The Poet, the Political Thinker, the Man,* London, 2006, pp. 43–44.

33 **a council of the Church:** Council of Vienne, 1311–12. The council, called by Clement V, dealt primarily with disbanding the Templars and dealing with the Spiritual Franciscans.

33 **a delegation arrived before the King Philip the Fair:** This occurred in Senlis, in October of 1301.

3. THE HOLY OFFICE

35 **Its mass of old stone and fortification fires the imagination of the susceptible:** Never once have I visited the Cité in the summertime without coming across little boys dueling with plastic swords in the principal square. For all I know, they could be municipal employees.

35 **Bastide St. Louis:** On its fourteenth-century reconstruction: Louis Fédié, *Histoire de Carcassonne, ville basse et cité* (orig. pub. circa 1890), Nîmes, 2000, pp. 98–103.

35 **England's Black Prince:** Known in his lifetime (1330–1376) as Edward of Woodstock, Prince of Wales. Commanded, at age sixteen, one of three English divisions at the Battle of Crécy (1346), then was victorious again at Poitiers (1356), this time as the brilliant commander in chief.

35 **older medieval Bourg:** A clarification is necessary here, which I thought too tiresome to include in the main text. Prior to 1240, there had been a hodgepodge town in this area. When the last of the Trencavels, Raymond, besieged the Cité in an attempt to win back his inheritance at midcentury, the inhabitants of this lower town sided with him. He lost, and French royal revenge was taken. Louis IX (St. Louis) ordered the town razed. This situation obtained for several years until, toward the end of the 1250s, Louis ordered the town rebuilt in a fortifiable, grid-like fashion. It would be populated by burghers, not nobles, beholden to the king. The Cité was royal; the Bourg was to be royal. It was also to be the French king's main city in Languedoc. At the time the other two main centers of the region, Toulouse and Montpellier, escaped royal control, the former held in arm's-length appanage by the Capetians (it would not become fully French until 1271), the latter held by the Kingdom of Majorca, based in Perpignan (Montpellier would not be French until 1349). Louis thus envisaged two distinct royal Carcassonnes: the military Cité and the commercial Bourg. He endowed the latter with impressive churches, two of which (St. Michel and St. Vincent) still stand; invited in the mendicants; and encouraged commerce. This is the Bourg in which Bernard Délicieux lived, and which the Black Prince destroyed in 1355. Last, Louis' logic in this matter coincided with his maritime strategy: lacking a port on the Mediterranean, he ordered the construction of the magnificent Aigues-Mortes in the Camargue. Thus the Bourg of Carcassonne and Aigues-Mortes stood as testament

to his desire to consolidate his hold on the newly acquired lands of the
Midi. Fédié, *Histoire de Carcassonne,* pp. 25–58.

35 **a marine infantry parachute regiment:** 3e Régiment de Parachutistes
d'Infanterie de Marine. Settled in Carcassonne in 1962, at the conclusion of the Algerian War, in which it saw a lot of action. Deployed to
southern Lebanon in the late 1970s. As of this writing, elements of the
regiment are in Afghanistan. On June 30, 2008, it caused a national
uproar during a military demonstration in Carcassonne watched by ci-
vilians: a soldier playing a terrorist infiltrated the crowd, toward which
eight soldiers then advanced, guns firing. But one of them had mistak-
enly loaded his assault weapon with live ammo. Result: seventeen
wounded, some gravely, including two children. Then, less than two
months later, its brother parachute regiment, the 8th, based in nearby
Castres, had ten killed and twenty-one wounded in a Taliban ambush
in the Uzbin Valley near Kabul on August 18, 2008, the worst single
day for the French army since deploying to Afghanistan in 2001. The
French, apparently, thought the sector was quiet, not having been informed by their NATO predecessors in the area, the Italians, that the
Italian secret services had been paying large bribes to rebel leaders. The
event, especially subsequent photos published in *Paris Match* of Taliban
wearing French insignia and uniforms as trophies, set off a political
firestorm in France. Together the two incidents, coming one after the
other, caused heads to roll at the top of the French military hierarchy.

36 **fortress of the royal governor:** It is more usually called the Château
Comtal, after the Trencavel viscounts who lived in it prior to the Albigensian Crusade. I call it the governor's (or seneschal's) fort because that is
who resided there in the time of Bernard Délicieux. It is now a museum.

36 **as it may have been seven hundred years earlier:** There is considerable
uncertainty as to whether the right bank of the Aude between the river
and the Cité had been built up in Bernard's time. Certainly we know
the Wall and the King's Mill and several religious buildings were there,
but there could have been a type of no-man's-land, or a pastoral area,
between the two Carcassonnes that eventually filled up with usual medieval mishmash of huts and lean-tos. Today it is an interesting, arty-
immigrant area—www.trivalle-carcassonne.com—hardly ever glimpsed
by the three million or so who come to the Cité every year. The neigh-
borhood is also called the Faubourg St. Laurent.

36 **attacked here in the hot summer of 1209:** For a reconstruction of those dreadful days, O'Shea, *Perfect Heresy*, pp. 89–103; Michel Roquebert, *L'épopée cathare, 1198–1212: L'invasion*, vol. 2, Toulouse, 1970, pp. 267–278.

37 **tabula rasa:** The blank slate revealed some of its secrets just prior to the construction of the parking garage in 2007. Archaeologists were allowed in during the winter of 2006–7 to dig up the remains of the convent in order to assess its considerable size and importance in the medieval period. Several dozen sepulchers and skeletons were unearthed—no surprise there, given the outlandish story of Castel Fabre to figure in this present work. The convent stood near the Porte des Cordeliers, with lands between the town's fortifications and the left bank of the Aude (Cordelier is another name for a French Franciscan, supposedly from the *corde liée*, or knotted cord, adorning their simple habit). The land there was a fertile floodplain, so the Franciscans had gardens and orchards aplenty. Bernard's convent was burned to the ground by the Black Prince in 1355; its successor was a victim to France's sixteenth-century Wars of Religion. By the eighteenth century the place had become a wood and coal market, with the Franciscans living elsewhere in the Bourg. Following the Revolution, it became the place Ste. Cécile, then the Square Gambetta. Agnès Bergeret, Isabelle Rémy, and Hélène Réveillas, "Carcassonne, Le couvent des Franciscains," *Archéologie du Midi médiéval*, 25, 2007, pp. 166–170.

37 **The placid woad fields of medieval Languedoc:** In Bernard's time, this was a specialty of Languedoc. Indeed, the splendor of Toulouse can be attributed to the revenues of the woad (French: *pastel*) trade for cloth dyeing. With the latter-day expansion of Europeans to tropical and subtropical climes, particularly India, and the discovery and commercialization of the "true" indigo plant, which yields the same tincture but in greater concentration, woad cultivation in Languedoc fell off dramatically. (True indigo was later replaced with synthetic dyes.) Still, Languedoc can claim a face-saving victory: the blue of blue jeans is indigo, and the name given its type of cloth, denim, derives from *serge de Nîmes*, where it was first produced.

37 **The year 1229:** The Treaty of Meaux-Paris, signed by Count Raymond VII, after a humiliating flagellation at Notre Dame, and by King Louis IX, with his mother, the formidable regent Blanche of Castille, acting in his name. Under its terms, Raymond gave his daughter Joan of Tou-

louse to the king's brother Alphonse of Poitiers. The couple thus held Languedoc in appanage for the Capetians, and on their death, childless, in 1271, the region became a part of France proper. Raymond also gave up his lands in Provence, some of them to the papacy, which later became the Comtat-Venaissin in which the Avignon papacy was based (the Church had to fight to wrest these lands of Provence from the crown, only gaining real possession of them in 1274). The last Count of Toulouse was also obliged to found a university in Toulouse in 1229, and to pay its faculty for the first ten years. This institution became a breeding ground of inquisitors.

38 **the lady of Lavaur . . . her brother:** Respectively, Geralda of Lavaur and Aimery of Montréal. Their mother, after raising her children, became one of the most famous of the Cathar Good Women, Blanche of Laurac. Her three other children also became Good Men and Good Women. Neither the murdered Geralda nor the hanged Aimery, however, had received the *consolamentum*.

38 **no unified inquisition:** As mentioned in Usage, there is a scholarly fashion afoot claiming that the Inquisition itself never existed. As there is no institutional paper trail concerning a well-organized, duly chartered inquisition, the argument runs, there was no inquisition, just inquisitors. Richard Kieckhefer, "The Office of Inquisition and Medieval Heresy: The Transition from a Personal to an Institutional Jurisdiction," *Journal of Ecclesiastical History*, 46, 1995, pp. 36–61. This does not mean you have to throw the baby out with the bathwater. People at Bernard's trial—judges, accused, witnesses—referred repeatedly to the inquisition. And Bernard was convicted for interfering with the inquisition. The "Black Myth" of the Inquisition should be countered, not the existence of the inquisition itself.

38 **The phantasmagoric uppercase "Inquisition":** To cite all the works propagating this myth over the centuries would require the destruction of too many trees. The best one-volume historical examination, in English, of how *inquisition* became a byword for evil remains Edward Peters, *Inquisition*, Berkeley, 1989.

39 **leached memorably into popular culture:** The two examples given are television's *Monty Python's Flying Circus* and its 1970 sketch, "No one expects the Spanish Inquisition!" and Umberto Eco, *The Name of the Rose*, trans. William Weaver, New York, 1983.

39 Perusal of this more authoritarian past focused on the *inquisitio*: Peters, *Inquisition*, pp. 12–17.

39 **"formation of a persecuting society"**: R. I. Moore, *The Formation of a Persecuting Society: Authority and Deviance in Western Europe 950–1250*, Oxford, 2007. This is the latest edition of this landmark book in medieval studies.

40 **"Burdened with the weight of oriental apocalyptic literature"**: Jacques Le Goff, *The Birth of Purgatory*, trans. Arthur Goldhammer, Chicago, 1984, p. 205.

40 **Humbert of Romans . . . *On the Gift of Fear:*** Christine Caldwell Ames, *Righteous Persecution: Inquisition, Dominicans, and Christianity in the Middle Ages*, Philadelphia, 2009, p. 215.

40 **A late twelfth-century pope issued a bull**: Lucius III, *Ad abolendam*, 1184.

40 **the Fourth Lateran Council of 1215**: For an efficient and entertaining account of the momentous and much-studied meeting: Brenda Bolton, "A Show with a Meaning: Innocent III's Approach to the Fourth Lateran Council, 1215," *Medieval History*, 1, 1991, pp. 53–67.

41 **the Dominicans had decided to make the world their monastery**: Ames, *Righteous Persecution*, p. 146. She develops this point also made by André Vauchez, *The Laity in the Middle Ages: Religious Beliefs and Devotional Practices*, ed. Daniel Bornstein, trans. Margery J. Schneider, Notre Dame, 1993, p. 72.

41 **"foxes in the vineyards"**: Song of Songs, 2:15.

41 **most convents had a jail**: Ames, *Righteous Persecution*, p. 157.

41 **descend on a village they had targeted**: Peters, *Inquisition*, pp. 58ff. on the techniques of the early inquisition. The early inquisitor's manuals also give a fairly detailed account of how to proceed.

41 **wolves in sheep's clothing**: This is an expression we will come across frequently. It was a favorite of ecclesiastical heretic hunters and is taken from scripture: Matthew 7:15.

42 **counterfeit holiness**: On this notion and the Achilles' heel of the Dominicans—the overt holiness of the Cathar clergy—see Ames, *Righteous Persecution*, pp. 42–45.

42 *mala fama*: On the old Roman notion of infamy, Edward Peters, *Torture*, Philadelphia, 1985, pp. 30–31. On the legal and cultural revolution of the twelfth century, see Robert L. Benson and Giles Constable, eds., *Renaissance and Renewal in the Twelfth Century*, Cambridge, MA, 1982.

43 **the registers were systematically organized:** For a very clear explanation of the paperwork of the inquisition, see James B. Given, *Inquisition and Medieval Society: Power, Discipline, and Resistance in Languedoc*, Ithaca, 1997, pp. 25–51.

43 **the Tarragona checklist:** This is so odd (and informative) that it is quoted in almost all books on the inquisition. Here we go:

> *Heretics* are those who remain obstinate in error.
>
> *Believers* are those who put faith in the errors of heretics and are assimilated to them.
>
> *Those suspect of heresy* are those who are present at the preaching of heretics and participate, however little, in their ceremonies.
>
> *Those simply suspected* have done such things only once.
>
> *Those vehemently suspected* have done this often.
>
> *Those most vehemently suspected* have done this frequently.
>
> *Concealers* are those who know heretics but do not denounce them.
>
> *Hiders* are those who have agreed to prevent heretics being discovered.
>
> *Receivers* are those who have twice received heretics on their property.
>
> *Defenders* are those who knowingly defend heretics so as to prevent the Church from extirpating heretical depravity.
>
> *Favorers* are all of the above to a greater or lesser degree.
>
> *Relapsed* are those who return to their former heretical errors after having formally renounced them.

43 **The first was written in Carcassonne in 1248:** Translated into English and analyzed in Walter Wakefield, *Heresy, Crusade and Inquisition in Southern France, 1100–1250*, Berkeley, 1974. An excerpt of the most famous of the inquisitor's manuals, that of Bernard Gui, was recently published as a trade book in 2006: Bernard Gui, *The Inquisitor's Guide: A Medieval Manual on Heretics*, trans. Janet Shirley, London, 2006. This is not the first time I have found her work abundantly useful. Fifteen years ago, Dr. Shirley produced a splendid translation of the *Cansó de la crozada* entitled *The Song of the Cathar Wars, A History of the Albigensian*

Crusade, by William of Tudela and an Anonymous Successor, Aldershot, 1996. One can only hope that perhaps one day she will render the entirety of Bernard Délicieux's trial transcripts into her elegant English.

44 **"The third way of evading a question":** Cited in Given, *Inquisition and Medieval Society*, pp. 93–95.

44 **There were heretical Christians, particularly the Waldenses, who believed that capital punishment was prohibited:** Peter Biller, "Medieval Waldensian Abhorrence of Killing Pre-1400," in W. J. Sheils, ed., *The Church and War*, Oxford, 1983.

44 **Dominic, came to be seen above all else as an inquisitor . . . [through] layers of successive biographies:** The first life, by Jordan of Saxony (1233), makes no mention of Dominic as an inquisitor. The second (Pedro Ferrando, 1235–39), the third (Constantine of Orvieto, 1236) and especially the fourth and official life (Humbert of Romans, 1260) gradually "inquisitorialized" Dominic, until by Bernard Gui's day the saint had been transformed into a holy persecutor. Ames, *Righteous Persecution*, pp. 103–104. The Prado in Madrid displays a famous tableau demonstrating Dominic's posthumous transformation into inquisitor, Pedro Berruguete's "St. Dominic Presiding at an Auto-da-fé." The painting dates from the late fifteenth century. It also, curiously enough, was used as the cover art for Michel Roquebert's *Histoire des Cathares: Hérésie, Croisade, Inquisition du XIe au XIVe siècle*, Paris 1999, his summation of his five-volume masterwork, *L'épopée cathare*, Toulouse, 1970–98.

45 **he would be far more useful to the brothers dead than alive:** His first biographer, Jordan of Saxony, makes this clear. Jordan of Saxony, *A New Life of Saint Dominic, Founder of the Dominican Order*, ed. and trans. Louis Getino and Edmond McEniry, Columbus, 1926, p. 155.

45 **the document that refused to burn was in all probability an inquisition register:** Ames, *Righteous Persecution*, p. 103

45 **preferring the conversation of younger women to that of older ones:** Cited in George Bernanos, *Les prédestinés*, ed. Jean-Loup Bernanos, Paris, 1983, p. 77.

45 **Much use was made of the many violent, vengeful passages in the Old Testament, with their far fewer counterparts in the Christian scriptures also deployed for full homiletic effect:** Old Testament: Ex-

odus 22:18, Exodus 32:25–29, Joshua 7:20–26, Judges 15:15–17, Leviticus 20:27, Leviticus 24:16, I Maccabees 2:24–26, Numbers 25:6–1. New Testament: Acts 5:1–11, Acts 12:23, Acts 13:8–11, John 8:3–11. Ames, *Righteous Persecution,* pp. 190–99. To see the ingenious punitive mind at work, consider Moneta of Cremona's exegesis of the last passage cited above, John 8:3–11, which seems to argue against inflicting capital punishment. Professor Ames deserves to be quoted at length:

> A dramatic instance is Moneta's exegesis of the woman seized for adultery (John 8:3–11). Moneta's imagined opponents had pointed out that when the scribes and Pharisees asked Jesus whether she should be executed by public stoning, the penalty prescribed by Mosaic law, he had responded that the one without sin should cast the first stone. This, they argued, was an obvious expression of disapproval for her execution and thus condemned any death penalty. Moneta countered that for several reasons, Jesus' statement could not be interpreted either as a denial of her licit execution or as a universal, transhistorical ban of killing malefactors: although he spared her, it does not follow from this that she could not be justly killed. Jesus' words were rather applicable only to this particular case, which failed to meet the requirements of right jurisdiction, authority, and procedure. Jesus knew that he was not a legitimate judge over her and should not determine her punishment; her accusers had fled, crippling a fair trial. He should not judge by himself, but rather through appropriate ministers. The Jews who seized the woman were of equal or greater sin. Moneta responded tantalizingly to his opponents' riposte that Jesus knew very well that no human was "without sin," and thus prevented anyone— ever—from casting a stone in execution, with a blunt "prove it." After all, I John (1:7) referred to Christians as "cleansed of sin." Finally, Moneta argued that Jesus' invitation that the one without sin cast the first stone should be read with striking literalism, its tone stripped of the challenging irony that other readers might supply: "as the lord permits he who is without sin to stone her, it proves that it was not evil." On the contrary, Jesus wished the "minister of secular judgments" to perform the "good office" of execution (p. 196).

45 **God does not sin, God kills, therefore killing is not a sin:** Ames, *Righteous Persecution,* p. 199.

46 **Bernard of Clairvaux:** In *In Praise of the New Knighthood,* his influential letter extolling the warrior monks of the Temple in crusader Outremer,

Bernard claimed that killing an infidel was killing evil, not a man—
malecide, not homicide. The relevant passage, from Bernard of Clairvaux
(trans. Conradia Greenia), *The Cistercian Fathers Series, XIX, The Works
of Bernard of Clairvaux*, 7, 3, Kalamazoo, 1977: "The knight of Christ, I
say, may strike with confidence and die yet more confidently, for he
serves Christ when he strikes, and serves himself when he falls. Neither
does he bear his sword in vain, for he is God's minister, for the punishment of evildoers and for the praise of the good. If he kills an evildoer,
he is not a mankiller, but, if I may so put it, a killer of evil." An extraordinarily bloodthirsty epistle even for the mores of the day, *In Praise of the
New Knighthood* undoubtedly makes Bernard of Clairvaux the patron
saint of the armchair chickenhawks who afflict us still.

46 **Grand Inquisitor:** The brilliant passage from *The Brothers Karamazov*
contains the memorable admonition from the Inquisitor to Jesus:
"Know that I fear You not. Know that I too have been in the wilderness, I too have lived on roots and locusts, I too blessed the freedom
with which You had blessed men, and I too was striving to stand among
Your elect, among the strong and powerful, thirsting 'to make up the
number.' But I awakened and would not serve madness. I turned back
and joined the ranks of those *who have corrected* Your work. I left the
proud and went back to the humble, for the happiness of the humble.
What I say to You will come to pass, and our dominion will be built up.
I repeat, tomorrow You will see that obedient flock who at the first sign
from me will hasten to heap up the hot cinders about the pile on which
I will burn You for coming to hinder us. For if anyone has ever deserved
our fires, it is You. Tomorrow I will burn You. *Dixi.*" Fyodor Dostoevsky, *Notes from Underground and The Grand Inquisitor*, trans. Ralph
E. Matlaw, New York, 1960, p. 143.

46 **the use of torture had been papally approved:** Innocent IV, *Ad extir-
panda*, 1252. This bull specified that members of the clergy were not allowed to torture, being obligated to work through surrogates. That
tiresome inconvenience was eliminated in Pope Alexander IV's *Ut ne-
gotium* in 1256.

46 **the focus of inquisition gradually came to center on obtaining a confession:** My brief discussion of torture and confession and proof, and
the changing legal culture surrounding those matters, draws on Peters,
Torture, pp. 40-73, and Peters, *Inquisition*, pp. 58–67.

47 **"The house, however, in which a heretic had been received"**: Innocent III, *Cum ex oficii nostri*, 1207. Cited in Peters, *Inquisition*, pp. 49–50.

47 **"What the inquisitors had done"**: Given, *Inquisition and Medieval Society*, p. 65.

48 **the appropriate type of punishment**: A masterful discussion of this in Given, *Inquisition and Medieval Society*, pp. 66–90. I rely on Given for the discussion of the sentencing. As for the wearing of crosses, it inspired the title of a superb book of Cathar microhistory, René Weis, *The Yellow Cross: The Story of the Last Cathars 1290–1329*, London, 2000.

50 **it was clear whose show this was**: The argument of Christine Caldwell Ames' *Righteous Persecution* counters the defenders of the inquisitors in this matter. The *sermo* was the finale, the sacerdotal blessing given to the sacramental function of the entire *inquisitio*. The devout Dominican inquisitor would have absolutely no reason to assume the role of second fiddle at a burning. The whole point of the exercise was to show the workings of divine justice in saving souls—and in restoring integrity to the Christian community.

50 **The relapsed heretic was a finger in the inquisitor's eye**: Bernard Gui's manual is particularly useful for its detailing of the form to follow in a *sermo*. The question of relapsed heretics also covered those Jews who had converted to Christianity but subsequently returned to Judaism. For them, Gui provided a standardized text to be used by other inquisitors in getting a Jew to denounce his reversion and return to Christianity. It was entitled: "Form of adjuration for those who renounced the treachery of the Jews for the faith of baptism and then returned to the vomit of Judaism." Gui, *Inquisitor's Guide*, p. 164.

4. THE UNHOLY RESISTANCE

52 **"The development of [the] inquisitorial mentality"**: Ames, *Righteous Persecution*, p. 4.

52 **The inquisitor was dependent on the secular authorities**: Jean-Louis Biget, *Hérésie et inquisition dans le Midi de la France*, Paris, 2007, p. 194.

52 **the inquisition in Languedoc lay in tatters**: The pontifical inquisition there was suspended entirely from 1248 to 1255.

52 **a pope who needed the backing of Christendom's great lords, including the count of Toulouse:** Indeed, the inquisition was suspended in Toulouse from about 1238 to 1241 as well. Yves Dossat, *Les crises de l'Inquisition toulousaine au XIIIe siècle*, Bordeaux, 1959, pp. 137–145.

53 **A shady demimonde:** Among the petty officers of the inquisition, instances of corruption and blackmail were not rare. All our historians attest to this, but to my mind the most eloquent testimony is that of the letter of the men of Carcassonne about the Wall quoted further on in this chapter.

53 **developing medieval institutions:** Given takes pains to stress the imperfections of these institutions, which is a particularly useful observation, given the natural tendency to believe that whatever is found in a document faithfully reflects the reality on the ground. In *Inquisition and Medieval Society*, Given notes: "Efforts to manipulate governing institutions like the inquisition were unique neither to the inquisition nor to Languedoc. Wherever the records allow us to examine the workings of medieval governing institutions, which were under construction in this period, we discover people busily at work influencing and exploiting them for their own ends. Manipulation of these organizations for purposes other than those for which they had been created was perhaps more the rule than the exception" (p. 163).

53 **the warden . . . was found to be spectacularly corrupt:** Friedlander, *The Hammer*, pp. 20–21.

53 **Raymond Gros:** On April 2, 1240, Gros appeared at the inquisition headquarters in Toulouse and announced that he was ready to talk. The inquisitors, conducting an investigation in Montauban, rushed back to Toulouse on hearing the news. His testimony implicated a great many, dead or alive, including his own son and father. Jörg Feuchter, "L'Inquisition de Toulouse: Perre Sellan (1234–1242), un vieillard expérimenté," in Laurent Albaret, ed., *Les Inquisiteurs: Portraits de défenseurs de la foi en Languedoc (XIIIe–XIVe siècles)*, Toulouse, 2001, p. 51.

53 **eventually eviscerate the remnants of heresy in that city:** J. H. Mundy, *The Repression of Catharism at Toulouse: The Royal Diploma of 1279*, Toronto, 1985, pp. 45–50.

54 **Arnaud Cathala escaped within an inch of his life:** The story is graphically told by the Dominican chronicler Guillaume Pelhisson.

Cathala was intent on disinterring a dead woman named Boyssene; Albi's royal magistrate, fearing a riot, refused to cooperate. So the headstrong Cathala went to the graveyard himself and set to work. The magistrate had been right: a mob of Albigeois attacked the inquisitor and another priest—a few of their more orthodox brethren then rescued the clergymen in a running street fight. One of the cries recorded by Pelhisson went more or less like this: "Let's cut off their heads, stuff 'em in a bag and toss it in the Tarn!" Cathala, once back in the safety of a church, promptly excommunicated everybody in sight. Guillaume Pelhisson, *Chronique (1229–1244) suivie du récit des troubles à Albi*, ed. and trans. Jean Duvernoy, Paris, 1994, pp. 112–122. In English, Wakefield, *Heresy, Crusade and Inquisition*, pp. 226–228.

54 **an old woman on her deathbed:** Apparently she was the mother-in-law of a Good Man, Peytavi Boursier. The Dominican bishop of Toulouse was Raymond de Fauga. Pelhisson, *Chronique*, pp. 59–65; Wakefield, *Heresy, Crusade and Inquisition*, pp. 215–16. I flesh out the appalling incident in O'Shea, *Perfect Heresy*, pp. 191–193.

54 **hounds of the Lord had themselves been hounded out of town:** On the details of their humiliations, Pelhisson, *Chronique*, pp. 70–88. For a full treatment on all their tribulations, see Dossat, *Les crises*.

55 **Avignonet:** The massacre at Avignonet came as a major trauma to the party of the inquisition. In May 1244, two years after the event, a survivor of the fall of Montségur, Imbert de Salles, gave the most detailed account of the incident to the inquisitor Ferrer. It is well presented in Michel Roquebert, *Mourir à Montségur*, Toulouse, 1989, pp. 327–330. It's a corker of a story, with the leader of the commando seeking an inquisitor's skull as a drinking vessel, so it appears prominently in O'Shea, *Perfect Heresy*, pp. 207–210. The Dominicans, less impressed by the drama than by the martyrdom, have vainly tried to get these murdered inquisitors made saints over the centuries: Yves Dossat, "Le massacre d'Avignonet," *Cahiers de Fanjeaux*, 6, 1971, pp. 356–358.

55 **Etienne was to be the good cop:** On the belief that the Franciscans were the more humane of the two main orders of mendicants: Jean Duvernoy, ed. and trans., *Guillaume de Puylaurens. Chronique; Chronica magistri Guillelmi de Podio Laurentii*, Toulouse, 1996, p. 152.

56 **three lawyers of Carcassonne:** Guilhem Garric, Guilhem Brunet, Raimond Costa. All three were prominent men; all may have had ties to

heresy. It seems that Garric also had ties with Peire Autier, before the latter left for Italy to become a Good Man; see testimony of Sébelia Peyre and Arnaut Bédeilhac to the inquisitor/bishop Jacques Fournier, cited in Anne Brenon, *Pèire Autier, le dernier des cathares (1245–1310)*, Toulouse, 2006, p. 274. Both Garric and Brunet eventually ended up in the Wall for a decade or two, being able to buy themselves out of it (they were wealthy, well-connected men) toward the end of their lives. Raimond Costa, as noted in the main narrative, escaped all prosecution by taking up the position of bishop of Elne, in the neighboring Kingdom of Majorca. He allowed the enemies of the inquisition to use his townhouse as a sort of headquarters. On these men, see Friedlander, *The Hammer*, pp. 13–16.

56 **The first two appeals:** The best description of the events in Carcassonne in the 1280s and 1290s is in Friedlander, *The Hammer*, pp. 13, 21, 25, 30. On the various riots, Dossat, *Les crises*, pp. 137–145.

56 **"We feel aggrieved":** Cited in full in Given, *Inquisition and Medieval Society*, pp. 64–65, and Jean-Marie Vidal, *Un Inquisiteur jugé par ses "victimes": Jean Galand et les Carcassonnais (1285–1286)*, Paris, 1903, pp. 40–41.

58 **Opinion is divided over whether this actually happened:** All the germane sources feel compelled to mention this plot. The biggest doubter is Vidal, *Un Inquisiteur jugé*, pp. 26–30.

60 **a witness would claim under oath years later:** The person impugning the integrity of Pope Boniface VIII was Bernard Délicieux. Testimony of Délicieux, in Duvernoy (ed. and trans.), *Le procès*, p. 105. Brother Bernard specifies that the withheld bribe was in the amount of 10,000 florins.

5. The Ambush at Carcassonne

65 **Some weeks after the signing of the accord:** There is some confusion about the year of the ambush. Some place it as early as 1296. I have accepted Alan Friedlander's chronology, as he has relied on Joseph Strayer, *Les gens de justice du Languedoc sous Philippe le Bel*, Toulouse, 1970, p. 61, to build a convincing argument for 1299 or early 1300: the royal judge accompanying Foulques de Saint Georges, Estève Auriol of Capestang, held office in Carcassonne only from September 1298 to August 1300. See Friedlander, *The Hammer*, p. 38.

65 **The party arrived at the outer portal of the convent:** Details of the ambush were provided during the 1319 trial. Duvernoy, *Le procès*: testimony of Bernard Audiguier (p. 175) and Pierre Camelin (pp. 178–179).

66 **the names of those he sought:** Guilhem André and Arnaud Vilaudégut.

68 **Franciscans in Bernard's mold:** The major biographers of Délicieux have stressed his Franciscan identity. Indeed, Dmitrewski, a Polish Franciscan, was ideally placed to understand it. Yet it was his latest biographer, Friedlander, who has the most clearly underlined Bernard's identity as a Spiritual Franciscan. Part of this emphasis was enabled by a fourteenth-century Dominican memoir unearthed in 1965, in which its author, Raymond Barrau, called Bernard the leader of the Spirituals in Béziers. Friedlander's great contribution has been in stressing this underlying belief as a way of understanding the entirety of the Francisan's career. Alan Friedlander, "Bernard Délicieux, le 'Marteau des Inquisiteurs,'" *Hérésis*, 34, 2001, pp. 9–34, and Friedlander, "Jean XXII et les Spirituels: le cas de Bernard Délicieux," *Cahiers de Fanjeaux*, 26, 1991, pp. 221–236.

69 **"He did not consider the Cathars as diabolical enemies":** Biget, "Autour de Bernard Délicieux," p. 90. In this passage Biget used the historic present tense, a common device in French prose to avoid the overly literary *passé simple*, but I saw fit to change all the verbs to the preterite to avoid confusion.

6. The Bishop of Albi

74 **The man behind the monument was a theocrat:** Principal sources for Castanet's career are Julien Théry, "L'évêque d'Albi Bernard de Castanet (v. 1240–1317), une politique de la terreur," in Albaret, ed., *Les Inquisiteurs*, p. 71–87; Jean-Louis Biget, "Un procès d'Inquisition à Albi," *Cahiers de Fanjeaux*, 6, pp. 273–341; and Louis de Lacger, "Bernard de Castanet, évêque d'Albi (1276–1308)," *Bulletin de littérature ecclésiastique*, 1954, pp. 193–220.

74 **one historian has drily termed his approach as "terrorist":** Julien Théry, "L'évêque d'Albi," in Albaret, ed., *Les Inquisiteurs*, p. 78.

74 **ejaculation must occur in the vagina of one's wife:** The commission of 1307–8 charged by Pope Clement V to investigate the inquisition-received testimony that Castanet had specified that the action was

forbidden *nisi in instrumento debito* (outside the proper receptacle). Théry, "L'évêque d'Albi," in Albaret, *Les inquisiteurs*, p. 79. Jean-Louis Biget, in "Un procès d'Inquisition," p. 85, argues that Castanet was concerned with coitus interruptus, the sin of Onan in the Bible (Genesis 38:6–10), which the medieval French rabbi Rashi (RAbbi SHlomo Itzhaki) memorably defined as "threshing within, winnowing without."

76 **the Albi inquisition kept up a breakneck tempo:** Aside from Biget's "Un procès d'Inquisition," the other major source for this episode is Georgene Webber Davis, *The Inquisition at Albi 1299–1300*, New York, 1948. She delivered a measured judgment on the actions of Castanet: "We shall, perhaps, come closest to the truth in concluding that the defendants of this particular process were to a greater or lesser degree adherents of Catharism, as charged, but that their practices were occasional, hardly flagrant, and possibly not much out of line with those of many of their neighbors. Their transgression might have escaped detection and prosecution had it not been that the man in whose power it stood to bring them to justice happened to be avid for money and not very scrupulous, so long as he kept within the law, as to the means he used to satisfy the need" (p. 90).

7. THE DEAD MAN OF CARCASSONNE

78 **Fabre had been the royal seneschal's treasurer in Carcassonne:** His predecessor, the first royal treasurer, had been a rich Jewish merchant, Astruguetus of Béziers; his successors, a series of Lombard bankers. Friedlander, *The Hammer*, p. 42.

78 **his son Aimeri was a prominent trader:** Aimeri was an ally of Bernard's in the revolt. He did not, however, approve of Hélie Patrice, perhaps out of class resentment, and took no part in the plot to secede from France. The inquisition eventually caught up with him and imprisoned him in the Wall in 1318. His mother's bones were dug up and burned a decade after his father's remains had received the same indignity in 1319.

80 **(partly because defending a heretic cast a cloud of suspicion on the defender):** The inquisition was not the first, and will not be the last, tribunal or committee before whom testifying in favor of a target of prosecution amounts to an implicit admission of guilt. Once an enemy of the people has been designated, seeing his or her defenders as accom-

plices occurs as a reflex. A sterling example of this process concerns the seventeenth-century witch trials of Salem, Massachusetts, as dramatized by Arthur Miller in *The Crucible*.

80 **On July 4, 1300:** Testimony of Bernard Délicieux, in Duvernoy, *Le procès*, pp. 50, 124. Friedlander, *The Hammer* (pp. 55–56), relies as well on the Latin text of the appeal published in Hauréau, *Bernard Délicieux*, pp. 167–175.

82 **the Franciscan believed that the registers contained a mountain of lies:** See the Afterword.

82 **Bernard Délicieux . . . nailed his appeal to the door:** Dmitrewski, "Fr. Bernard Délicieux, O.F.M," *Archivum Franciscanum Historicam*, 17, p. 196. Citing Hauréau, *Bernard Délicieux*, p. 167.

82 **He then addressed the crowd that had gathered:** Hauréau, *Bernard Délicieux*, p. 7.

8. The Bishop of Pamiers

85 **They absented themselves frequently . . . , according to Bernard at his trial, laboriously recopying and "fixing" the registers:** Testimony of Bernard Délicieux, in Duvernoy, *Le procès*, p. 112.

85 **The leadership of the Bourg had lived up to the letter, if not the spirit, of its conditions:** Friedlander, *The Hammer*, p. 38.

86 **carved out of the diocese of Toulouse in 1295:** Jacques Paul, "Jacques Fournier inquisiteur," *Cahiers de Fanjeaux*, 26, 1991, p. 43.

86 **"more handsome than any man":** Cited in Read, *The Templars*, p. 257.

86 **a bastard, a counterfeiter, and a statue:** Georges Digard, *Philippe le Bel et le Saint-Siège de 1285 à 1304*, Paris, 1936, p. 53.

86 **"useless to the Church":** Digard, *Philippe le Bel*, p. 61.

87 **The first *enquêteurs* had been Franciscan friars:** Burr, *Spiritual Franciscans*, p. 5.

87 **the great magistrate from Amiens fell under the spell of the friar of Carcassonne:** Testimony of Bernard Fenasse, in Duvernoy, *Le procès*, p. 182. Fenasse stated that in 1302 Picquigny was, rather incredibly, dissuaded from rushing back to his king to help in the campaign in Flanders.

Délicieux came in on him as he was preparing his armor and persuaded him to stay and deal with the problems of Languedoc. Also, testimony of Arnaud Garsie (p. 78), Bernard Audiguier (p. 175), Peire Pros (p. 194: "You couldn't bring up any matter with [Picquigny] unless in the company of Brother Bernard").

88 **He first traveled to meet Picquigny and Leneveu in Toulouse:** Duvernoy, *Le procès*: testimony of Raimond Baudier (p. 179) and Bernard Fenasse (p. 183).

89 **The dwelling still belonged to Raimond Costa:** Friedlander, *The Hammer*, p. 16.

89 **one of their recalcitrant witnesses emerged from the dungeon to testify with both arms irredeemably broken:** Digard, *Philippe le Bel*, p. 59.

9. THE KING AT SENLIS

93 **a series of accusations concerning his sexual proclivities:** These accusations were amplified by the people of Albi during the investigation of the inquisition called by Pope Clement V in 1307–8.

94 **Bernard possessed a trump, in the person of Jean de Picquigny:** Alone among Bernard's biographers, Friedlander makes the case that Picquigny and Délicieux crafted the friar's manner of presentation beforehand. The inference makes perfect sense: the stakes were high, no expense had been spared, this was the south's one best chance. *The Hammer*, p. 93.

94 **Picquigny, Délicieux, and the men of Albi and Carcassonne entered the great hall in Senlis:** Details of the audience contained in Duvernoy, *Le procès*: testimony of Guillaume Fransa of Albi (p. 59), Pierre de Castanet of Albi (p. 65), Bernard Délicieux (pp. 106, 125).

95 **An inquisitor had even preached that heresy had spread through the malevolence of the king of France:** Duvernoy, *Le procès*, Charge #6 of the forty-four-item accusation drawn up by Castanet (p. 35), testimony of Guillaume Fransa (p. 60).

96 **Bernard cited the swath cut by Foulques de Saint-Georges through the honest womanhood of Languedoc:** Duvernoy, *Le procès*, Charge #4 of the forty-four-item accusation drawn up by Castanet (p. 35), testimony of Guillaume Fransa (p. 60).

96 the king did not consent to receive the Dominicans until five days after the friar's speech: Final judgment on Bernard Délicieux, in Duvernoy, *Le procès*, p. 125.

96 Délicieux testified that when they had tried to enter the hall earlier, the king shooed them away with an angry gesture: Testimony of Bernard Délicieux, in Duvernoy, *Le procès*, p. 109.

97 The constable of France and the archbishop of Narbonne, Gilles Aycelin . . . were charged with the investigation: Testimony of Bernard Délicieux, in Duvernoy, *Le procès*, p. 125.

97 "Fr. Foulques, of the Order of the Preaching Friars": King Philip's letter cited in Hauréau, *Bernard Délicieux*, p. 39, and Friedlander, *The Hammer*, p. 96.

10. Aftermath

101 the king's displeasure with their bishop was so great as to render any further inquisition in Albi unlikely: Testimony of Arnaud, Duvernoy, *Le procès*, p. 201 ("Yes, and since then [Senlis] no one's been arrested for heresy in Albi").

101 His flock awaited him in the square before the construction site of Ste. Cécile . . . the portraits of St. Dominic and St. Peter Martyr were torn down by a mob: The source for Castanet's return and the woes of the Dominicans of Albi is Bernard Gui, *De fundatione et prioribus conventum Provinciarum Tolosanae et Provinciae ordinis Praedicatorum*. Duvernoy translated the relevant passages and thoughtfully included them in an appendix to the trial of Bernard Délicieux. *Le procès*, pp. 219–224.

102 If the transfer of the famous friar was meant as a diplomatic sop thrown to the Dominicans: Dmitrewski, "Fr. Bernard Délicieux, O.F.M.," 17, p. 198.

103 he set about increasing his renown . . . by going on extensive preaching tours to the smaller centers of Languedoc and Périgord: Hauréau, *Bernard Délicieux*, p. 51.

103 The people of Albi, however, had no doubt that Fresquet had been murdered on Castanet's order: Given, *Inquisition and Medieval Society*, p. 132. Also, testimony of Peire Pros, in Duvernoy, *Le procès*, p. 193.

103 **Once settled near the royal court:** Testimony of Bernard Délicieux, in Duvernoy, *Le procès*, p. 115.

104 **Bernard had been delegated to attend the Estates General in place of the Franciscan provincial of Languedoc:** Testimony of Bernard Délicieux, in Duvernoy, *Le procès*, p. 125.

11. THE WEAVER OF BRUGES

107 **"I thought that I alone was Queen":** George William Thomson Omond, *Belgium*, London, 1908, p. 41.

107 **one itinerant preacher of Antwerp . . . stated that the rich man, even if he be virtuous, was no better than a whore:** Henri Pirenne, *Histoire de Belgique*, vol. 1, Brussels, 1909, p. 373.

107 **Leliaert, or "Lilies" . . . Clauwerts, or "Claws:"** David Nicholas, *Medieval Flanders*, London, 1992, p. 190.

108 **"a violent and haughty man":** Pirenne, *Histoire de Belgique*, vol. 1, p. 406.

108 **the thick muck riddled with waterlogged traps set by the Flemish:** The great Belgian historian Pirenne complained that almost immediately after the debacle French chroniclers began making excuses for their defeat by claiming that the Flemings had set traps, of which there was no evidence aside from the assertions made by these sore-loser apologists. Worse, these stories launched a French historiographical tradition in which Flemish trickery is often cited as the main cause of the setback for Philip the Fair. However annoying that tradition, there really is no reason why the Flemings would *not* have set traps. They were the underdogs faced with heavily armed knights, they knew the terrain, and, as had been shown in the Bruges Matins, the townsmen were clever and ruthless.

109 **five hundred of these items retrieved from the fallen noblemen:** Nicholas, *Medieval Flanders*, p. 193.

109 **Pieter de Coninck . . . was now King Peter of Flanders:** Pirenne, *Histoire de Belgique*, vol. 1, p. 425. Also, testimony of Albert de Lavalette at Bernard's trial, in Duvernoy, *Le procès*, p. 167.

109 **holding on to only the prizes of Lille, Béthune, and Douai:** By the Treaty of Athis-sur-Orge, June 23, 1305, thereby ensuring the existence of a French Flanders.

12. The Sermon

116 **King Philip sent a letter in the spring of 1303 to his subjects in Cordes and Albi:** Friedlander, *The Hammer*, p. 113.

116 **Riot and murderous assault were by no means uncommon in the rough-and-tumble medieval city:** Given devotes a large section to the use of riot as a means of resistance in *Inquisition and Medieval Society*, pp. 112–117.

116 **The grand civic processions on holy days . . . which was hard-won but extremely fragile in the face of seething jealousy and status envy:** A civic procession of the eighteenth century, a descendant of the medieval iteration, is brilliantly taken apart by Robert Darnton in the chapter "A Bourgeois Puts His World in Order: The City as Text" of *The Great Cat Massacre: And Other Episodes of French Cultural History*, New York, 1985, pp. 145–190.

117 **the Church sponsored a Truce of God movement:** The first such agreement was signed in the year 1027, in the Roussillon village of Toulouges, the church of which proudly bears a plaque celebrating the Peace and Truce of God (*Pau i Treva de Deu*, in Catalan).

117 **Henry II's harsh penance over the killing of Thomas Becket:** Walking barefoot, in sackcloth and ashes, to Canterbury, whipped by monks along the way. A similar public flogging was administered to him in Caen.

118 **The inquisitor Bernard Gui contemptuously called Patrice "the little king":** Gui, *De fundatione, Le procès*, p. 223.

118 **witnesses described the high-handed tactics and royal pretensions of Patrice:** Duvernoy, *Le procès*: testimony of Albert de Lavalette (p. 167) and Drouin de Montchevrel (p. 169).

118 **Picquigny summoned his guests to the house of Raimond Costa, the absentee troublemaker turned bishop in the Kingdom of Majorca:** Testimony of Bernard Délicieux, in Duvernoy, *Le procès*, p. 131.

119 **"My good fellow, here is your agreement":** Testimony of Gui Sicre in Duvernoy, *Le procès*, p. 163. In this deposition Sicre said he was about to leave the house when Délicieux entered and asked to see the document.

120 **Each household of the town was instructed to have one or two members present to hear what Brother Bernard had to say:** Hauréau, *Bernard Délicieux*, pp. 53–54.

120 **His listeners were medieval men and women, prone to outbursts of emotion and sudden accesses of depair or joy:** One of the foundation texts of medieval mentality remains Johan Huizinga, *The Autumn of the Middle Ages*, trans. Rodney J. Payton and Ulrich Mammitzsch, Chicago, 1996. (Its original English publication is entitled: *The Waning of the Middle Ages: A Study of Forms of Life, Thought and Art in France and the Netherlands at the Dawn of the Renaissance*.) Although nearly a century old (it was first published in Dutch in 1919) with some of its conclusions debated, Huizinga's study opens an imaginative window into the mind and emotions of late medieval man.

121 **A tear welled up, then slowly rolled down his cheek:** The remarkable sermon was clearly remembered in 1319. Duvernoy, *Le procès*: Charges #20, #21, and #22 of the sixty-item accusation drawn up by Gui (p. 42), evidence entered in the court record (p. 49), testimony of Bernard Délicieux (p. 53), Pierre Vital (p. 153), Arnaud Marsend (p. 170) and Raimond Arnaud (p. 176).

122 **A group of rams, he recounted, inhabited a verdant meadow:** On the ram exemplum, Duvernoy, *Le procès*: Evidence entered in the court record, pp. 49–50.

123 **Gui Sicre and two confederates from the town jumped on their horses:** Testimony of Arnaud Marsend, in Duvernoy, *Le procès*, p. 170.

13. THE INQUISITOR GIVES A READING

124 **Bernard then began repeating a strange story of an extraordinarily unflappable fellow:** Two lessons can be taken from this tale. First, wrongful prosecution must have been distressingly common in Carcassonne for such a story to gain traction. This lesson underscores how Bernard's career was possible. If the inquisitors had acted all along with impeccable respect for the truth, then it would not have been credible for the unflappable fellow to have been faced with the baseless accusation of heresy in the first place. That he was, and that Bernard's listeners immediately understood his plight, speak plainly of the abuse of inquisitorial power at the turn of the century. Délicieux was not a

fantast—there was something deeply rotten within the inquisition, no matter how sincere individual persecutors might be.

On a tactical level, the story of the unflappable man also shows a shift toward more robust resistance. Violence is not meted out by some talking ram on a hillside; it is a punch thrown in the street by a man angry with his lying neighbor. More important, it is not an allegory. In his sermon Bernard had spoken of two butchers leading sheep to the slaughter. That, after all, is what butchers do, so the metaphor works. But with this placid, collected man, there is no metaphor. The actions take place in a town that could be, or most certainly is, Carcassonne; the actors are Bernard's listeners. The story hinges on one word: *heresy*. Heresy was the raison d'être of the inquisition, and the charges of heresy in the tale were *necessarily* without foundation. Bernard here is directly taking on the inquisitors and their helpers. The story is not a veiled attack—it is a bald invitation for the people of the town to roll up their sleeves and fight.

124 "'Once there was a town in which there lived a good man, of whom it was said that nothing could anger him or make him angry'": Testimony of Guillaume Rabaud, Duvernoy, *Le procès*, p. 165.

125 "the other was lying through his teeth": The French reads "*il mentait par sa gorge*," meaning, literally, "he was lying in his throat." The phrase appears again in the trial transcript, when Arnaud de Nougarède testified that Délicieux spat out the expression on hearing it suggested that he had bribed Picquigny (Duvernoy, *Le procès*, p. 192). I am not familiar with an English expression using "throat" for lying—though I have seen Délicieux's remark translated as "Thou liest in the throat." In both instances I judged it better to change the expression to the more familiar "teeth." As the Italians famously say of translation: *traddutore, traditore* (translator, traitor).

125 "'Draw your own conclusions'": Another vexed translation question. The French reads, elegantly, *Me comprenne qui voudra*, which may be translated any number of ways, none of them very satisfactory, such as "Understand whatever you want," or perhaps even "Know what I'm sayin'?"

125 "Good people, if anyone calls you a heretic, defend yourself as best you can, because you have the right to defend yourself": Testimony of Giraud de Meaux, Duvernoy, *Le procès*, pp. 166.

125 **They would later say at his trial that he encouraged the people to murder them:** Duvernoy, *Le procès*: Testimony of Arnaud Marsend (p. 171) and Bernard Trèves (p. 202).

125 **the city's bishop, of an old Carcassonne family, who had been conspicuously silent in the dispute between the brash Franciscan and his Dominican foes:** Peire de Rochefort. Friedlander, *The Hammer*, p. 129.

125 **his ancestor had been a famously live-and-let-live bishop who counted several Good Men and Good Women in his immediate circle of kinship:** Bernard-Raymond de Roquefort, bishop of Carcassonne at the time of the Albigensian Crusade. His mother was a Good Woman; three of his brothers were Good Men. Michel Roquebert, *L'épopée cathare, 1198–1212*, pp. 148–149.

126 **Scholarly examination of what remains of the secret agreement of 1299 has determined that Picquigny was right:** The consensus is solid among Bernard's biographers.

126 **As a jurist of Carcassonne sniffed at Bernard's trial:** Testimony of Peire Guilhe, Duvernoy, *Le procès*, p. 207.

127 **the word *abjure* appears but once in the document, in a passage of ecclesisastical boilerplate:** Friedlander, *The Hammer*, p. 34.

127 **The inquisitor Geoffroy d'Ablis:** On his background: Charles Peytavie, "L'Inquisition de Carcassonne, Geoffroy d'Ablis (1303–1316), le Mal contre le mal," in Albaret, ed., *Les Inquisiteurs*, pp. 89–100.

127 **The moment for disclosure had arrived:** On the reading and its riotous aftermath: Duvernoy, *Le procès*: Testimony of Pierre Vital of Carcassonne (p. 154).

128 **he hadn't started the riot; the inquisitor had:** Showing remarkable chutzpah, Bernard asserted this at his trial. Duvernoy, *Le procès*, pp. 116, 134.

14. THE WALL

129 **"*Cohac! Cohac!*":** Testimony of Bernard Trèves, Duvernoy, *Le procès*, p. 203.

129 **Masked men burst into their church, smashing windows and statu-ary:** Duvernoy, *Le procès*: charge #26 of the sixty-item accusation drawn up by Gui (p. 43), testimony of Guillaume Olivède (p. 160), Bernard Trèves (p. 203), Pons Siméon (p. 208), Alice L'Alayrague (p. 211).

130 **the townspeople saw that Picquigny's company included a lawyer who had advised the consuls in 1299:** The unfortunate fellow was Guiraud Guiart. On the general chaos and disorder in Carcassonne in August 1303: Duvernoy, *Le procès*: testimony of Drouin de Montchevrel (p. 169) and Arnaud Marsend (p. 171).

131 **the Franciscan convent had welcomed several dozen guests from Albi:** Duvernoy, *Le procès*, charge #32 of the forty-four-item accusation drawn up by Castanet (p. 38), testimony of Guillaume Fransa (p. 62), Pierre de Castanet (p. 64), Bernard Bec (p. 68).

131 **Several witnesses at Bernard's trial vividly remembered the morning:** Duvernoy, *Le procès*: testimony of Guillaume Fransa (p. 59), Jean Laurent (p. 173), Jacquet Barquinhan (p. 174), Bernard Audiguier (p. 175), Pierre Camelin (p. 178), Pons Siméon (p. 208), Pierre Ardit (p. 211), Pierre Guilhem (p. 212), Jean Gauthier (p. 212).

132 **formal appeals to the pope to reverse the injustice of this day:** Duvernoy, *Le procès*: testimony of Jacquet Barquinhan (p. 174), Pierre Camelin (p. 178), Pons Siméon (p. 208), Jean Gauthier (p. 212).

133 **"When the existence of the Church is threatened":** The author of this remarkable passage was the bishop of Verden in Lower Saxony, Dietrich von Nieheim, in his *De schismate libri III*, in 1411. It is cited as the epigraph of the chapter entitled "The Second Hearing" in Arthur Koestler, *Darkness at Noon*, trans. Daphne Hardy, London, 1940, p. 97.

134 **"Behold, the Lord has sent down an angel to help us!":** Testimony of Raimond Arnaud, Duvernoy, *Le procès*, p. 177. In his testimony, Arnaud, a Dominican, relates an exemplum that Délicieux is supposed to have uttered from the pulpit. It concerns an owl-king that does nothing as his bird subjects are serially snatched away, so the beleaguered birds he is supposed to protect think of switching allegiances. Bernard is supposed to have repeatedly given a full public explanation of the story's meaning, naming names and, essentially, unveiling the secret treasonous plot. It strikes me as a contrived, after-the-fact invention— the Dominican is alone in mentioning the tale, which he exposes

with suspicious eloquence. The story seems crafted expressly for the purposes of further damning the Franciscan at his trial. Although other studies of the Carcassonne revolt accept and analyze it, I deemed the narrative's other two exempla—the rams and the unflappable man—sufficient and credible enough to give a flavor of Bernard's preaching.

15. TORTURE EXPOSED

135 **the nearly indignant references to it contained in the formal charges against him at his trial:** Charges #15 and #16 of the forty-four-item accusation drawn up by Castanet, in Duvernoy, *Le procès*, p. 36.

135 **the torture in common use in his day:** Peters, *Torture*, p. 68.

137 **he had suggested bringing along the prisoners who had been freed from it so that the monarch could see the marks of torture and mistreatment:** Duvernoy, *Le procès*: Testimony of Bernard Délicieux (pp. 129, 133), Arnaud Garsie (p. 202).

138 **the identity of Picquigny's ghostwriter:** Further evidence of Bernard's behind-the-scenes handiwork comes at the end of the letter, where its author takes a somewhat gratuitous swipe at the Dominicans for not living in poverty. This kind of mendicant indignation would not have been the work of a layman, Picquigny, but of a friar. Friedlander, *The Hammer*, p. 154.

138 **"There are no words, no expressions that We could use":** Entered as evidence in the court record, accompanying the testimony of Peire Pros, in Duvernoy, *Le procès*, pp. 197–198.

138 **who in reality do not preach, but rather breach divine law:** Another instance of *traddutore, traditore*—the Latin wordplay in the original can be rendered effortlessly into French as *prédicateur* and *prévaricateur*. "Preacher" and "prevaricator" do not work at conveying the wordplay in English, nor, for that matter, do "preacher" and "breacher," as the latter word is unusual and awkward. Hence the choice to switch the nouns to verbs.

139 **at one point Philip informed Délicieux and Picquigny that their oft-extended invitation had finally been accepted:** Duvernoy, *Le procès*: testimony of Arnaud Garsie, p. 76.

16. The King and Queen in Languedoc

144 **In 1988, the Maison Seilhan . . . was purchased and lovingly restored by a group associated with the modern-day Dominican order:** The people running the Maison encourage passers-by to drop in and take a tour, free of charge. On my visit there in the summer of 2009, a demurely dressed woman in her late thirties—a Dominican nun, I assumed—took me through the rooms and expertly explained the exhibits and the restorations. Toward the end of the tour, I pointed through a window at a half-timbered dwelling and said that I had just read in a glossy magazine about the Inquisition (the French newsstand is a thing of beauty) that the house across the way was, in fact, where the inquisitors tortured people. Her smile vanished, and she exclaimed with wounded pride, "Oh non, monsieur, c'est bien ici que les supplices ont eu lieu!"—you're mistaken, sir, this is where the torture happened!

145 **The king made this journey only once in his thirty-year reign:** Favier, *Roi de marbre*, p. 305.

145 **In the months and years to follow this tour, several senior officials were dismissed and replaced:** Friedlander, *The Hammer*, p. 154–157.

146 **At once, he was met by a near hysterical mob, the handiwork of Délicieux:** There is no eyewitness account of this welcome. However, from references made to it at Bernard's trial, it seems to have been a notorious event at the time. Délicieux claimed that it was not his handiwork, but that assertion is clearly unbelievable. Duvernoy, *Le procès*: testimony of Arnaud Garsie (p. 78), Bernard Délicieux (p. 117), Gui Sicre (p. 165).

146 **A biographer of the great Capetian monarch states that Philip had two religions:** Strayer, *Reign*, p. 13.

146 **Dominicans, Franciscans, bishops, royal officials, and a delegation from Carcassonne and Albi led by Délicieux were invited to a large hall:** The Dominicans gamely tried to prevent Bernard from attending the meeting by complaining to his hierarchy that he had impeded the work of the Holy Office and was thus ineligible to speak. The Franciscan leadership conducted a speedy review and concluded he was innocent of the charge and thus could speak for them before the king (testimony of Bernard Délicieux, in Duvernoy, *Le procès*, p. 84). As for the sequence

of speakers at the meeting, I have found that, among all the friar's biographers, the chronology established by Friedlander in *The Hammer* (chap. 5) to be the most convincing. There is a possibility that the leader of the Dominicans of Languedoc may have spoken to the king at a separate meeting, but that eventuality would not have affected the tenor or content of the discussion at the main meeting. The details of the presentations are found in *Le procès*.

147 **As one witness recalled at Bernard's trial: "[Picquigny] had found the whole country to be in a very bad state":** Testimony of Arnaud Garsie, in Duvernoy, *Le procès*, p. 78.

148 **Unexpectedly, the Dominican superior then veered back to the case of Foulques de Saint-Georges:** Testimony of Arnaud Garsie, in Duvernoy, *Le procès*, p. 201.

148 **The head of the Dominicans in Languedoc had admitted there could be no more than forty or fifty heretics in all of the country around Carcassonne and Albi:** Testimony of Bernard Délicieux, in Duvernoy, *Le procès*, p. 117.

149 **"I said that if Saint Peter and Saint Paul":** Testimony of Bernard Délicieux, in Duvernoy, *Le procès*, p. 118.

150 **The inquisitors, Aycelin continued, would still be under the control of their local bishops:** Testimony of Bernard Délicieux, in Duvernoy, *Le procès*, p. 118.

151 **"should be congratulated in many ways, honored like golden candelabras of the church, to the sound of trumpets":** Testimony of Bernard Délicieux, in Duvernoy, *Le procès*, p. 118.

152 **It was a wonder, he exclaimed, that the people of Languedoc did not rise up against the French who ruled them and shout as one: "Get out!":** Testimony of Peire Pros, in Duvernoy, *Le procès*, p. 195.

152 **Arnaud had it on good authority that Brother Nicolas was in the pay of the Flemish rebels:** Testimony of Arnaud Garsie, in Duvernoy, *Le procès*, p. 201.

153 **Bernard Délicieux, who had in turn heard it from a high-placed cardinal in Paris the year before:** He had been told this inflammatory gossip by Cardinal Jean Lemoine, Boniface's ambassador to the

French court. Lemoine stayed on in Paris, founding a famous college there. His name still graces a street and a Métro stop in the Latin Quarter.

154 **One witness claimed Patrice said to the king, "My lord, you must do us justice quickly":** Testimony of Arnaud Marsend, in Duvernoy, *Le procès*, p. 172.

154 **"Lord! Lord! Have pity on your wretched city which suffers so!":** Testimony of Bernard Audiguier, in Duvernoy, *Le procès*, p. 176.

154 **"Throw them out of here!":** Testimony of Bernard Audiguier, in Duvernoy, *Le procès*, p. 176.

154 **Patrice ordered them to rip down the garlands and banners:** Testimony of Bernard Audiguier, in Duvernoy, *Le procès*, p. 176.

154 **Witnesses at Bernard's trial tell a strange tale of two large silver vases:** Duvernoy, *Le procès*: testimony of Arnaud Garsie (p. 79), Bernard Délicieux (p. 96), Guillaume Fransa (p. 185).

155 **The men of Carcassonne now looked, as one historian notes, "ridiculous":** Favier, *Roi de marbre*, p. 308.

155 **Guillaume de Nogaret finally took the Franciscan aside:** Testimony of Bernard Délicieux, in Duvernoy, *Le procès*, p. 101.

155 **Wait, he advised Bernard, until circumstances became more favorable:** Testimony of Bernard Délicieux, in Duvernoy, *Le procès*, p. 101.

17. INTRIGUE IN THE ROUSSILLON

156 **Once past the border town of Salses, they had left the kingdom of France:** Testimony of Bernard Délicieux, in Duvernoy, *Le procès*, p. 93. Bernard gave details of his itinerary to the court: he left Carcassonne, passed by Roubia, Fontfroide, and Salses, and then on to Perpignan.

156 **its fertile bounty a source of amazement for visitors from arid Languedoc:** Once past Salses, the modern-day visitor immediately comes across the famous vineyards that produce Muscat de Rivesaltes, a sweet wine that was first produced in the Roussillon by none other than Arnaud de Vilanova.

157 **Testimony at Bernard's trial . . . states that the Franciscan was seen twice conferring with the thirty-year-old prince:** Duvernoy, *Le procès*: testimony of Arnaud Garsie (p. 79).

157 **"sinister words":** Testimony of Arnaud Garsie, in Duvernoy, *Le procès*, p. 80.

157 **The same reaction, only stronger, occurred in Albi:** Testimony of Arnaud Garsie, in Duvernoy, *Le procès*, p. 81.

157 **Other towns they approached, such as Limoux and Cordes, had turned them down, too:** Duvernoy, *Le procès*: for Cordes, testimony of Bernard Délicieux (p. 100); for Limoux, Gui Sicre (p. 164), Pierre Gaytou (p. 213), Jean Laures (p. 214), Pierre Raimond Salavert (pp. 214–215), Michel Sartre (p. 215), Isarn Servel (p. 216), Raimond de Niort (p. 217). Gaytou, Laures, and Sartre stated that when the consuls of Limoux turned down Bernard's offer, he called them swine.

158 **the town of Elne:** Although it has no bearing whatsoever on this story, Elne provides a golden nugget of useless knowledge from the French language's always interesting trove of *gentilés*, that is, the names given to inhabitants of particular localities. Taking its derivation from the old Iberian name for the town, the word for a man of Elne is an *Illibérien*; a woman, an *Illibérienne*.

158 **judged the plan "silly" and "hopeless":** Strayer, *Reign*, p. 14.

159 **Perthus Pass:** At 290 meters, one of the lowest passes of the Pyrenees. Standing on the Franco-Spanish border (the Roussillon became French in 1659 with the signing of the Treaty of the Pyrenees), it has witnessed much drama, particularly in 1939, when the defeated Republicans fled Catalonia via Perthus at the close of the Spanish Civil War.

159 **Bernard and his companion called in at a local church and found lodging:** Most of the information about this visit, including the prevarications over matter of fact, come from the same source, the testimony of Bernard Délicieux, in Duvernoy, *Le procès*, pp. 87, 93–94, 97 (the urination story), 100, 103 (full confession).

160 **Two Catalans who testified at Bernard's trial:** Duvernoy, *Le procès*: Bérenger d'Oms (p. 155) and Raimond Guilhem of Perpignan, who was King Jaume's chancellor (p. 157). They provided the colorful details of the beating of Ferran.

161 **Bernard hotly replied that he had met with sons of far more important kings:** Testimony of Raimond Guilhem, in Duvernoy, *Le procès*, p. 158.

161 **"We have heard reports about Fr. Bernard Délicieux":** Original letter in Hauréau, *Bernard Délicieux*, pp. 190–191. Translated in Friedlander, *The Hammer*, p. 219.

18. SURVIVAL

165 **Peyre-Cavaillé had been picked up on suspicion of heretical leanings in late 1304:** Brenon, *Pèire Autier*, pp. 276–278. The information on this interview and on the subsequent raid at Limoux comes from the depositions made at the inquisition of Jacques Fournier a decade and a half later. The inquisition register has been translated in its entirety into French: Jean Duvernoy, ed., *Le Régistre d'Inquisition de Jacques Fournier, évêque de Pamiers*, 3 vols., Paris, 1978.

165 **an established Church, run by a dozen or so well-trained and much beloved Good Men:** Details of the revival come from Brenon, *Pèire Autier*, and Weis, *Yellow Cross*.

167 **"There are two Churches":** Testimony of shepherd Pierre (Peire) Maury in Duvernoy, *Le Régistre*, p. 925. In Weis, *Yellow Cross*, p. xxviii. Brenon, who uses Duvernoy's French translation, speculates (*Pèire Autier*, p. 262) that Autier's description of the Roman Church that *"possède et écorche"* is directed at shepherds who, when shearing their sheep, must take care not to skin (*écorcher*) them. Thus a less elegant translation might be the Church "that owns and skins/scorches."

168 **"As Bernard Gui observes with savage exultation":** Henry Charles Lea, *A History of the Inquisition of the Middle Ages*, vol. 2, New York, 1887, p. 106. Lea's masterly three-volume work has been mostly superseded by subsequent scholarship, his full-throated indignation at the crimes of inquisition toned down by subsequent revisionists and less passionate, more detached specialists. However unfashionable Lea's humanity, the work remains a wonderful read, with passages of stirring prose. On the risks run by the peasantry sheltering the Good Men of the Autier revival: "Few more touching narratives can be conceived than those which could be constructed from the artless confessions extorted from the peasant-folk who fell into the hands of the inquisitors—the humble alms which they gave, pieces of bread, fish, scraps of cloth, or

small coins, the hiding-places which they constructed in their cabins, the guidance given by night through places of danger and, more than all, the steadfast fidelity which refused to betray their pastors when the inquisitor suddenly appeared and offered the alternative of free pardon or the dungeon and confiscation" (vol. 2, p. 61).

168 **When, at last, on July 6, 1304, the vicar of the Franciscan provincial of Aquitaine arrived in Carcassonne to arrest him:** Duvernoy, *Le procès*: charge #49 of the sixty-item accusation drawn up by Gui (p. 45), testimony of Bernard Délicieux (p. 86).

169 **the sheer number of people aware of the plot:** Among those at the trial, in Duvernoy, *Le procès*, to have heard of the treasonous plot, aside from Délicieux himself: Arnaud Garsie, who believed King Jaume told Philip of the failed plot (p. 80), Pierre Vital (p. 154), Bernard Amat (p. 154), Jean Marsend (p. 159), Raimond Delpech (p. 161), Albert de Lavalette (p. 167), Philippe Perry (p. 169), Drouin de Montchevrel (p. 170), Arnaud Marsend, who believed Nicolas de Fréauville told Philip of the plot (p. 171), Guillaume Fransa (pp. 185–189), Bernard Trèves (pp. 203–204), Raimond Arnaud-Terré (pp. 209–210).

169 **they somewhat impudently requested that she elicit some pillow talk from her husband:** Duvernoy, *Le procès*: testimony of Arnaud Garsie (p. 83) and Guillaume Fransa (p. 186).

169 **they, innocent or guilty, would later have to pay a huge bribe to Jean d'Aunay:** Duvernoy, *Le procès*: testimony of Arnaud Garsie (p. 81) and Bernard Fenasse (p. 183).

170 **The great Arnaud de Vilanova, whose advice Philip is known to have solicited in other matters:** Dmitrewski, "Fr. Bernard Délicieux, O.F.M.," 17, p. 206.

170 **But a more plausible conjecture is the queen:** Friedlander, in *The Hammer* (pp. 223–224), is of the same opinion.

170 **Testimony at Bernard's trial demonstrates that the seneschal Jean d'Aunay came across the plot independently of any royal instructions:** The seneschal's interrogations have not survived. But witnesses at Bernard's trial revealed that Jean d'Aunay stumbled across the plot when Guillaume Brunel, a Carcassonnais called to testify about Bernard's revolt, became so nervous and agitated that the shrewd seneschal

offered him immunity if he would reveal the reason for his unease. Duvernoy, *Le procès*: Testimony of Albert de Lavalette (p. 167) and Bernard Trèves (p. 204).

171 **a new grasping boomtown rose on the banks of the Rhône:** The poet Petrarch, writing from the city at the height of the Avignon papacy in midcentury, famously confided his disgust to a friend: "Now I am living in France, in the Babylon of the West . . . Instead of holy solitude we find a criminal host and crowds of the most infamous satellites; instead of soberness, licentious banquets; instead of pious pilgrimages, preternatural and foul sloth; instead of the bare feet of the apostles, the snowy coursers of brigands fly past us, the horses decked in gold and fed on gold, soon to be shod with gold, if the Lord does not check this slavish luxury. In short, we seem to be among the kings of the Persians or Parthians, before whom we must fall down and worship, and who cannot be approached except presents be offered."

172 **He dispatched envoys to investigate the newly invigorated inquisition:** This investigation of 1307–8 was conducted by two prelates favorable to Bernard's cause: Bérenger de Frédol, his longtime protector from Béziers, and, interestingly, Pierre de la Chapelle-Taillefer, the former bishop of Toulouse so scathingly criticized by Bernard Saisset for being a Parisian. It seems that the northern bishop sided with the south in the matter of the inquisition and had perhaps gone native. This was also the investigation that uncovered Bishop Castanet's anti-onanistic legislation.

172 **Three powerful cardinals, friends and protectors of his, eventually felt compelled to take Bernard aside:** Bérenger de Frédol, who would shelter Bernard in Béziers, Pietro da Colonna, of the family that had raided Anagni alongside Guillaume de Nogaret, and a cardinal of Bruges, Etienne de Suisy. Testimony of Bernard Délicieux, in Duvernoy, *Le procès*, p. 89.

173 **Pope Clement had forgiven him all, as had King Philip:** The king pardoned Bernard at Chartres in 1310, according to Dmitrewski, "Fr. Bernard Délicieux, O.F.M.," 17, p. 463.

19. CATHARS AND SPIRITUALS, INQUISITORS AND CONVENTUALS

175 **"I'll tell you why they call us heretics":** Testimony of shepherd Pierre Maury in Duvernoy, *Le Régistre*, pp. 924–926. Cited in Brenon, *Pèire Autier*, p. 259.

175 **"Those who adore such images are idiots"**: Testimony of Sébélia (Sibylle) Peyre in Duvernoy, *Le Régistre*, p. 580. Cited in Brenon, *Pèire Autier*, p. 261.

175 **"Oh no, it's a fine thing"**: Testimony of Sébélia Peyre in Duvernoy, *Le Régistre*, p. 581. Cited in Brenon, *Pèire Autier*, p. 262. Sébélia, a woman, did not have this said to her. She was present when Autier made the quip in answer to a question asked by the shepherd Maury. Spirited to the last, Sébélia, who was to be burned at the stake, then told the inquisitor-bishop Fournier that they had all had a good hearty laugh at the joke.

176 **A large theoretical framework had been built around the notion of Franciscan poverty**: David Burr, *Olivi and Franciscan Poverty: The Origins of the Usus Pauperus Controversy*, Philadelphia 1989. The foremost English-language specialist on the Spirituals, Professor Burr also hosts a very informative Web site: http://www.history.vt.edu/Burr/OliviPage/Olivi_Page.html.

177 **Francis' injunction to eat what was put before them**: Burr, *Spiritual Franciscans*, p. 139.

177 **"So it goes, there is no more religion"**: Jacopone da Toda, cited in Burr, *Spiritual Franciscans*, p. 103. The details of the Conventual-Spiritual controversy are drawn from the two works of Burr cited here.

178 **"saints of God and the foundation of His church"**: The exasperated Dominican was Raimond Barrau, writing in the 1330s. Pierre Botineau, "Les tribulations de Raimond Barrau, O.P. (1295–1338)," *Mélanges d'archéologie et d'histoire de l'Ecole française de Rome*, 77, 1965, pp. 465–528.

179 **The heterodoxy of the later Spirituals arose from a lush forest of apocalyptic and mystical thought**: The scholarship on the subject is also a lush forest. Of particular use for my brief evocation of the topic was Marjorie Reeves, *The Influence of Prophecy in the Later Middle Ages*, Oxford, 1969.

180 *Stupor Mundi*—**who was christened in the same baptismal font in Assisi that had served to christen Francis**: Julien Green, *God's Fool*, p. 21.

182 **That proceeding has come down to us because the transcripts of Fournier's activities survived in the archives of the Vatican**: The

story of the villagers of Montaillou became internationally known with the publication of Emmanuel Le Roy Ladurie's superb microhistory *Montaillou: The Promised Land of Error*, trans. Barbara Bray, New York, 1978. Their story was brought to its bitter end by Weis, *Yellow Cross*.

183 **And the last Good Man of Languedoc was lured across the Pyrenees:** The story of the Good Man, Guillaume Bélibaste, is told in O'Shea, *Perfect Heresy*, pp. 239–246.

184 **"quills upon a fretful porcupine":** H. K. Mann, *Tombs and Portraits of the Popes of the Middle Ages* (originally 1928), Whitefish, MT, 2003, p. 56.

184 **"For poverty is good, and chastity is greater, but obedience is greatest of all":** Cited in Burr, *Spiritual Franciscans*, p. 196.

185 **Two eyewitnesses left accounts of what happened next:** Angelo Clareno and Raimond de Fronsac.

20. The Trial

187 **Bonagratia de Bergamo, questioned and tortured Bernard throughout late 1317 on his relation to the Spirituals:** Friedlander, *The Hammer*, p. 256.

188 **During the last months of Cardinal de Castanet's life in 1317, he drew up the initial list of forty charges against his Franciscan foe:** Dmitrewski, "Fr. Bernard Délicieux, O.F.M.," 17, p. 474.

188 **A second, more comprehensive list of sixty-four charges:** Dmitrewski, "Fr. Bernard Délicieux, O.F.M.," 17, p. 486.

189 **"I will not respond to the question":** Declaration of Bernard Délicieux, in Duvernoy, *Le procès*, p. 52.

190 **"Whereas inaction before those who cause harm to others must rightly be odious to all men of good sense":** Entered into the court record, in Duvernoy, *Le procès*, p. 33.

191 **"You lie through your teeth!":** Testimony of Arnaud de Nougarède, in Duvernoy, *Le procès*, p. 192. Once again, as explained above, French "in your throat" has been changed to English "through your teeth."

191 **As the friar was expected to be available at almost all times during his trial, holding him here was only a matter of convenience, as well as security:** I am indebted to Cathar expert Jean-Louis Gasc for this insight. Jean-Louis took me on a tailor-made "Bernard Délicieux tour" of the Cité in the summer of 2009.

192 **The trial at Carcassonne began on September 12, 1319, and concluded on December 8:** Extremely useful to me in making sense of what is often a confusing document, especially with regard to procedural matters, was the introduction in Friedlander, *Processus Bernardi Delitiosi*.

193 **had little time for the self-inflicted woes of the self-important mendicants:** Etienne Baluze, a seventeenth-century French historian, minced no words in his 1693 work on the Avignon popes: "He [Fournier] obviously hated the mendicant orders. He promoted very few of them . . . He willingly listened to their quarrels, but he seemed strangely inclined to side with subordinates against their leaders." Cited in introduction to Duvernoy, *Le procès*, p. 22.

194 **Three men of Albi—those who were deposed in Avignon in June 1319—claimed to have been in Bernard's presence in the spring of 1304:** Duvernoy, *Le procès*: testimony of Guillaume Fransa (p. 63), Pierre de Castanet (p. 66) and Bernard Bec (pp. 68–69).

195 **no bird could fly to Rome fast enough from Languedoc to see the pontiff alive:** Comment attributed to Bernard Délicieux in all three testimonies cited immediately above.

195 **As with the story of treason, Bernard made implausible denials. The book was not his, or perhaps it was:** Testimony of Bernard Délicieux, in Duvernoy, *Le procès*, pp. 54, 92–93, 122 (confession).

195 **He told a lengthy and entirely credible story of a Dominican friar, no less, warning a prelate of Narbonne of their outright falsehoods:** Testimony of Bernard Délicieux, in Duvernoy, *Le procès*, pp. 106–107, 109. Bernard stated that the Dominican friar Jean Marty, in the 1280s, warned Archbishop Pierre de Montbrun that something was terribly awry with the inquisition at Carcassonne. Other Dominicans, according to Bernard, suggested that the Order be relieved of inquisitorial duties until the culprits were removed. The archbishop did not act. Bernard stated that the matter was raised again with Pope Clement V by other scandalized Dominicans.

195 Bernard named the inquistion clerks he believed behind what was essentially a scheme to keep the inquisition active in Carcassonne: Testimony of Bernard Délicieux, in Duvernoy, *Le procès*, p. 109. The clerks were southerners, Jean Falgous and Guillaume de Malviès. Bernard claimed that Jean Marty, the Dominican pleading with the archbishop of Narbonne, believed these men decided to hoodwink the credulous northerner, inquisitor Jean Galand, with invented tales of widespread heresy—all in the interest of keeping the inquisition alive and their positions intact.

196 He enumerated once again his complaints about imaginary Good Men, then recited a devastating taxonomy of the type of people whom the inquisitors of the 1280s and 1290s convicted and despoiled: Testimony of Bernard Délicieux, in Duvernoy, *Le procès*, p. 108. It is a magisterial demolition. We can conjecture that Fournier must have seen that Délicieux was on solid ground here. There had indeed been reason to take action against the inquisitors.

196 anyone who causes to be released from the custody of the inquisition any duly convicted prisoner . . . is automatically, as a result of that action, excommunicated: The written "monition" of the judges to Bernard, in Duvernoy, *Le procès*, pp. 122–123.

197 "to ensure the inquisition was completely paralyzed and persuade the king of France to abolish it altogether": Testimony of Bernard Bec, in Duvernoy, *Le procès*, p. 67.

197 who, at time of the disputation of Toulouse in 1304, were the inquisitors at Carcassonne and Toulouse?: Questioning of Bernard Délicieux, in Duvernoy, *Le procès*, p. 130. Adroitly detecting and underlining the importance of this seemingly trivial question is Friedlander, *Processus Bernardi Delitiosi*, p. 22.

198 "[The judges], seeking and attempting to effect the conversion of Brother Bernard and the salvation of his soul, warned him once, twice, thrice": Duvernoy, *Le procès*, p. 138.

198 "Despite the justifications and excuses put forth by me in my statements and responses on favoring and obstructing, I now admit my guilt": Duvernoy, *Le procès*, p. 138.

199 On Saturday, December 8, 1319, crowds jammed the market square of the Bourg of Carcassonne: Dmitrewski, "Fr. Bernard Délicieux, O.F.M.," 18, p. 18.

199 there were prelates and noblemen and notables in their splendid finery, among them: Duvernoy, *Le procès*, p. 146. The list of distinguished
guests is included in the final judgment.

200 "Having finally assigned him to strict confinement in the Wall": The
request for mercy appears at the end of the final judgment, in Duvernoy, *Le procès*, p. 147.

200 "He [Bernard] committed or encouraged others to commit many
great and shameful crimes": The royal appeal is included with the
court documents, in Duvernoy, *Le procès*, pp. 148–150.

201 The pope had no such scruples: I use the word advisedly. In institutional settings, particularly one as fraught with intrigue as the medieval
papal curia, *scruple* can mean one thing—and its opposite.

201 "My Lord the Most Holy Pope John XXII": Duvernoy helpfully added
this information in a footnote at the end of the trial document. *Le
procès*, p. 151.

AFTERWORD

203 "It should be noted that in all the arguments put forth by the reformers": Hauréau, *Bernard Délicieux*, p. 27.

204 he was no saint, either: At Bernard's trial, a consul of 1299, and thus a
foe of the friar, testified that the Franciscan had enjoyed the favors of
a mistress—until reprimanded by his superior. Despite its source, I
find the accusation plausible. A commanding man in his late thirties, adored by the crowds, at the height of his powers: the nature of
many men makes such dalliance possible; the nature of many women,
for whom the cassock or collar presents a challenge, even more so.
However, all the specialists of Délicieux—Biget, Dmitrewski, Dossat, Duvernoy, Friedlander, Hauréau—ignore or dismiss the allega-
tion. (Testimony of Guillaume de Villeneuve, in Duvernoy, *Le procès*,
pp. 161–162.)

204 "This little book contains many characters": Cited in the final judgment (sentencing), in Duvernoy, *Le procès*, p. 144.

205 John Paul II, felt compelled . . . to apologize on behalf of the Church
for the excesses of its inquisitors: On March 12, 2000, in Rome. The pope
also let it be known he was alluding to the Crusades, anti-Semitism,

and a few other matters large and small. In the very next breath, however, he pardoned those who had attacked the Church over the centuries. So John Paul's extraordinary initiative pioneered a new genre: the forgiving apology.

BIBLIOGRAPHY

Abulafia, David. *Frederick II: A Medieval Emperor*. London: Penguin, 1988.

———. *A Mediterranean Emporium: The Catalan Kingdom of Majorca*. Cambridge: Cambridge University Press, 2002.

Albaret, Laurent, ed. *Les Inquisiteurs: Portraits de défenseurs de la foi en Languedoc (XIIIe–XIVe siècles)*. Toulouse: Privat, 2001.

———. *L'Inquisition: Rempart de la Foi?* Paris: Gallimard, 1998.

———. "Les Prêcheurs et l'inquisition." *Cahiers de Fanjeaux*, 36, 2001, pp. 319–41.

Ames, Christine Caldwell. "Does Inquisition Belong to Religious History?" *The American Historical Review*, 110, 1, 2005, pp. 11–37.

———. *Righteous Persecution: Inquisition, Dominicans, and Christianity in the Middle Ages*. Philadelphia: University of Pennsylvania Press, 2009.

Baraz, Daniel. *Medieval Cruelty: Changing Perceptions, Late Antiquity to the Early Modern Period*. Ithaca: Cornell University Press, 2003.

Barber, Malcolm. *The Trial of the Templars*. Cambridge: Cambridge University Press, 1978.

Beck, H. G. J. (trans.). "William of Hundlehy's Account of the Anagni Outrage." *Catholic Historical Review*, 32, 1947, pp. 190–220.

Benson, Robert L., and Giles Constable (eds.). *Renaissance and Renewal in the Twelfth Century*. Cambridge, MA: Harvard University Press, 1982.

Bernanos, Georges (ed. Jean-Loup Bernanos). *Les prédestinés*. Paris: Seuil, 1983.

Bergeret, Agnès, Isabelle Rémy, and Hélène Réveillas. "Carcassonne, Le couvent des Franciscains." *Archéologie du Midi médiéval*, 25, 2007, pp. 166–170.

Biget, Jean-Louis. "Autour de Bernard Délicieux. Franciscanisme et société en Languedoc entre 1295 et 1330." *Revue d'histoire de l'Eglise de France*, 70, 1984, pp. 75–93.

———. *Hérésie et inquisition dans le Midi de la France*. Paris: Picard, 2007.

———. "Un procès d'inquisition à Albi en 1300." *Cahiers de Fanjeaux*, 6, 1971, pp. 273–341.

Biller, Peter "Medieval Waldensian Abhorrence of Killing Pre-1400." In W. J. Sheils, ed., *The Church and War*. Oxford: Basil Blackwell, 1983.

Blanc, Jean, Claude-Marie Robion, and Philippe Satgé. *La Cité de Carcassonne*. Paris: Grancher, 1999.

Bolton, Brenda. "A Show with a Meaning: Innocent III's Approach to the Fourth Lateran Council, 1215." *Medieval History* 1, 1991, pp. 53–67.

Botineau, Pierre. "Les tribulations de Raimond Barrau, O.P. (1295–1338)." *Mélanges d'archéologie et d'histoire de l'Ecole française de Rome*, 77, 1965, pp. 475–528.

Brenon, Anne. *Pèire Autier, le dernier des cathares (1245–1310)*. Paris: Perrin, 2006.

———. *Le vrai visage du catharisme*. Portet-sur-Garonne: Loubatières, 1988.

Brown, E. A .R. "The Prince Is Father of the King: The Character and Childhood of Philip the Fair of France." *Medieval Studies*, 49, 1987, pp. 282–334.

Burnham, Louisa A. *So Great a Light, So Great a Smoke: The Beguin Heretics of Languedoc*. Ithaca: Cornell University Press, 2008.

Burr, David. *Olivi and Franciscan Poverty: The Origins of the Usus Pauperus Controversy*. Philadelphia: University of Pennsylvania Press, 1989.

———. *The Spiritual Franciscans: From Protest to Persecution in the Century After Saint Francis*. University Park: Pennsylvania State University Press, 2001.

Canning, Joseph. *A History of Medieval Political Thought 300–1450*. London: Routledge, 1996.

Cantor, Norman F. *Inventing the Middle Ages: The Lives, Works, and Ideas of the Great Medievalists of the Twentieth Century*. New York: William Morrow, 1991.

Carayon, Charles. *L'inquisition à Carcassonne* (orig. pub. circa 1900). Nîmes: Lacour-Ollé, 1997.

Cohn, Norman. *The Pursuit of the Millennium: Revolutionary Millennarians and Mystical Anarchists of the Middle Ages*. Oxford: Oxford University Press, 1957.

Darnton, Robert. *The Great Cat Massacre: And Other Episodes of French Cultural History*. New York: Vintage, 1985.

Davis, Georgene Webber. *The Inquisition at Albi 1299–1300*. New York: Columbia University Press, 1948.

Davis, Natalie Zemon. *The Return of Martin Guerre*. Cambridge: Harvard University Press, 1983.

Delumeau, Jean. *La Peur en Occident (XVIe–XVIIIe siècles)*. Paris: Fayard, 1978.

Digard, Georges. *Philippe le Bel et le Saint-Siège de 1285 à 1304*. Paris: Recueil Sirey, 1936.

Dmitrewski, Michel de. "Fr. Bernard Délicieux, O.F.M. Sa lutte contre L'Inquisition de Carcassonne et d'Albi, son procès, 1297–1319." *Archivum Franciscanum Historicam*, 17, 1924, pp. 183–218, 313–337, 457–488; 18, 1925, pp. 3–32.

Dossat, Yves. "La crise de l'Inquisition toulousaine en 1235–1236 et l'expulsion des Dominicains." *Bulletin philologique et historique (jusqu'à 1715)*, pp. 391–398. In *Eglise et hérésie en France au XIIIe siècle*. Aldershot: Ashgate, 1982.

————. *Les crises de l'Inquisition toulousaine au XIIIe siècle*. Bordeaux: Bière, 1959.

————. "Guillaume de Nogaret, petit-fils d'hérétique." *Annales du Midi*, 53, 1941, pp. 391–402. In *Eglise et hérésie en France au XIIIe siècle*. Aldershot: Ashgate, 1982.

————. "Le massacre d'Avignonet." *Cahiers de Fanjeaux*, 6, 1971, pp. 343–359.

————. "Les origines de la querelle entre Prêcheurs et Mineurs provençaux." *Cahiers de Fanjeaux*, 10, 1975, pp. 315–354.

Dostoevsky, Fyodor. *Notes from Underground and The Grand Inquisitor*. Trans. Ralph E. Matlaw. New York: Penguin, 1960.

Duvernoy, Jean (ed., trans.). Guillaume Pelhisson. *Chronique (1229–1244) suivie du récit des troubles à Albi*. Paris: CNRS, 1994.

———— (ed., trans.). Guillaume de Puylaurens. *Chronique; Chronica magistri Guillelmi de Podio Laurentii*. Toulouse: Pérégrinateur, 1996.

———— (ed., trans.). *Le Procès de Bernard Délicieux 1319*. Toulouse: Pérégrinateur, 2001.

———— (ed., trans.). *Le Registre d'Inquisition de Jacques Fournier, évêque de Pamiers*. Paris: Mouton, 1978.

Eco, Umberto. *The Name of the Rose*. Trans. William Weaver. New York: Harcourt Brace Jovanovich, 1983.

Eliot, T. S. *Collected Poems, 1909–1962*. New York: Harcourt Brace Jovanovich, 1991.

Favier, Jean. *Un Roi de Marbre, Philippe le Bel, Enguerran de Marigny*. Paris: Fayard, 2005.

Fédié, Louis. *Histoire de Carcassonne, ville basse et cité* (orig. pub. circa 1890). Nîmes: Lacour-Ollé, 2000.

Feuchter, Jörg. "L'Inquisition de Toulouse: Perre Sellan (1234–1242), un vieillard expérimenté." In Laurent Albaret, ed., *Les Inquisiteurs: Portraits de défenseurs de la foi en Languedoc (XIIIe–XIVe siècles)*. Toulouse: Privat, 2001.

Frale, Barbara. "The Chinon Chart, Papal Absolution to the Last Templar, Master Jacques de Molay." *Journal of Medieval History*, 30, 2, 2004, pp. 109–134.

Friedlander, Alan. "Bernard Délicieux, le 'Marteau des Inquisiteurs.'" *Heresis*, 34, 2001, pp. 9–34.

———. *The Hammer of the Inquisitors: Brother Bernard Délicieux and the Struggle Against the Inquisition in Fourteenth-Century France.* Leiden: Brill, 2000.

———. "Jean XXII et les Spirituels: le cas de Bernard Délicieux." *Cahiers de Fanjeaux*, 26, 1991, pp. 221–236.

———. *Processus Bernardi Delitiosi: The Trial of Fr. Bernard Délicieux, 3 September–8 September 1319.* Philadelphia: American Philosophical Society, 1996.

Galbraith, Georgina Rosalie. *The Constitution of the Dominican Order, 1216 to 1360.* Manchester: University of Manchester Press, 1925.

Galiana, Charles. *L'Inquisition.* Portet-sur-Garonne: Loubatières, 2002.

Ganshof, François L. *The Middle Ages: A History of International Relations.* Trans. Rémy Inglis Hall. New York: Harper & Row, 1970.

Getino, Louis, and Edmond McEniry (eds., trans.). *A New Life of Saint Dominic, Founder of the Dominican Order.* Columbus: Aquinas College, 1926.

Gies, Joseph, and Frances Gies. *Life in a Medieval City.* New York: Harper, 1981.

Given, James B. *Inquisition and Medieval Society: Power, Discipline, and Resistance in Languedoc.* Ithaca: Cornell University Press, 1997.

Girou, Jean. "Bernard Délicieux." *Bulletin de la Société d'Etudes Scientifiques de l'Aude*, 51, 1950, pp. 10–14.

Gosman, Martin. *Les Sujets du Père: Les Rois de France face aux Représentants du Peuple dans les Assemblés de Notables et les États Généraux 1302–1615.* Leuven: Peeters, 2007.

Green, Julien. *God's Fool: The Life and Times of Francis of Assisi.* Trans. Peter Heinegg. San Francisco: Harper & Row, 1985.

Greenia, Conradia (trans.). *The Cistercian Fathers Series, XIX, The Works of Bernard of Clairvaux*, vols. 7, 3. Kalamazoo: Cistercian Publications, 1977.

Griffe, Elie. *Le Languedoc cathare et l'Inquisition (1229–1329).* Paris: Letouzey & Ané, 1980.

Gui, Bernard. *The Inquisitor's Guide: A Medieval Manual on Heretics.* Trans. Janet Shirley. London: Ravenhall, 2006.

Guilaine, Jean, and Daniel Fabre, eds. *Histoire de Carcassonne.* Toulouse: Privat, 1984.

Haag, Michael. *The Templars: History and Myth*. London: Profile, 2008.

Hamilton, Bernard. *The Medieval Inquisition*. New York: Holmes & Meier, 1981.

Hauréau, Jean-Barthélemy. *Bernard Délicieux et l'inquisition albigeoise (1300–1320)*. Paris: Hachette, 1877.

Heer, Friedrich. *The Medieval World*. Trans. Janet Sondheimer. New York: Penguin, 1961.

Hetherington, Paul. *Medieval Rome: A Portrait of the City and Its Life*. New York: St. Martin's, 1994.

Hillgarth, J. N. *Ramon Lull and Lullism in Fourteenth-Century France*. Oxford: Clarendon, 1971.

Horne, Alistair. *La Belle France*. New York: Knopf, 2006.

Huizinga, Johan. *The Autumn of the Middle Ages*. Trans. Rodney J. Payton and Ulrich Mammitzsch. Chicago: University of Chicago Press, 1996.

Joulin, Marc. *Petite Vie de saint Dominique*. Paris: Desclée de Brouwer, 1989.

Kantorowicz, Ernst H. *Frederick the Second, 1194–1250*. Trans. E. O. Lorimer. New York: F. Ungar, 1957.

Kelly, J. N. D. *The Oxford Dictionary of Popes*. Oxford: Oxford University Press, 1986.

Kessler, Herbert L., and Johanna Zacharias. *Rome 1300: On the Path of the Pilgrim*. New Haven: Yale University Press, 2000.

Kieckhefer, Richard. "The Office of Inquisition and Medieval Heresy: The Transition from a Personal to an Institutional Jurisdiction." *Journal of Ecclesiastical History*, 46, 1995, pp. 36–61.

Koestler, Arthur. *Darkness at Noon*. Trans. Daphne Hardy. New York: Macmillan, 1941.

Krautheimer, Richard. *Rome: Profile of a City, 312–1308*. Princeton: Princeton University Press, 1980.

Lacger, Louis de. "Bernard de Castanet, évêque d'Albi (1276–1308)." *Bulletin de littérature ecclésiastique*, 1954, pp. 193–220.

Lambert, Malcolm. *The Cathars*. Oxford: Blackwell, 1998.

———. *Franciscan Poverty: The Doctrine of the Absolute Poverty of Christ and the Apostles in the Franciscan Order, 1210–1323*. London: S.P.C.K., 1961.

———. *Medieval Heresy: Popular Movements from the Gregorian Reform to the Reformation*. Oxford: Blackwell, 2002.

Lawrence, C. H. *Medieval Monasticism: Forms of Religious Life in Western Europe in the Middle Ages*. London: Longman, 1984.

Lea, Henry Charles. *A History of the Inquisition*. 3 vols. New York: Harper & Brothers, 1887.

Le Goff, Jacques. *The Birth of Purgatory*. Trans. Arthur Goldhammer. Chicago: University of Chicago Press, 1984.

——. *L'imaginaire médiéval*. Paris: Gallimard, 1985.

Le Roy Ladurie, Emmanuel. *Montaillou: The Promised Land of Error*. Trans. Barbara Bray. New York: George Braziller, 1978.

Mann, H. K. *Tombs and Portraits of the Popes of the Middle Ages* (orig. 1928). Whitefish, MT: Kessinger Publishing, 2003.

Manselli, Raoul. "De la *persuasio* à la *coercito*." *Cahiers de Fanjeaux*, 6, 1971, pp. 175–97.

——. *Spirituels et Béguins du Midi*. Trans. Jean Duvernoy. Toulouse: Privat, 1989.

Martel, Philippe. *Les cathares et l'Histoire: Le drame cathare devant ses historiens (1820–1992)*. Toulouse: Privat, 2002.

McGinn, Bernard. "Angel Pope and Papal Antichrist." *Church History*, 47, 1971, pp. 155–173.

McNamara, Jo Ann. *Gilles Aycelin: The Servant of Two Masters*. Syracuse: Syracuse University Press, 1973.

Menache, Sophia. *Clement V*. Cambridge: Cambridge University Press, 1998.

Moore, R. I. *The Formation of a Persecuting Society: Authority and Deviance in Western Europe 950–1250*. Oxford: Blackwell, 2007.

——. *The Origins of European Dissent*. Toronto: University of Toronto Press, 1994.

Mundy, J. H. *The Repression of Catharism at Toulouse: The Royal Diploma of 1279*. Toronto: Pontifical Institute of Medieval Studies, 1985.

——. *Studies in the Ecclesiastical and Social History of Toulouse in the Age of the Cathars*. Aldershot: Ashgate, 2006.

Murray, Alexander. *Reason and Society in the Middle Ages*. Oxford: Clarendon, 1978.

Nicholas, David. *Medieval Flanders*. London: Longman, 1992.

Nirenberg, David. *Communities of Violence: Persecution of Minorities in the Middle Ages*. Princeton: Princeton University Press, 1996.

Oakley, Francis. *The Medieval Experience*. Toronto: University of Toronto Press, 2005.

——. *The Western Church in the Later Middle Ages*. Ithaca: Cornell University Press, 1979.

Omond, George William Thomson. *Belgium*. London: A. & C. Black, 1908.

O'Shea, Stephen. *The Perfect Heresy*. London: Profile, 2000.

——. *Sea of Faith: Islam and Christianity in the Medieval Mediterranean World*. London: Profile, 2006.

Partner, Peter. *The Murdered Magicians: The Templars and Their Myth*. Oxford: Oxford University Press, 1982.

Paul, Jacques, "Jacques Fournier inquisiteur." *Cahiers de Fanjeaux*, 26, 1991, pp. 39–68.

Peters, Edward. *Inquisition*. Berkeley: University of California Press, 1989.

———. *Torture*. Philadelphia: University of Pennsylvania Press, 1985.

Pinsky, Robert. *The Inferno of Dante: A New Verse Translation*. New York: Farrar, Straus & Giroux, 1994.

Pirenne, Henri. *Histoire de Belgique*, vol. 1. Brussels: H. Lamertin, 1909.

Poux, Joseph. *La Cité de Carcassonne, précis histoirique, archéologique et descriptif*. Toulouse: Privat, 1923.

Read, Piers Paul. *The Templars: The Dramatic History of the Knights Templar, the Most Powerful Military Order of the Crusades*. London: Weidenfeld & Nicolson, 1999.

Reeves, Marjorie. *The Influence of Prophecy in the Later Middle Ages: A Study in Joachimism*. Oxford: Oxford University Press, 1969.

Reynolds, Barbara. *Dante: The Poet, the Political Thinker, the Man*. London: I. B. Tauris, 2006.

Romer, Lucien. *A History of France*. Trans. A. L. Rowse. New York: St. Martin's, 1953.

Roquebert, Michel. *L'épopée cathare, 1198–1212: L'invasion*, vol. 2. Toulouse: Privat, 1970.

———. *L'épopée cathare, Les cathares, de la chute de Montségur aux derniers bûchers (1244–1329)*, vol. 5. Paris: Perrin, 1998.

———. *Histoire des Cathares: Hérésie, Croisade, Inquisition du XIe au XIVe siècle*. Paris: Perrin, 1999.

———. *Mourir à Montségur*. Toulouse: Privat, 1989.

Scholem, Gershom. *Origins of the Kabbalah*. Trans. Allan Arkush. Princeton: Princeton University Press, 1987.

Selfe, Rose E. (trans.).*Villani's Chronicle, Being Selections from the First Nine Books of the Croniche Fiorentine of Giovanni Villani*. London: Archibald Constable, 1906.

Soule, Claude. *Les États Généraux de France (1302–1789), Étude historique, comparative et doctrinale*. Heule: UGA, 1968.

Southern, R. W. *Western Society and the Church in the Middle Ages*. Harmondsworth: Penguin, 1970.

Strayer, Joseph R. *Les gens de justice du Languedoc sous Philippe le Bel*. Toulouse: Association Marc Bloch, 1970.

————. *The Reign of Philip the Fair*. Princeton: Princeton University Press, 1980.

Théry, Julien. "Les Albigeois et la procédure inquisitoire: Le procès pontifical contre Bernard de Castanet, évêque d'Albi et inquisiteur (1307–1308)." *Heresis*, 33, 2000, pp. 7–48.

Ullmann, Walter. *A Short History of the Papacy in the Middle Ages*. Abingdon: Routledge, 2003.

Vauchez, André. *Laity in the Middle Ages: Religious Beliefs and Devotional Practices*. Ed. Daniel Bornstein, trans. Margery J. Schneider. Notre Dame: University of Notre Dame Press, 1993.

————. (ed.). *Mouvements franciscains et société française XIIe–XXe siècles*. Paris: Beauchesne, 1984.

Vicaire, Marie-Humbert. "La maison de Pierre Seila, à Toulouse, où l'ordre fut fondé." *Cahiers de Fanjeaux*, 1, 1966, pp. 159–66.

Vidal, Jean-Marie. *Bernard Saisset, évêque de Pamiers (1232–1311)*. Toulouse: Privat, 1926.

————. *Un Inquisiteur jugé par ses "victimes": Jean Galand et les Carcassonnais (1285–1286)*. Paris: A. Picard, 1903.

Vilandrau, Céline. "Inquisition et 'sociabilité cathare' d'après le registre de l'inquisiteur Geoffroy d'Ablis (1308–1309)." *Heresis*, 34, 2004, pp. 35–66.

Wakefield, Walter. *Heresy, Crusade and Inquisition in Southern France, 1100–1250*. Berkeley: University of California Press, 1974.

Walsh, William Thomas. *Characters of the Inquisition*. Rockford, IL: Tan, 1940.

Weis, René. *The Yellow Cross: The Story of the Last Cathars 1290–1329*. London: Viking, 2000.

Wood, Charles T., ed. *Philip the Fair and Boniface VIII*. New York: Holt, Rinehart & Winston, 1967.

Wright, Jonathan. *Heretics: The Creation of Christianity from the Gnostics to the Modern Church*. New York: Houghton Mifflin Harcourt, 2011.

Yoo, John. *War by Other Means: An Insider's Account of the War on Terror*. New York: Atlantic Monthly Press, 2006.

INDEX

Page numbers followed by an "n" indicate a note.

A NOTE ON THE AUTHOR

STEPHEN O'SHEA is a historian and the acclaimed author of *Sea of Faith: Islam and Christianity in the Medieval Mediterranean World*, *The Perfect Heresy: The Revolutionary Life and Death of the Medieval Cathars*, and *Back to the Front: An Accidental Historian Walks the Trenches of World War I*. He lives in Providence, Rhode Island.